FROM BOARDING HOUSE TO BISTRO

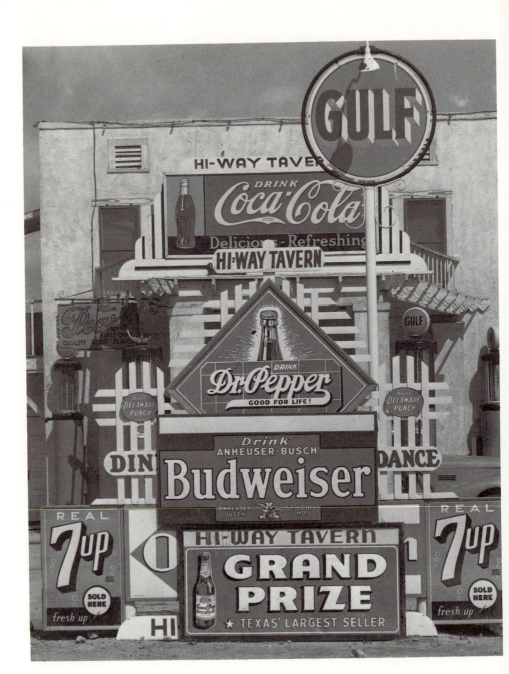

FROM BOARDING HOUSE TO BISTRO

The American restaurant then and now

Richard Pillsbury

Boston
UNWIN HYMAN
London   Sydney   Wellington

Unwin Hyman, Inc.,
955 Massachusetts Avenue, Cambridge, MA 02139, USA

Published by the Academic Division of
Unwin Hyman Ltd
15/17 Broadwick Street, London W1V 1FP, UK

Allen & Unwin (Australia) Ltd,
8 Napier Street, North Sydney, NSW 2060, Australia

Allen & Unwin (New Zealand) Ltd in association with the
Port Nicholson Press Ltd, Compusales Building, 75 Ghuznee Street,
Wellington 1, New Zealand

First published in 1990

Library of Congress Cataloging-in-Publication Data

Pillsbury, Richard.
    From Boarding House to Bistro: the American
restaurant then and now/Richard Pillsbury.
        p.   cm.
    Includes bibliographical references (p.).
    ISBN 0–04–445680–8: $35.00 (est.)
        1. Restaurants, lunch rooms, etc. – United
States – History.   2. Fast food restaurants
– United States – History.   3. Diet – United
States.   I. Title.
    TX909.P55   1990
    647.95'0973–dc20   90–12311 CIP

British Library Cataloguing in Publication Data

Pillsbury, Richard, 1940–
    From Boarding House to Bistro.
1. United States. Restaurants
I. Title
647.9573

ISBN 0–04–445680–8

Typeset in 10 on 13 point Melior by Computape (Pickering) Ltd,
North Yorkshire
and printed in Great Britain by
the University Press, Cambridge

Contents

		page
Acknowledgments		ix
Introduction		1
1	Taverns and boarding house rows	13
	Woodward Inn	19
	The Plate House	32
2	Street vendors to diners	35
	Bert's Diner	41
3	Castles and queens	55
	White Tower	69
4	America transformed	83
	French Fries	83
	Western Cafe	89
5	Sprouts and baked beans	107
6	Cornucopia becomes smorgasbord	135
	Kenny's Kitchen	145

7 The patchwork quilt   161

   Norske Nook   168
   Studio Inn   185

8 "Parts is parts"   189

9 Feeding the soul: some last thoughts   225

   Bibliographic sources   231

   General index   243

   Geographical index   246

Acknowledgments

HUNDREDS OF PEOPLE allowed me to come into their lives for a few moments over the last few years and there would have been no book without their patience and forbearance. I appreciate their assistance, and, more importantly, acknowledge that their contributions come first to mind in this recounting of assistance received. Because of the nature of these encounters, however, I have taken the liberty of altering the names of several of the vignetted individuals and restaurants to protect the privacy of those portrayed, though all incidents and individuals existed as described. While this book represents a great deal of traditional scholarship, it also is very much the product of those encounters, and I am grateful to have been allowed into their lives for those few moments.

It is a rare privilege in academia to be given the opportunity to create a work that is so divergent from academic tradition. Roger Jones of Unwin and Hyman must be acknowledged at the beginning of this recounting of debts for his role in that process. Roger listened to my half-formed ideas and gave me the faith and freedom to mold them in my own style. He encouraged me to go forward when I began to lose my way, while simultaneously helping curb those tendencies that detracted from the project as a whole. This book could never have come into being without his assistance.

I also owe a great debt of gratitude to a variety of individuals and institutions who contributed more concrete items to the finished product. The Actors Theater of Louisville has given permission for the use of Jane Martin's poignant "French Fries," but readers are reminded that all rights are reserved on this material and no recorded, printed, or performance-use is allowed without the express written permission of Samuel French Inc., the play's New York agent. James Collins loaned me several personal photographs of the original Hamburger Handout for use here and the Krystal Company took the time to tabulate the data for me on the diffusion of Krystal restaurants, as well as loaning me their last copy of the original Krystal photograph. The Philadelphia Free Library, the Special Collections Department, Georgia State University Library, and the New York Historical Society also graciously granted permission to utilize their materials as well.

Many others also assisted in the completion of the book. I owe a special debt of gratitude to my brother Robert and to June Stout for putting me up as I did field work in their respective cities and to my daughters Sandra, for introducing me to Jane Martin's work, and Meredith for giving up several summer vacations to help map restaurants. Assistance from academic colleagues includes the encouragement of Clyde Faulkner, Dean of the College of Arts and Sciences, Georgia State University, as well as Margaret Sullivan of Brenau College, Gainesville, Georgia. The maps were made by Jeffery McMichael and Elizabeth Cheney who transformed my crude original drawings in order to create what you see here. I must also thank William Carstensen for allowing me to use his unpublished maps of the spread of McDonald's in the United States and Joe Manzo for the use of his materials on Greek-Americans and diners. Many of the concepts expressed here were first formulated while giving lectures and seminars at several universities, and I am grateful to my friends at the University of Oklahoma, Oklahoma State University, Francis Marion (SC) State College, the University of South Carolina, and most importantly Randall Detro's fabulous annual meeting of the Society for the North American Cultural Survey in Thibidoux, Louisiana.

Several people reviewed the typescript and gave their comments. Wilbur Zelinsky, of the Pennsylvania State University, read the early draft, while John Florin, of the University of North Carolina, got the dubious opportunity to read the early, middle, and final drafts. John Rooney, of the Oklahoma State University, and Philip Langdon read the final draft and I appreciate their comments and criticisms as well.

Finally, I must express my gratitude to my wife Patricia who patiently encouraged me throughout this process, while putting up with endless oral renditions of the successive drafts, my frequent absences as I traveled gathering material to use in the final typescript, and my many mental absences as I became consumed with the project. This book would never have been possible without her encouragement and love.

Richard Pillsbury
Sandy Springs, Georgia

Your stomach is growling and in Marietta you head for the Big Chicken
to fuel the body.

Introduction

WE DIDN'T EAT out much when I was growing up. Actually, there weren't many restaurants back then. Certainly all our family celebration meals were consumed at home. My grandparents' orgiastic gatherings of the generations around the three groaning Thanksgiving tables transcended even Norman Rockwell's most vivid imagination. My mother, however, would periodically attempt to civilize us and drag the family downtown so that we would learn how to eat in polite society at the Park Hotel. Mostly we learned to eat by ourselves, the occasional salesman and traveler being the only others who still dined at this anachronistic leftover of another time. The hotel dining room was stuffy, cold, and formal—much like the food. The Park is gone now, torn down long ago for that ultimate urban land use—the parking lot.

My very earliest memory of dining out was at Hoyt's late one night while returning from a family vacation. Hoyt's was a seedy cafe on the wrong side of town where truckers stopped and the police had their late-shift coffee breaks. My genteel mother told us, "Nice people don't eat here," but late at night it was the only place open and we were hungry. My father, something of a misanthrope, of course knew all of the waitresses by their first names. He told mother that he knew them from his days as a teacher, but even my brother and I knew that he ate at Hoyt's after playing poker with his old baseball cronies down at the Elks Club on Wednesday nights. Mother ignored all this, of course, and went to Hoyt's only that one time, as far as we could tell.

How can I describe Hoyt's? In Providence or Newark it would have been a diner. In small-town California it was just a greasy spoon occupying an ugly, old wooden building squatting along US 99. It was known mostly for its pie and coffee as it fed truckers and ex-baseball players, and occasionally even families who came home after all the "nice" places had closed.

Kouchi's Candy was the other great restaurant in our almost

mythical post-war small-town America. Kouchi's was a soda fountain and candy shop slipped in between the bank and the White Palace barbershop. Located in the heart of Main Street, my mother and I used to stop there on Saturday shopping trips and have a fresh lemon coke, and once in a great while a tuna fish sandwich, at their genuine, old-time soda fountain. Old Mrs Kouchi, that stereotypical short, stout Greek lady, stood in the center of the store welcoming all her customers from behind her clanging brass cash register on those Saturday afternoons. Between times she bustled about hurrying the fountain girls making phosphates and floats, and sold colorful delights from the wall of glass jars containing homemade chocolates and bright hard candies.

Several roadhouses and other questionable places hung out along the edge of town in those days, but nice people usually didn't go to those places. The most famous of these was the Rice Bowl Chinese/American Food, featuring exotic fare such as bird's nest soup and hundred-year-old eggs, or so one heard. My mother always wanted to go there, and once my father relented on her birthday. The food looked as exotic as we had heard. My chop suey platter certainly was too exotic for me. My mother was happy, though, as she had managed to take her brood one more small step forward toward civilization.

The arrival of Stan's Drive-In in the 1950s—with 19-cent hamburgers, shakes in paper cups, and fries in a bag—changed the face of our town forever. You could eat for less than a dollar and feel big-time in this harbinger of *American Graffiti*. We teenagers flocked to this bastion of haute cuisine as we cruised Main Street looking for excitement. Stan's was soon joined by the A & W, Foster's Freeze, and the Dairy Kone, to complete our picture of early American fast food, but these latecomers never held the fascination of Stan's—now also a parking lot.

Other adventuresome restaurateurs soon recognized this new phenomenon of families eating out by opening up more new places in our "mythical" home town. Pizano's Pizza, reputedly featuring real Roman rats scurrying across the dimly lit, sawdust-strewn floor, opened on the edge of town. A Mexican place appeared behind the church pew factory, not far from Hoyt's, on the south side. The restaurant boom was on its way, and we were a part of it.

Since those days Garrison Keillor has immortalized these places with his Chatterbox Cafe, which has become an integral part of our image of the small towns where once so many of us lived. Like most self-images, the reality of this one is far more complex than a mythical mom-and-pop cafe in a mythical Lake Wobegon. We need to go beyond the Chatterbox and Hoyt's to understand the changing nature of the world around us, especially to understand how the restaurant came to be a part of our image and reality of place.

Grappling with chaos

A casual drive down any American city street quickly leads one to believe that chaos rules our palate today. Chinese, Italian, fast Indonesian, gourmet French, breakfast places, sub shops—the range of restaurants seems to be without end. About the only thing that is difficult to find in the average city today are those steamy mom-and-pop cafes which once dominated our restaurant life. Worse yet, drive down that same street in a few months and it will be very different. Urban restaurants appear and disappear like mushrooms after a rain.

There seems to be an endless parade of new restaurants and concepts. Gourmet hamburgers, nouvelle Southern, northwestern chic, Cajun, fern bars, the "Soup Plantation"—the list seems to be without end. The range of apparent restaurant cuisines in a typical American city today tops more than 100, and that includes stuffing many into categories where they barely fit.

But are there really more than 100 restaurant cuisines in a typical city today? Or, to turn the question around, if there are really so many kinds of restaurants, why is it so difficult to find a new dining experience? This problem isn't a consequence of the availability of so many different cuisines; rather, it's a product of the expectations we carry with us when we dine out.

Body food, soul food

The answer lies in matters of time, money, and intent. How much time am I willing to spend? No more five-minute drives to Hoyt's in today's sprawling cities. You can't order Peking Duck when you have only a twenty-minute lunch. No point considering Peking Duck, either, when you have a $3.00 lunch budget. Indeed, no point in thinking of Peking Duck without first asking yourself about intent: am I here to fuel the body or fuel the soul?

It could well be argued that all restaurant food should be divided not on the basis of cuisine, but on the basis of intent. From this vantage point the two great cuisines are body food and soul food. McDonald's is the ultimate restaurant to fuel the body. No one over the age of eight waxes eloquently about the savory aroma and flavors of a Big Mac, fries, and Coca Cola. Some would even argue that the McDonald's regular hamburger without the pickle and catsup would have no flavor at all—but that's begging the question.

We are not arguing for culinary snobbism here. McDonald's is easily the very best at what it sets out to do—filling the stomach with cheap, non-offending food as quickly as possible while providing clean rest rooms and easy parking. McDonald's and all of its brethren are our quintessential body food restaurants. We patronize them—and we *all* patronize them if we travel or eat out much—because they are clean, they are efficient, they are ubiquitous, their bathrooms are acceptable, and they are fast.

Most pizza parlors, mom-and-pop cafes, coffee shops, diners, sub

A mug of coffee mysteriously appears with a spoon peeping from
its depths. That's body food.

shops, and luncheonettes are body food emporiums. Walk into your favorite small-town cafe at breakfast and sit down. A cup of mysterious black liquid covered with specks of grease and a spoon peeping out of the depths pops up in front of you as a disembodied voice asks, "Coffee?". That's body food.

Soul food restaurants are places that serve the inner person. One dines at New York's Luchow's, or Chicago's Morton's, or the Blue Fox in San Francisco, for reasons which have little to do with that growling in the abdomen—in fact, the abdomen seldom growls for soul food eaters. We dine on soul food to celebrate, to reward, to impress, or to create a mood.

There is an almost endless variety of soul food restaurants, but all have something in common. The very thought of dining there raises expectations of pleasure in the mind. The decor brings a sense of satisfaction. The food must be beautiful, but not necessarily gourmet. It must evoke a sense of pleasure in the mind of the diner. Thus, the 57th Fighter Group chain operated by Specialty Restaurants, Inc. is a quintessential soul food restaurant. The food is adequate, but the decor of a bombed-out World War II French farmhouse sited at the edge of an airport runway is superb. Big band music plays in the background, World War II memorabilia covers the walls, and large windows overlook parked World War II relics and modern airplanes which land and take off in the distance. All this creates a distinctive and pleasurable image, especially if you are dining with an acquaintance who loves airplanes or the war, or any of the other images this restaurant tries to evoke.

Soul food places are not for singles. Going to a soul food restaurant alone is one of the truly horrible experiences of life. The fun in going to these places is in sharing. Alone you feel like an outsider stranded on a darkened beach forced to watch others laugh and cloy and impress. You are left to sip your wine too slowly and feel sorry for yourself.

Location and environment are important elements in creating these body food and soul food atmospheres. Some locations murmur images of pleasure, others scream "fuel and go." Location may be the most critical element in restaurant success, but location means more than how many cars pass a site each day or how many potential customers live within a three-mile radius of a site. Soul food restaurants must consider neighborhood image, the pace of activities that take place around a proposed site, and its environmental mood.

Diners at the 57th Fighter Group restaurant feed the soul in a cacophony of World War II and contemporary aircraft images.

The complexity of these needs and the array of elements which relate to them make the concept of a good or bad restaurant location difficult to define.

Almost all restaurants cluster together today. The isolated restaurant has almost disappeared in most cities. There are many reasons for this, but mostly it has to do with the disappearance of the independent restaurant and the independent diner. When the cost of starting restaurants was less and the competition not as keen, the owner/chef could start his new venture where he thought it should be. If he served good food, the restaurant prospered. The urban explosion of the post-war era has changed all that. There is a restaurant for about every 1,000 people in the average American city in the 1980s—that means more than 2,200 restaurants in Atlanta and more than 10,000 in metropolitan Chicago. The competition is keen; the bankers are steely eyed about their money.

Body food restaurants and soul food restaurants don't make good neighbors. Each has a mutually exclusive mission. One must be efficient, the other sets a mood. How do you wax romantic sitting on the garish plastic seats of a Whataburger? How do you calm your nerves as you dodge hot rods tearing out of the Dairy Queen parking lot? What is calm about Sonic?

Body food restaurants do make good neighbors for each other. It's lunch time; your stomach is growling as you are driving down the street. You head for the nearest fast-food strip and make a quick decision. The fast-food stores are lined up like Burma Shave signs. Your first choice is crowded and there is a line waiting to get into the parking lot. Do you push your way through the crowd? Of course not; you change your destination. Like all convenience stores, these places sell time, not food.

Convenience has little to do with the best locations of your favorite soul food store. Milieu is more important than traffic count when one wishes to fuel the soul. We associate pleasurable experience with very specific kinds of environments and dining experiences. Italian neighborhoods ought to have the best Italian foods, Black neighborhoods the best "soul" food, fishing villages the best seafood, expensive elite neighborhoods the best gourmet foods, and gentrifying neighborhoods exquisite, chic little cafes providing exotic new dining experiences.

Restaurants that feed the soul tend to cluster for much the same

Cappy's, located in a John's Island salt marsh near Charleston, South Carolina, draws diners from many miles to enjoy the food, the atmosphere, and the sun setting across the marsh.

The Willow Inn of Waynesburg, Pennsylvania, exudes a sense of the past, from its folk art decor to its warm and gracious hosts. (Painting by Pat Varner)

reasons as fast-food chains, but they also search for some soul-satisfying magnet to draw them together. Each magnet tends to draw its own unique collection. The gentrifying neighborhood draws ersatz cafes and the ethnic food of the week. It prefers independent hamburger stands and pseudo-grubby bars to McDonald's and Bennigan's. It shuns corporate links of all kinds, for the patrons of these places spend their lives searching for reality in mass culture. My favorite is the puckishly named, and now shuttered, Cafe Erehwon ("Nowhere" spelled backwards).

The restaurant has unwittingly become a symbol of contemporary American life.

Urban soul food restaurants are not confined to the city by any means. The Sunday drive into the country to admire the changing scene demands a stop at an inn for a meal of traditional favorites. Mother–daughter days out need an extra special place to prop up the often lagging conversation. And an expedition to the darkest, most remote, secret country hideaway to one-up your business colleagues, who think they know all the best places, is always fun.

The Willow Inn is one of my favorite such restaurants. It's located in a charming old house filled with antiques and old furniture, and is decorated in a folk art style harking back to a simpler time. It feels warm and cozy. It must be one of the least likely city restaurants in all of America. Situated on a narrow, barely paved road several turns and many miles out of Waynesburg, Pennsylvania, it offers everything but convenience. Each night it offers a single, fixed-price meal with guests served by reservation only. Don't plan to go unless you can make reservations more than a week in advance, because there won't be space. How to find it? Follow the cars from Pittsburgh wending their way southward some fifty miles into the heart of the rural Greene County, Pennsylvania countryside. The experience? One to be remembered for a lifetime. Your gracious hosts greet you at the door and create a perfect evening of wine in front of the crackling fire, amusing conversation, and a little homemade music. Unsurpassed food? Possibly not, but then the Willow Inn doesn't set out to astound you with its cuisine; rather the goal is to nurture your soul. At that it is unsurpassed.

The search continues

The restaurant has unwittingly become a symbol of contemporary American life. Our love affair with the automobile, the flight to the suburbs, the return to the city, disposable materialism, and even the counterculture—all are reflected in this constantly changing milieu of Alice's Restaurant, McDonald's, and Clarisse's Soul Vegetarian Cafe. Dinks, yuppies, an increased disposable income, moving away from the mother-in-law, car pools, Little League, the long trek to the exurbs, hating to empty the dishwasher, and that continuing societal evil, television—have made their contributions to the restaurant revolution as well. As time has passed and those changes have become more pervasive, it has grown to be increasingly difficult to separate the reality from the mythology of this process.

Living in a small town, my family, along with all of my aunts, uncles, and cousins, went to dinner at grandma's house every Saturday night for more than forty years. Appearance was mandatory, the baked beans menu unchanging. The essence of family tradition and the continuity of a New England heritage relocated to California remain steadfast. However, those meals, that sense of continuity, and a life defined by tradition are impossible in our modern urban world. Contemporary society has become restless, changing without reason or direction in its search for meaning and continuity. The chapters that follow inspect the history and geography of one aspect of our contemporary life, in an attempt to reach a better understanding of the change that is taking place around us. The restaurant is only a surrogate measure of this change, but it clearly has become a mirror of ourselves, our culture, and our new geography.

The Philadelphia wharves presented a chaotic scene of taverns, boarding houses, ship chandlers, and suppliers. (The Free Library of Philadelphia)

1

Taverns and boarding house rows

MOST COLONIAL AMERICANS never dined in a restaurant even once. The typical seventeenth- and eighteenth-century American had little reason to partake of meals in a commercial establishment, even if one was available. Prior to the Industrial Revolution most of them lived on relatively isolated farms, traveling to town only to attend weekly markets and transact business at the courthouse. Even their churches were usually in the country, not in town as today. They did indeed dine away from home—at church socials, funerals, weddings, and the like—but few had either the cash, the reason, or the interest to sample the rough fare available at most inns and taverns of this period.

Meals were for sale to travelers and others away from home as early as the seventeenth century in taverns, inns, and boarding houses, but few early Americans frequented these places without the excuse of being away from home. Pleasure travel was the province of the very rich. Our image of a constantly moving population holds credence only when seen within the context of a century or two's perspective. Most individuals stayed in the vicinity of their birth, and those that did migrate generally did so only once. Certainly, the concept of eating out for the pleasure of the event is essentially a twentieth-century phenomenon.

A night at the tavern was not your romantic interlude in colonial times.

Taverns as restaurants

The tavern is easily the most romanticized restaurant form in American history. Like its contemporary the log house, it is likely that the romance of this institution is best partaken at some temporal distance. Taverns were rude affairs by any standard, and their travel-weary patrons in rural areas were a captive audience with little choice as to their accommodation. Sleeping arrangements were basic—typically, several people would share a bed and many a single room. Meals were considered a necessary evil. Isaac Weld, for example, describes uncounted meals of "salt pork boiled with turnip tops", with little variation, in his travels in central Appalachia in the 1780s. Featherstonhaugh found worse in Arkansas in the 1840s as he dined on "little pieces of pork swimming in hog's grease, some very badly made bread and much worse coffee."

Meals were offered at set times and consumed quickly in the taverns along frequently travelled roads. Travelers who arrived after the dining hour in these places were out of luck. Innkeepers in less busy areas tended not to prepare meals at all until the traveler actually arrived. One reads of cooks fetching the chicken from the yard after the traveler entered the inn seeking refreshment. Speed was not of the essence in these environments.

The most fortunate of this period may have been those traveling on the frontier, beyond the reach of commercial establishments. John Audubon described a chance meeting with a newlywed couple while traveling in the West. Having become lost from the main road in the rain, he and his companion encountered a house in the woods. The householder sent servants out to lead them in and then said to them:

"A bad night this, strangers; how came you to be along the fence? You certainly must have lost your way, for there is no public road within twenty miles . . . Eliza," turning to his wife, "see about some victuals for the strangers . . ."

Audubon and his companion were taken forthwith to his benefactors' log cabin, where they found:

Bread was prepared by the fair hands of the bride, and placed on a flat board in front of the fire. The bacon and eggs already murmured and spluttered in the frying-pan, and a pair of chickens puffed and swelled on a gridiron over the embers, in front of the hearth.

The first licensed public house in America is reputed to have been the White Horse Tavern in Newport, Rhode Island, although there are other places that would disagree with that assertion. Most eighteenth-century villages and small towns had at least one tavern located on the main through road, while most cities had literally hundreds of them. A 1799 Philadelphia city directory, for example, lists 248 taverns, while the 1805 directory of New York indicates a mere 121, plus 42 combination taverns and boarding houses (Figs 1 & 2). The urban taverns provided food and overnight accommodation for travelers, although their principal business seems to have been purveying alcoholic beverages.

It shouldn't be imagined that there were no taverns serving adequate food during this period. The Fraunces Tavern in lower Manhattan, which is still in operation in name if not in fact, was famous for its venison, bear meat, and cherry bounce. The less famous Ephraim Smith, a Tory from London, announced during the British occupation that he would reopen his tavern "at the desire of many gentlemen of the Royal Army and Navy to be a Steak and Chop House in the London Stile, much wanted in the City. The best of wines, punch, and draft porter, with steaks, chops and cutlets will be served every day from one o'clock til four." Other examples also can be found, but they seem to be the exceptions to the general abysmal rule of awful tavern food.

Over the ensuing years, the tavern has become such a part of the American self-image and our search for roots in this essentially rootless society that the rural tavern (read "bed and breakfast") is undergoing a revival. Norman Simpson's Berkshire Traveller Press has found an almost bottomless market of new readers searching for this new way of "getting away" from it all. Literally hundreds of deserted houses, inns, and small hotels along the nation's by-ways have been refurbished as frustrated urban America has sought to flee from the pressures of urban life and discover a new easier and simpler life in small-town America. The trend has even been given attention in recent years by the popular Bob Newhart television show which idealizes the existence of this urbane expatriate getting away from it all as an innkeeper-cum-writer, living in a quaint Vermont village surrounded by real people and a few "innocent" town characters.

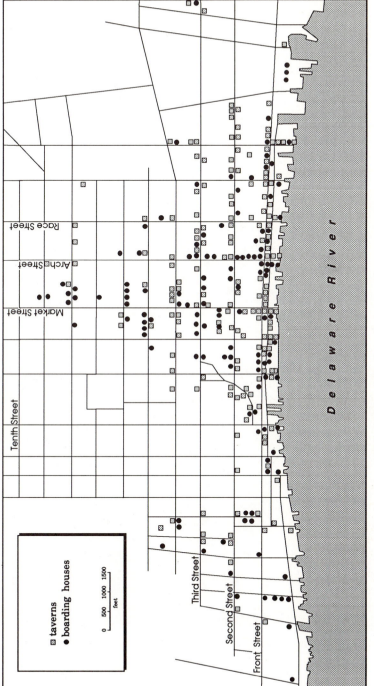

Figure 1. Philadelphia boarding houses and taverns, 1799

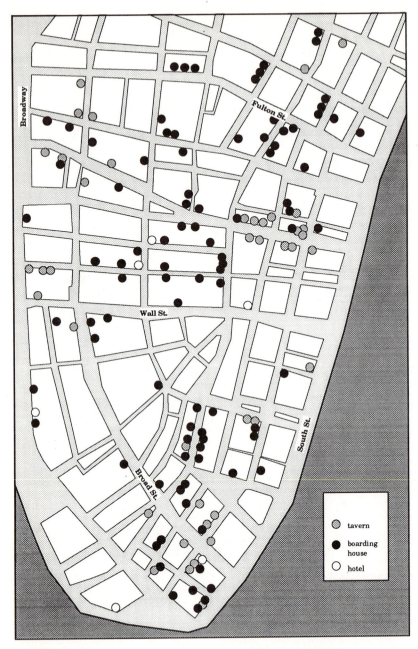

Figure 2. Manhattan eating establishments, 1805

Woodward Inn

The Woodward Inn nestles at the end of Penn's Valley in central Pennsylvania, seemingly little touched by modern life. It is an unpretentious stone house of the kind so common in every central Pennsylvania village. A large sign still announces that it serves the passing public, but time and experience have immutably changed it.

Once, a Friday night trip to the Woodward with friends was the high point of our monthly ritual of graduate school survival. I don't remember how we found it, but it soon became our favorite "treat." Leaving State College, we drove up Pennsylvania 45 through the corn fields, pastures, and villages of this little changed Appalachian landscape. The newest homes in most villages dated from the 1920s, but neglect and bad times had made them look as battered as their century-old neighbors. It was much like a drive back in time to visit the Woodward in those days.

Woodward is a street village lying along the old road connecting Altoona and Lewisburg. It is Amish country at this end of the valley, and the sight of Amish farms and buggies was a continuing delight to our alien eyes. A few of them would always be stopped in the Woodward store on those evenings, while from the road over the mountain lying next to the inn came the clip-clop of horses hurrying home in the failing light, and this brought a touch of romance to many a dinner.

The inn itself was a warm and comforting sight. Run by an elderly woman who never seemed to change, it was a vestige of a past that we outsiders had never encountered before. There were two dining rooms filling half of the first floor, which were furnished with unmatched wooden tables and chairs. The charm of those evenings came as much from an immersion in the atmosphere of those two great rooms, with their massive, open fireplaces and views of the rugged mountains disappearing into the night, as it did from the food.

The choices were limited, but, like many such places, the entrée selection was secondary to the remainder of the meal. Selecting the least expensive item on the menu, we would sit back and await the feast. And what a feast it was. The serving girls brought steaming bowls of vegetables and potatoes, relishes and breads, sauerkraut and more to the table. Fresh green beans to savor; despised creamed corn to ignore. A gourmand feast to be remembered for a lifetime.

Discoveries were as much a part of the meal as the food. Gypsy graduate students, we came from everywhere except Pennsylvania. The meals became a culinary geography lesson. German potato salad and cole slaw as my mother would never imagine. Our first dinner introduced a dark brown substance which mystified us all. After ignoring it for a while, I finally gathered courage and took a great spoonful to test it. A mouthful of apple butter cooked over an open fire in an iron pot is a memory never forgotten. The deserts and the ice tea and coffee stopped coming only when we could eat no more.

I stopped at the Woodward Inn a while back for a nostalgic return to that simpler time. The inn and the wide boards and the dining rooms are still there, but not the meals. New food codes and restrictions have forced the proud Woodward—"open since 1834"—into that now ubiquitous bed and breakfast pigeonhole. The weekly auctions down the street too are only a memory, though the clip-clop of the Amish hooves along the road beside the inn still echo across the lawn and into the now empty dining room.

Boarding houses as restaurants

Boarding houses have been a part of the American dining-out scene probably as long as taverns. Traditionally, most artisans, craftsmen, and businessmen outside the largest cities worked out of their homes, with the owner and any apprentices living on site. The infant Industrial Revolution came to mark the end of that age-old practice soon after Samuel Slatter's mill began attracting more and more young men and women from family farms in the surrounding rural areas into towns to find work. The new factories were not responsible for lodging their employees, and thousands of single men and women soon lived and ate in boarding houses throughout the industrial cities of the nation.

Many boarding houses served the traveling public as well, even after the invention of the "hotel." Most city directories continued listing boarding houses in sections dealing with accommodations for travelers well into the nineteenth century. It is impossible to determine today how many people each of these establishments served at a time, although the surviving structures are relatively small in size. Large numbers were operated by widows who apparently converted their family homes to commercial use after the death of their husbands.

Boarding houses numbered in the hundreds in the larger cities during this period. The 1799 directory for Philadelphia lists 203 such establishments, slightly fewer than the numbers of taverns during this same period. The 1805 directory for New York lists 206 regular boarding houses, 26 additional "sailor" boarding houses, and 42 combination taverns and boarding houses. The establishments tended to be highly concentrated in only a few areas of the city (Fig. 1). More than half of those found in Philadelphia were within a block of the Delaware River waterfront, often located side by side.

The Fraunces Tavern, New York

Short Elbow Alley, for example, had four boarding houses in pairs on each side of the street and another three taverns (Fig. 1). Similarly Arch Street had four between Front Street and the river, while Spruce Street had six boarding houses and a tavern in the same distance.

Boarding house food was universally reviled and received almost unanimous scathing reviews from all that described such fare. Three meals were served at most boarding houses during the early nineteenth century: breakfast, dinner, and tea. Generally meals were served at set times which were announced by the sound of a bell or gong. The early dining hour for "dinner" (lunch) received endless complaints from the largely rural population, however, and the supper hour was steadily pushed later and later into the early evening.

Meals were served "family" style, and woe to those who arrived late. Speed was the one element which all boarding house meals seem to have had in common. Buckingham's description of the meals endured in the boarding house in which he resided in the 1830s was typical:

> The boarding house life was to us, however, extremely disagreeable from the beginning . . . The early hour at which all are rung out of bed by the sound of a great bell, as if at school; the rapidity with which persons rush to the table exactly at eight o'clock; the certainty that if you are five minutes after this, the breakfast will be half consumed, and what remains will be cold and unpalatable . . . the earliness of the dinner hour, three o'clock, with a repetition of the same hurry and bustle over again . . .

The rise of restaurants

Restaurants—that is, stores specializing solely in the selling of food for on-the-premises consumption—began appearing in the late eighteenth century. The earliest examples probably were lodging houses and taverns that rented rooms only as a sideline and began specializing in the sale of food. Coffee houses and oyster houses began appearing in the largest cities during the late eighteenth century. The late introduction of this simple concept was due largely to the European guild traditions, which regulated who prepared food for sale and under what conditions such food could be sold.

The term "restaurant" was coined by the French in the 1760s. Earlier the term had referred simply to "fortifying" oneself in respect to food. Specifically, it referred to the consumption of bouillon, a dish of boiled chicken with coarse salt, and some types of eggnogs which were often served in refreshment rooms called "bouillons." M. Boulanger, a Parisian operator of such a bouillon establishment, advertised in 1765 that "Boulanger serves divine restaurants." This event in itself might not have caused too much comment among any except connoisseurs of the origins of words, except that M. Boulanger also served a dish made of sheep's feet covered with a poulette sauce. The caterer's guild immediately brought suit that M. Boulanger was selling a "ragout", which was specifically protected under guild laws solely for its own sale. The courts studied the matter at length, as one might expect of a French court in such matters of the palate, and eventually determined that such a dish was not a stew. The matter was ultimately resolved by a June 8, 1786 decree that authorized caterers and restaurateurs to receive people in their public rooms for food service.

The term "restaurant" came into general use in America in the nineteenth century. A variety of regional names designated what would now be called restaurants. The term "eating house" was common as late as 1830 in New York City, while "restorator" was widespread in Boston and elsewhere. The term "dining room" was also commonly used in various cities, while "dining hall" and "victualing house" were less frequent. "Coffee houses" and "oyster houses" also appeared in many American coastal cities in the late eighteenth century. None of these places were numerically important in the eighteenth century, and they were rarely listed in business directories until the 1820s.

The question of the site of America's first restaurant has fascinated food historians, and many attribute John and Peter Delmonico with founding the first such establishment. Although this is obviously untrue, it is interesting that the Delmonico brothers played such an important role in early American restaurant history that the myth would continue in the face of such conclusive evidence to the contrary. John Delmonico, an ex-sea captain, opened a wine shop in lower Manhattan in the 1820s. He soon brought over his pastry-chef brother Peter from Switzerland and they opened their first coffee and pastry shop on South William Street in 1827. They continually expanded their offerings and in 1831 opened a full-scale restaurant, reputedly complete with a French chef. They apparently did extremely well almost from the beginning, as they continued moving northward with the elite of Manhattan.

Delmonico's went on from this simple beginning to become one of the nation's most famous and elegant restaurants, as well as one of the best documented from the period. Charles Ranhofer, a chef at Delmonico's for many years, published *The Epicurean*, an 1,183-page cookbook, recounting many of the recipes and famous soirées of his former employer over his thirty-two-year tenure in the late nineteenth century. The menus and recipes are scrumptious to read. A typical menu for a large private party might consist of ten courses, including *croquettes à la comtesse* for hors d'oeuvre, *saumon à la royale* for the fish course, *filet de boeuf Chateaubriand* for the *relèves*, *filets de grouse à la Dauphine* for the entrée, and on and on. Examining the full range of menus presented in this remarkable book makes one marvel at the skill of kitchen staff to have presented such foods in days when transportation was slow and refrigeration hardly known. Unfortunately, Mr Ranhofer neither dealt with that aspect nor gave us a clear idea as to the cost of these fabulous repasts.

Little is generally known about the food served in the restaurants of this period because menus were either called out or written on chalk boards. An 1834 menu from "Delmonico's" at 494 Pearl Street (a location never attributed to the famous Delmonico brothers) is reputed as being the first printed menu in America. The bill of fare is interesting in that it closely parallels the descriptions for the typical middle-class restaurants of the city, such as the later famous Brownivoriums. A "regular dinner" (which is not delineated) is listed at 12 cents. Individual items range from the expected—hash, beef or mutton stew, and corn beef and cabbage—to the unexpected—pig's head with cabbage, fried or stewed heart, and, interestingly, a hamburger steak.

The restaurant revolution thus had gotten underway in the early nineteenth century, with the first of such establishments appearing in the larger cities along the eastern seaboard as coffee houses, oyster houses, eating houses, tea gardens, and restorators. Their numbers remained small until the 1840s, however, as most boarding houses and taverns sold rooms on the American plan—including meal service—and there was little reason regularly to partake meals elsewhere.

The revolution began when the larger cities grew to a size that made

⚔DELMONICO'S⚔

RESTAURANT
494·PEARL·STREET.

BILL OF FARE.

Cup Tea or Coffee,	1	Pork Chops,	4
Bowl " "	2	Pork and Beans,	4
Crullers,	1	Sausages,	4
Soup,	2	Puddings,	4
Fried or Stewed Liver,	3	Liver and Bacon,	5
" " Heart,	3	Roast Beef or Veal.	5
Hash,	3	Roast Mutton,	5
Pies,	4	Veal Cutlet,	5
Half Pie,	2	Chicken Stew,	5
Beef or Mutton Stew,	4	Fried Eggs,	5
Corn Beef and Cabbage,	4	Ham and Eggs,	10
Pigs Head " "	4	Hamburger Steak,	10
Fried Fish,	4	Roast Chicken,	10
Beef Steak,	4		

Regular Dinner 12 Cents.

Smith & Handford Printers 23 and 25 Dey St N. Y.

Menus generally were called out to entering patrons or written on blackboards prior to the appearance of printed ones in 1834. This Delmonico's (Pearl Street) is reputedly the first printed menu in America. (New York Historical Society)

it increasingly difficult for working people to return home for their noon meals, the largest meal of the day. Also, many residents were tired of boarding house culinary fare by this time and increasingly were seeking furnished rooms without meal service. Most factory workers continued to carry their food to work, but the increasing numbers of white-collar workers in the labor force, the higher levels of disposable income that these occupations provided, and the limited variety of foods that could be carried to the work-place prior to the widespread use of refrigeration made the new restaurants increasingly attractive.

There was a much wider variety of eating houses available to the general public in the northeastern cities than is generally assumed at this time. The 1805 edition of the *New York Mercantile and General Directory* listed a number of free-standing emporiums, including four coffee houses, four oyster houses, four tea gardens, two victualing houses, and a cookshop. Additionally, thirteen establishments identified as hotels presumably had dining rooms. Similarly, the somewhat later *Philadelphia As It Is & Citizens Advertising Directory* of 1834 lists eight coffee houses, along with a variety of other establishments. This same directory also lists the Café Francais, one of the nation's earliest "French" restaurants. Finally, an 1825 advertisement for the Franklin Restorator in the *Boston Annual Advertiser* stated that "The subscriber respectfully informs his friends and the public that he continues his Establishment . . ."

Coffee houses began appearing in American cities in the 1790s. The Tontine Coffee House was founded in New York in 1794 with more than 200 nominees. Literally hundreds of other references are found to coffee houses during the late eighteenth and early nineteenth centuries, as they were often patronized by many of the city's most wealthy businessmen. Coffee houses tended to be widely scattered throughout the business sections of the post-colonial cities, although they were most often found near the financial districts and public markets. The Merchants and Tontine Coffee Houses were located on opposite sides of Wall Street. They were the scene of many important events, including the founding of the New York Insurance Company, the Bank of New York, and, under a buttonwood tree outside these two facing businesses, the New York Stock Exchange itself.

Much less is known about the oyster houses, or cellars, of the period. Most cities of the eastern seaboard seem to have had large numbers of these ubiquitous establishments which served a filling meal for a small price. The trademark of oyster cellars in New York City was a lighted red and white striped balloon hung out front during open hours. Oysters were cheap and plentiful and most were sold on the "all you can eat" basis for a few cents. Those who

The Tontine Coffee House about 1787

consumed more than the operator felt fair soon discovered a "bad" oyster on their plate and quickly lost interest in continuing the orgy. While raw oysters were a menu favorite, fried oysters and oyster stew were also served. Fifteen cents bought a stew of at least three dozen oysters in New York City in the 1840s.

Thomas Downing's, at 5 Broad Street in lower Manhattan, was the most famous oyster house in that city during this period. Downing, a Black man, ran an elegant house that was as sumptuous as the later more famous Delmonico Brothers' restaurant a few blocks away. He attracted large numbers of bankers, traders, politicians, and notables. Even properly chaperoned women were welcomed in his establishment, located near the Custom House. The menu included a much wider variety of dishes than was typical of oyster houses at this time, including oyster pie, scalloped oysters, and a variety of game items stuffed with oysters.

The oyster house period in New York came to an end in the second half of the nineteenth century as the nearby oyster beds became overfished and polluted. Although it was still possible to bring oysters in from both Raritan Bay in New Jersey and the more southerly Chesapeake Bay, the higher prices created by the increased shipping costs eventually brought an end to this venerable institution as a major restaurant type.

Oyster houses were not as concentrated as might be assumed in the typical city of the period. Direct access to water had little to do with their location. The largest concentration of such eating houses in Manhattan in 1850, for example, was found near the junction of Catherine, Bowery, and Canal Streets, not far from what is now Greenwich Village. This famous concentration was not the only cluster of oyster houses, however, and four were to be found in the 400 block of Broadway, six at Oliver slip, and seven at the Catherine Market (Fig. 3). Others were even more scattered throughout the city. Downing's, for example, was located just off Wall Street on Broad. Oyster houses were widely scattered throughout Philadelphia and Boston as well, although they tended to be located in the seedier parts of town where large numbers of laborers could be found.

George Foster, of the New York *Herald Tribune*, evaluated the dining possibilities of that city in 1848 and gave us some additional insight into the kinds of eating houses which were open to the public. He recognized three types of "eating houses" in his survey, including the Sweeneyorium, the Brownivorous and the Delmonican. The lowest order of these was Daniel Sweeney's on lower Ann Street, which was relocated the following year to the somewhat better site at 46 Chatham. A short-order restaurant known as a six-penny house, it served breakfast, dinner, and tea. The changing menu was continually shouted out by a barker at the door who listed the day's fare. Diners sat on benches and ate at long tables from which they ordered their meals.

George Brown's Eating House, the progenitor of the terms "Brownivorous", was located on Water Street, just a few doors from Wall Street. It was a modernized tavern with a written bill of fare, fixed prices, and waiters who actually waited. Brown's is reputed to have served 2,000 customers a day.

Delmonico's has been described previously, but it should be noted that the confusion over the location of this famous restaurant stems from the constantly changing sites. In the 1820s John Delmonico opened his first shop at 2 South William near Hanover Square. The site was then shifted to 21–23 William Street near Exchange Place. The brothers continued relocating as fashionable New Yorkers

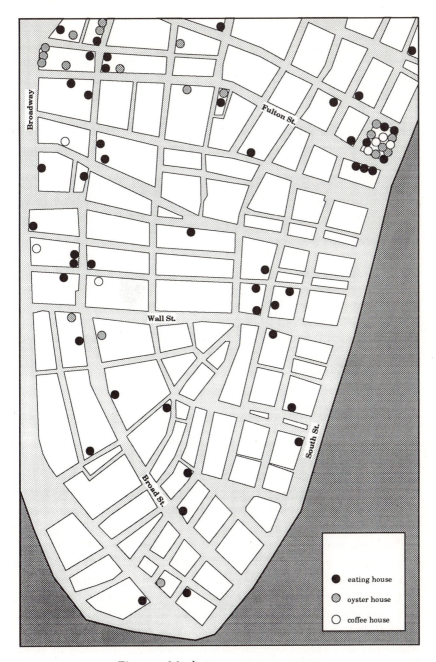

Figure 3. Manhattan restaurants, 1857

moved northward until a total of ten known locations had been used. Restaurant historians have suggested that the Delmonico's constantly shifting locations meant that they operated the nation's first chain restaurant, as several restaurants often were operated simultaneously. This is a clear misinterpretation of the facts. Restaurant owners were little different at that time from now. As soon as an operator got one restaurant running satisfactorily, he typically began considering expansion to new locations. City directories for New York, Philadelphia, and Boston all indicate examples of multiple restaurants under common ownership before the Delmonicos operated such units. The Delmonico mystique was as real in the mid-nineteenth century as Howard Johnson's in the 1920s and Ray Kroc's McDonald's today. If there was an innovation in the industry, it must have been theirs.

The number of restaurants increased rapidly during this period in the larger American cities, but their distribution remained relatively restricted because of the continuing lack of cheap, fast transportation. The 1857 map of New York, for example (Fig. 3), demonstrates only a few clusters, especially around Broadway and Fulton, the aforementioned oyster house clusters near Canal on Catherine and Bowery, and around Wall Street. Possibly of more interest is the presence of several similar clusters well outside the mapped zone, indicating that "pre-hamburger alleys" were already beginning to form in the mid-nineteenth century.

Markets were important centers for eating houses throughout the early nineteenth century. Business directories list oyster houses, eating houses, and dining rooms both within the market houses and in the buildings around them. In 1851 New York's Fulton Market was found to have four eating houses, four coffee houses, and six oyster houses inside the market, while an additional four eating houses were located on the blocks facing the market.

The turnover of restaurants during this period was little different from today's constantly changing milieu. Of the 497 different addresses that housed a restaurant in 1850 and 1860 in New York City, only 11 were open under the same proprietor during both years. At an additional 20 addresses restaurants were in operation in both years, but had different proprietors. Thus, only 6 percent of the addresses and only 2 percent of the restaurants operating in 1850 survived the ten-year period, a failure rate even higher than that experienced in the industry today. Similarly, a survey of Charlestown, Massachusetts, indicated that less than half of the restaurants listed for 1858 were still operated at the same site by the same proprietor two years later in 1860. About 15 percent were still open with a different proprietor, while one proprietor had moved his store to a new location across the street. This failure rate is not as surprising as it might seem. The nineteenth-century restaurant had far less specialized equipment and modifications than those found today. Most fixtures were mobile, and, unlike today, health codes did not demand substantial structural modifications.

The numbers and the sophistication of the urban restaurant began increasing rapidly after 1850. Philadelphia, for example, had eight coffee houses, twenty-one oyster houses and 254 restaurants, as well as uncounted porter (beer and ale) houses, boarding houses, and hotels. Specialty American restaurants were beginning to appear in larger numbers by this time, and French cuisine was now readily available in the city. Other cities had similar numbers of restaurants, although what has become the standard pattern of the greatest numbers of restaurants per person being found in western cities, slightly fewer per person in eastern industrial cities, and the fewest per person in the South was already beginning to emerge.

The increasing number of restaurants was brought about by the explosive suburbanization of the urban areas accompanied by a rapid expansion of a new affluent middle class. The longer commutes of these workers made it increasingly difficult for them to return to their homes for the traditional large midday meal. This market was further enlarged when lodging house and hotel owners began to phase out the previously standard American (meals included with room) rental plan in favor of the European (room only) plan. This forced (allowed) thousands more of those renting rooms to purchase their meals at restaurants.

Of course, most people did not participate in the revolution, as they continued to carry lunches, return home for their midday meal, eat at taverns and saloons, or buy from street vendors. The market for a substantial number of restaurants was created, however, and this trend would continue until the post World War II boom of the industry.

Some significant changes were also taking place in the nature of the dining establishments. The concept of the coffee house had expanded significantly. These places were much more genteel than their ruder brethren and were comparable to the nicer "coffee shops" of today. The French restaurant was also in full flower by mid-century. French restaurants were found in most larger cities and tended to serve the most elegant food of the day outside of the massive hotel dining rooms. Finally, the Sweeneyorium of the 1840s was replaced in name, if not in kind, by the newly evolving "plate houses." Plate houses were the antecedents of today's lunchrooms, and indeed, a period description of one could easily be mistaken for the description of an innovative type of lunchroom today.

The Plate House

We entered a long, narrow, and rather dark room . . . with a row of boxes on each side made just large enough to hold four persons and divided into that number by fixed arms . . . Along the passage, or avenue between the row of boxes, which was not above four feet wide, were stationed sundry little boys, and two waiters, with their jackets off—and good need, too, as will be seen. There was an amazing clatter of knives and forks, but not a word audible to us was spoken by any of the guests. The silence, however, on the part of the company, was amply made up for by the rapid vociferations of the attendants, especially of the boys, who were gliding up and down, inclining their heads for an instant, first to one box, then to another, and receiving the whispered wishes of the company, which they straight way bawled out in a loud voice . . . It quite baffled my comprehension to imagine how the people at the upper end of the room, by whom a communication was kept up in some magical way with the kitchen, could contrive to distinguish between one order and the other . . . The multiplicity and rapidity of these orders and movements made one giddy. Had there been one set to receive and forward the orders and another to put them to execution, we might have seen better through the confusion; but all hands, little and big together, were screaming out with equal loudness and quickness—"Half plate beef, 4!"—"One potato, 5"—"Two apple pie, one plum pudding, 8" and so on.

There could not be, I should think, fewer than a dozen boxes, with four people in each; and as everyone seemed to be eating as fast as he could, the extraordinary bustle may be conceived. We were not in the house above twenty minutes, but we sat out two sets of company at least.

Captain Hall, 21 May 1827

Although New York, Philadelphia, and Boston were at the leading edge of restaurant innovation, changes were taking place elsewhere, albeit somewhat more slowly. Presaging the future western bias of restaurants generally, 1860 San Francisco was replete with sixteen oyster houses and forty-eight restaurants, more eating houses per person than many of its larger eastern brethren. A local newspaper advertisement for Messrs Harris & Garcia's "Magnificent Dining and Ice Cream Saloon" indicates that "This magnificent establishment will surpass anything of the kind on the Pacific Coast, and it is the intention of the proprietors to make it the most desirable for Ladies and Families of any in this City". In contrast, the significantly larger city of Pittsburgh had a total of only seventy restaurants in the same year, while Rome and Utica (New York) had only seventeen and twelve. Similarly, only seventeen restaurants and, amazingly, twenty-nine oyster and refreshment saloons were found in Providence in 1860.

The basic pattern was set. The restaurant forms and locational preferences of the mercantile age had come into focus by 1860. The restaurant would increase in number and elaborate its form over the next decades, but real change must await the now-emerging Industrial Revolution before bringing in a new set of operational assumptions and parameters.

The Riverside Diner, The Home Of Perfect Food. (Library of Congress)

2

Street vendors to diners

THE INDUSTRIAL REVOLUTION brought a new economic base and social order, as well as setting the stage for a restructuring of the demographic character of the nation. It also fostered a new attitude about how things should be done. Clothes, houses, machines, and virtually every other element of daily life became mass-produced in the name of efficiency. Mass production was the right way to do things.

The mass production of food was accomplished through the invention of restaurant buildings that could be built in factories, the development of national restaurant chains to allow the mass distribution of food, and the invention of a host of new types of restaurants to serve the hungry hordes flocking to the cities to work in the factories. Most importantly, the Industrial Revolution created the demand for new foods suitable for mass production which also began appearing during this period. The result was an explosion of the types, numbers, and patronage of restaurants, creating an entirely new industrialized dining landscape by 1920.

Mass-produced restaurants

It is intriguing that the diner—at least as important a symbol of our national dining mythology as the roadside tavern—developed just a few miles from Newport's White Horse, the nation's first licensed tavern. The setting is Providence, Rhode Island; the impetus is the invention of the factory system itself. Samuel Slater introduced the

Street vendors were an important source of fare for the working-class, boarding house residents when they could not meet the rigid meal schedules imposed by their lodgings. (Philadelphia Free Library)

spinning jenny, the textile mill, and the factory system to America in Pawtucket, Rhode Island, in the 1790s. Providence/Pawtucket became one of the nation's most important industrial centers by the late nineteenth century, with many textile, jewelry, and other factories. This led to an unparalleled need to feed the multi-shift factory workers at all times of the day and night. Boarding houses and taverns continued to maintain their rigid dining schedules, leaving the street vendor to feed the thousands of hungry factory workers on irregular shifts. This situation created both a market for the development of independent restaurants to serve the middle- and lower-class society and a need to mass-produce in as short a period as possible these units to meet the overwhelming demand for them.

The diner story begins in 1872 when Walter Scott, a street vendor, traded in his hand-carried basket of food one night for a horse-drawn wagon. The wagon allowed him to serve a large number of customers without having to return home for more provisions, as well as giving him a place to stand protected from the weather. No accommodation was provided for the customers, who stood in the street while being served through a window. He continued his nightly beat with little change for forty-five years until he retired in 1917. Scott's menu was very simple. The most important items were boiled eggs with buttered bread, frankfurters, and what may have been some of the earliest chicken salad sandwiches, each for a nickle, and sliced chicken for thirty cents. Scott was proud of the quality of his food, and during a retirement interview with the local newspaper commented that his success was due largely to the consistent quality of the food that he served.

Scott's lunch-wagon was an instant success in Providence, and the concept was quickly adopted by many others in that city and throughout southern New England. Ruel Jones, a competitor in Providence, was the first to order a lunch-wagon specifically designed for that purpose, in 1883. Jones soon had a chain of seven of these vehicles operating throughout the streets of the city.

Samuel Messer Jones, a cousin of Ruel, moved to Worcester, Massachusetts, in 1884 to set up business. Having saved $800 in his new business by 1887, Jones carried the evolution of the diner one step further by ordering a new wagon which allowed patrons to be seated inside while consuming their meals. He had several wagons built to this new design. These proved to be so popular that his competition soon adopted the innovation. He sold all but one of his wagons two years later to his competitor Charles H. Palmer.

Palmer perceived the rugged competition of the Worcester lunch-wagon trade as an opportunity and decided to begin building the vehicles. He patented a new wagon design in 1891, and the factory era for lunch-wagons had begun. A variety of builders eventually entered the lunch-wagon business, although production of these "vehicles" was generally restricted to greater New England. T. H. Buckley, the lunch-wagon king, was also located in Worcester, Massachusetts, where he employed 55 craftsmen by 1898. The factory built about 650 wagons over ten years, each taking about a day or two, exclusive of paint, to construct. These restaurants were sold to complete turnkey operations with all furnishings, from tables to plates and silverware. The fancier models came with tile-covered interiors and were equipped with marble counters and brass cash registers. The Buckley company sold lunch-wagons in more than 275 communities, primarily in New England.

Mobile lunchrooms caused their share of problems. They were considered eyesores by the "polite" people in town, who thought they were the hangouts for bad sorts. They also caused inconvenience by their sheer numbers. There were more than fifty working the night streets of Providence in 1912 when a new law was enacted to make sure they were off the streets by 10 a.m. The proprietors' solution was to find off-street parking and locate semi-permanently on empty building lots. Skirts were soon added to hide the wheels, and utilities were hooked up, consequently creating a new sense of permanence at these stationary locations. One hesitates to call these locations truly permanent, as the wheels remained, so that if the site rent were raised too much the operator could simply lift his restaurant's skirts, pick up his steps, and move on.

Lunch-wagons evolved into diners during the first decades of the twentieth century. The principal difference between the earliest diners and the lunch-wagons of this transition period was in the name alone. As a result, it is impossible to reconstruct the geography of diners for this time; many eateries that utilized the term "diner" in their name were not true diners, while not all true diners chose to include that term in their appellations.

Some inferences about the distribution of diners can be made on the basis of the location of factories. P. J. Tierney & Sons Company of New Rochelle, New York started in Tierney's garage soon after the turn of the century and soon became the world's largest manufacturer

The Modern Diner in Pawtucket, Rhode Island, is a classic example of
the streamlined period of diner design.

of these unique assemblages. By 1925 the company, under the
management of his sons, worked on as many as forty diners simultaneously, finishing at least one a day. The O'Mahony Company of
Bayonne, New Jersey, was the second largest manufacturer in the
inter-war years and produced almost as many as Tierney's. The
Worcester Lunch Car Company of Worcester, Massachusetts, was
somewhat smaller than its two competitors, but did a lively business
in southern New England. Virtually all of the other manufacturers of
note were located in greater New York and southern New England,
including Sterling Diners of Merrimac, Massachusetts, Ward &
Dickinson of Silver Creek, New York, and the Kullman Dining Car
Company of Newark, New Jersey, to name a few. While it was
possible to ship diners long distance—some were even shipped by
sea to California—most traveled either over local roads at ten miles
per hour on their iron unsprung wheels, or by rail. Few diners of the

lunch-wagon tradition were established south of Virginia or west of Ohio. New England and "Megalopolis"—the urbanized Northeast—contained the largest concentrations of these restaurants, although two recent movies, *Diner* and *Tin Men*, interestingly, are set in 1960s Baltimore.

Trolleys, streetcars, and railroad dining cars were also converted to this use after 1900. The end of the streetcar era in the larger cities of the nation was especially important in this trend, but most tended to be too small for continued use. A number of these cars are still found around the nation, including a comparatively recent one improbably located in Portland, Oregon. Diners are still manufactured, most notably by the Mobile Module Company of Atlanta, Georgia, but their numbers are insignificant in the greater scheme of contemporary restaurants.

The menus of the diner remained simple through time and were

The newly constructed restaurants of the Mobile Module Company of Atlanta, Georgia, look little different from those of the 1920s.

This Bordentown, New Jersey, diner interior well illustrates the simple interiors and menus characteristic of the 1920s. (FSA, Library of Congress)

one of the contributing factors to the decline of this American institution. The rise of the true diner in the 1920s allowed a tremendous expansion of the menu, but in practice, even today it remains oriented toward the meat-and-potatoes audience that was its original clientele.

Bert's Diner

The silver tube lay along the small southern New England side-street like a giant discarded lipstick case. Even at ten o'clock in the morning the word "Diner" glowed in green neon from a sign which hung on a small iron pipe-stand over the sidewalk. Sitting amidst the yawning parking lot of the surrounding jewelry factories, the diner seemed lonely and forlorn, as if dropped by accident by someone hurrying down this side-street.

Entrance through the heavy stainless steel and glass doors brought one face to face with the past. The smell of grease filled the air. The stainless steel kitchen lined the rear wall as if it had grown there. A great iron grill covered with a once-silver hood coated with grime, a refrigerated pie case, and a milk case gave the cooking area a unique sense of class. The counter stretched almost the entire length of the tube, cut off at the end so you could follow the grubby arrow pointing to the rest room. The booths were pleasant enough, though somewhat older than my grandmother. The Wurlitzer Juke Box module hanging on the wall looked tired. So did the music. Sam Cook, Frank Sinatra, the Boss, and the Sherelles still sang for a dime at Bert's Diner.

The place appeared deserted at first. Bert was standing at the grill smoking the last drags of a cigarette butt. In his early fifties, he was blessed with a splendid belly peeking out from beneath his yellowing T-shirt. Tattoos dotted his hairy arms; his giant calloused hands nicked and scarred in a hundred ways. His slow and purposeful movements were those of a man who spent as much time standing before a bar as before a grill. He looked as tired as his shirt.

A pimply faced teenager of seventeen or so with a black Motley Crue T-shirt came out of the back carrying some boxes. They exchanged a few unpleasantries as they passed. If looks could kill, Bert would have been a goner. The kid put the boxes on the counter and began filling the napkin holders while he bounced to some hidden tune from his Sony Walkman.

The menu was basic. Breakfast twenty-four hours a day. Hamburg, Coney Island, grilled cheese sandwich, french fries, and an assortment of sandwiches appeared on the one-page laminated plastic menu. The specials of the day were found on the black menu board over the grill. They appeared to have been unchanged since VJ Day. Meat loaf, liver and onions, hamburg steak, breaded veal cutlet, flounder filet. Mash potatoes and gravy or french fries and a salad or cole slaw came with the meal, though it looked like it had been a while since Bert's had served anything green that wasn't still living.

The kid wandered over and sullenly asked what we wanted. I decided on the breakfast special—after all, how badly could you ravage two scrambled eggs, toast, hash browns, and coffee? My companion's cheese omelet and raisin toast was more daring. The coffee came in a few moments and was passable, if you were accustomed to used motor oil. I was.

Three young men, apparently of Portuguese descent, wearing repairmen jump suits burst in during the middle of the ordering, taking the kid's mind off his work. They shouted at Bert, gave a wave to the kid, and settled in a booth. They continued telling jokes and teasing each other in mixed English–Portuguese about their male prowess, ancestry, and any other topic that came to mind. This kept them in stitches while they devoured their coffee and stale pie. Eventually the plumbers' attention shifted to some newly arrived Italian electricians. Both groups *good naturedly began to yell insults at each other over the backs of the booths as they drank their coffee. Clearly this was a mid-morning ritual.*

Soon the diner was filling with the early lunch crowd. Bert began moving a little faster as the hamburger patties started popping onto the grill and the fryer baskets dipped in rapid succession. Things were soon flying—if one overlooked the Motley Crue.

Breakfast arrived, and I knew that the crowd did not come here for the food. The eggs were unique: burned brown with a smell that turns the stomach on the outside; runny white dripping from the inside. Grease spread out from the hash browns like the Johnstown flood, threatening the toast with instant drowning. It was too late. The lake of liquid imitation margarine slopped on by the cook had already done that job. I would have written off the whole thing and just had a second cup of coffee, but didn't have time to wait for the dinner meal for my refill.

I always knew there had to be some reason why McDonald's did such a big breakfast trade while offering Egg McMuffins and the like. Now I realized what it was.

Diners and their menus are chic today and are making something of a comeback. The Fog City Diner of San Francisco popularized a nouvelle greasy-spoon cuisine without the grease, and has made gourmet food of chicken fried steak, mashed potatoes, and meat loaf. New "diners" are opening throughout the nation as suburbanites search for their lost roots. Anyone even casually interested in the diner should read R. J. S. Gutman and E. Kaufman's *American Diner*, a graphic exploration of this American phenomenon.

Chains: mass management

The second important innovation ushered in by the Industrial Revolution was the chain restaurant. Multi-unit operations were hardly an industrial-age invention. Restaurant operators such as the Delmonico brothers, Lovejoy, and Brown all operated several restaurants at different locations as early as the 1830s. The innovation was to operate multiple restaurants which functioned as a complex organism—usually meaning the use of the same name, almost duplicate menus, and similar genetic consistencies—to create clones, rather than a group of diverse operations under the same general management. Chain restaurants began appearing throughout the major eastern cities during the mid-nineteenth century, and by the

1880s examples could be found in virtually every city of any size. The most famous of these early chains and an early model for many who followed, was the Harvey House.

Fred Harvey emigrated to New York from his native England in 1850. He worked first at the Smith McNeill Cafe, but soon moved on to New Orleans and finally to St Louis, where he married. He and a partner operated a restaurant there until his partner joined the Confederacy with the company's funds. Harvey worked for a time as a mail clerk, but by 1875 he was operating three restaurants on the Kansas Pacific Railroad in Kansas and Colorado. In the spring of 1876 he signed a contract with the Atchison, Topeka and Santa Fe railroad to provide food service, and soon was on his way to creating an empire.

Harvey expanded rapidly from his first Sante Fe railroad lunch-room in Topeka. He bought his first hotel in 1878 in Florence, Kansas, and five years later owned seventeen restaurants and/or hotels primarily serving meals to the railroad's patrons, although many were important in their local communities as well (Fig. 4). The Harvey Houses became a legend in southwestern dining lore for their efficiency, their quality, and their waitresses.

Harvey's restaurants had a number of advantages over the local "town" competition, not least free freight to ship his goods on the railroad. The railroad access not only provided foods which would

Figure 4. Fred Harvey hotels and eating houses, 1876–1907

Harvey's success was due partially to the quality of the competition, if this period Colorado drawing can be believed. (Library of Congress)

not otherwise be available in many of these communities, but also allowed him to maintain reasonable prices even in the most isolated locations. Thirty-five cents bought a full meal in those days of a quality seldom seen previously in many of these communities at any price.

The Harvey operation is atypical of most chains in many respects. The distribution of the restaurants was more or less predetermined by the railroad schedules, which brought trains to locations far removed from any reasonable local market at dining hours. Communities such as Wallace, Kansas, and Ash Fork, Arizona, existed almost entirely because of the railroad, and there the Harvey units operated virtually without competition. In contrast, hotels and restaurants in communities such as Topeka, Albuquerque, and Los Angeles faced severe competition, although it is said that the most severe critic of the chain's operations was Fred Harvey himself.

Harvey introduced several important innovations into the industry which were crucial in the development of chain restaurants. Although the buildings varied architecturally, the vast majority adopted a southwestern style which made them easily identifiable.

Patrons knew that these businesses were Harvey Houses, even without seeing the signs. Waitresses and other help were also dressed identically to help continue the sense of association with the Harvey name.

The apparent diversity of offerings along the rail routes was another important element in the company's success. Menus were centrally developed and printed to ensure that a traveler riding across the country would never encounter exactly the same fare for two meals in a row. The central commissary achieved this goal by maintaining a variety almost unknown in chains prior to that time. Local managers could purchase locally, but most food was shipped from the commissary. Harvey House supervisors rode the trains constantly to ensure quality control, and were famous for walking into units where food quality and service had fallen below company standards and firing the manager and cooks on the spot. The result was a consistency of product that probably was not matched again until Bill Marriott and Ray Kroc came into the restaurant business many years later.

New restaurants for a factory age

The rapidly expanding restaurant market demanded new types of establishments to feed the exploding market. The lunchroom, the cafeteria, and the previously described diner were the most important of these. Lunchrooms began appearing as early as 1869, although it is difficult to pinpoint the origin of this form of restaurant. The lunchroom became one of the most common restaurant types of the late nineteenth century and was found in almost every city in the nation. Serving simple food quickly and inexpensively, the lunchroom was that period's equivalent of the fast-food hamburger store.

The cafeteria appeared somewhat later than the lunchroom and was an early attempt to cut down on labor costs and make food available both inexpensively and quickly. The all-male Exchange Buffet was founded in 1885 in New York and may have been the earliest restaurant utilizing the self-service innovation. William and Samuel Childs are also occasionally given credit for the first cafeteria. The Childs brothers opened their first restaurant in 1873 and introduced the tray about 1898. The tray concept was considered so revolutionary that the *Caterer's Monthly* thought to include an

The lack of personal transportation kept most lunchrooms and cafes concentrated along the principal trolley tracks before World War I. (Philadelphia Free Library)

Many restaurants during the 1920s adopted an in-between position about the roles of cafeterias, lunchrooms, and restaurants, as can be seen in the Brilliant Lunch Bar Restaurant. (FSA, Library of Congress)

account of the innovation that year. Wherever the cafeteria started, the most important adopter of the concept was the 1893 Chicago World's Fair, which instituted "Conscience Joints." This name stemmed from the practice of having the customers itemize their own bills. The cafeteria concept was introduced to such a wide audience in this arena that cafeterias began opening in scattered locations throughout the nation.

On the origins of fast food

The last element in the "revolution" was the development of a new menu which lent itself to the needs of this new genre of food service. The basic menu items must be tasty while appealing to everyone. Or, more importantly, they must offend as few as possible. These culinary delights must also have a good inherent profit margin. The ingredients must be easy to obtain. Finally, they must be so simple to prepare that the most ill prepared neophyte chef is able to cook them with virtually no training, interest, or innate ability. The hamburger, the hot dog, the milk shake, french fries, and the pizza met these requirements, and all appeared for the first time in America at about the same time.

Little is known about the real origins of the food items that powered the fast-food revolution. There are several "true" stories about the origin of each. The term "hamburger" may derive from the German city of Hamburg where pounded beefsteak was served in the nineteenth century, although even that bit of information is far from certain. The first apparent use of the term "hamburger steak" was at Delmonico's restaurant on Pearl Street in 1834 (Fig. 1.5). The later date of 1884 for a newspaper reference in Boston is also often used as the first occurrence of this term. Other writers claim, however, that these early references describe pounded beefsteak, rather than ground meat. These sources claim that the earliest reference for a ground-meat patty is 1902.

The origin of the hamburger sandwich is even more controversial. The best-known claim is Billy Ingram's assertion that his partner Walter Anderson created the modern hamburger by searing ground meat on an iron griddle for a sandwich in 1916 in Wichita, Kansas. This new food item was later used as the cornerstone menu item of the partners' White Castle hamburger chain. Louis' Lunch of New Haven, Connecticut, is also cited as the home of the hamburger at a somewhat earlier date. Additional scattered references to ground beef sandwiches are also found in the Midwest in the first decades of the twentieth century. Clearly, there is no definitive answer to this question. We can infer, however, that the hamburger sandwich probably evolved independently throughout the country in the first or second decade of the twentieth century. The plethora of regional names for this food, including "hamburg," "hamburger," and "burger," and from the numerous regional methods of preparation ranging from grilling to frying, from serving it on plain bread to serving it on buns, and from cooking it plain or adding onions and other vegetables, tend to support this belief. The cheeseburger developed almost simultaneously with the hamburger. The gourmet burger also apparently has been around for many years; the Hamburg

Heaven chain in 1956, for example, featured Heavenly Hamburgs, Wine Hamburgs, and Tartar Sandwiches (raw steak, raw egg, and onion).

The hot dog's origins are just as confused. Street vendors in Providence and many other industrial cities served frankfurters on bread as early as the 1860s. The date of development of the distinguishing concept of using a specially designed bun is unknown, but the term "hot dog" apparently originated in 1906 from cartoons drawn by a T. A. Dorgan, a Hearst sports columnist. The *Oxford English Dictionary* dates the term even earlier at 1900. Clearly, New York was the early center of this food, although versions of it were found throughout the industrial northeast at about the same time. Unrelated local terms for this food abound and include "hot dog," "frankfurters," "frank," "wiener," "wienie," "dog," "coney," and "red hot," suggesting that this food probably appared in widely scattered locations, with only limited reference to any center of innovation.

The pizza apparently originated in Naples, Italy, but, as any traveling American will attest, the European version of this standard dish bears faint resemblance to what is generally served in this country. Pizza had long been a staple food in Italian homes throughout the late nineteenth century, but was always limited in distribution because of the requirements of special ovens. Home pizza was served and continued to be served in Italian–American homes long before the first commercial examples appeared.

The first pizzeria was opened in New York City in 1888. Gennaro Lombardi also opened one on Spring Street in 1905. Both are credited with the innovation. New York was the most important early center of the pizza concept, but it spread rapidly throughout the northeast into the areas where large numbers of Italians were found. There are a number of varieties of American pizzas, including the standard New York (Neapolitan) thin crust style, the thicker crusted Sicilian, and the Chicago version cooked in a skillet and created in 1947.

Possibly the most interesting element of the pizza parlor revolution was that all of the major early national chains started in small Midwestern cities, well away from significant centers of Italian population. Pizza Hut (Wichita, Kansas), Godfather's (Omaha, Nebraska), and Mazzio's (Wichita, Kansas) come to us from the depths of the Midwest, where traditional American foods generally reign without competition. Even the later entries, such as Domino's, Little

Caesar's, and Pizza Inn, developed far from the hearth of this quite distinctive food.

Little is known about the origins of the French fry other than it obviously has little to do with France. French-fried potatoes first appeared as early as 1894, although it was not until the post World War II era that this food really took on its current popularity. Interestingly, the first national notice of the McDonald brothers drive-in in San Bernardino, California, came in the form of a two-page advertisement by Primex shortening telling of their small drive-in which sold 30,000 orders of french fries a month (using Primex, of course), in *American Restaurant* magazine in May 1952.

Restaurants and cities

The Industrial Revolution increasingly dominated American life in the late nineteenth century and is largely responsible for the restaurant as we know it today. Set hours, greater and greater distances between workers' homes and their jobs, and increasingly higher concentrations of hungry potential patrons contributed to the explosion of restaurants after 1880. This revolution, however, must be viewed in context. There were 33,844 restaurant keepers in 1880, only slightly more than the numbers of journalists and livery stable keepers (Fig. 5).

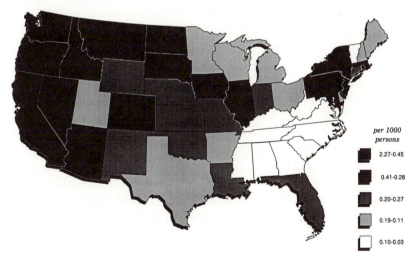

per 1000 persons

2.27–0.45

0.41–0.28

0.20–0.27

0.19–0.11

0.10–0.03

Figure 5. American restaurant keepers, 1879 (US Census, 1880)

The pattern of restaurants began assuming a more modern look during this period, although the dependence upon public transportation and the lack of a "restaurant" tradition among most Americans kept most of them concentrated in the central business district. Providence's twenty-three restaurants in 1889 well illustrates the point. Almost all were highly clustered within a few city blocks of the business or factory districts. Interestingly, many of the addresses occupied in 1889 are still occupied by restaurants a hundred years later in the 1980s, although not necessarily continuously or under related management. Providence appears to be highly under-restauranted in the 1880s, but it must be recalled that the previously discussed lunch-wagons roamed the streets throughout the nights and into the morning hours for the breakfast trade without being tabulated by the directories of the period.

Oklahoma City had far more restaurants per capita during this period than Providence, although its overall concentration of restaurants within the central business district mirrored that of Providence. Ten restaurants were tabulated in 1894 and fifteen in 1896. Five of the restaurants survived the two-year period and two more were replaced by others when a new building was placed on the site. Six of the latter year were in association with hotels, two were boarding houses serving meals, and two were lunchrooms. The Far West had the most restaurants per person then, as now.

Ethnic restaurants were also beginning to appear during this period. Most western cities had one or more Chinese restaurants, including the not so western Dubuque, Iowa. Chinese restaurants were found in East Coast cities, but in far fewer numbers. French restaurants and French restaurant proprietors were found throughout the nation from San Francisco to Boston, while German, Viennese, and Italian restaurants were also beginning to appear. Many of the new emigrants from southern Europe came from traditions where alcohol and food were regularly consumed away from the home, which created further markets for exotic foods.

More typical of America was Buffalo, New York. In 1926 the Restaurant Association of America held its annual convention in Buffalo and published a map of the locations and character of the restaurants near the hotel as encouragement for potential conventioneers. Thirty-five restaurants were listed, including ten cafeterias, seven lunchrooms, four sandwich shops, three coffee shops, and eleven full-service restaurants. Of the latter, two each specialized in seafood and German cuisine, one featured Spanish cuisine, and one, rotisserie chicken and turkey. Possibly of greater interest was the structure of these places. A number of the "restaurants" featured several kinds of service—full-service, cafeteria, and sandwiches. Three of the remaining were lunchrooms and two were cafeterias. All of the sandwich shops were associated with chain operations. The remaining 69 percent were independently operated.

Little had changed in the restaurant trade for most Americans by this time. Life in Dubuque, Oklahoma City, and Johnstown, Pennsylvania, was much like it had been a century before. Hotels, boarding houses, and taverns continued to provide the vast majority of the food service in the smaller places. Lunchrooms and occasionally even Chinese restaurants were entering the smaller communities of America, but continuity was still the order of the day. Restaurant dining was an unknown experience for most Americans as late as 1900. While restaurants were common in the larger cities, there were only 200 restaurants tabulated for the entire state of Mississippi in the 1900 Census.

The foundations for the current restaurant landscape were in place by World War I, however. Change was sweeping out from the cities, and it is easy to select examples of sophisticated restaurants in such places as New York and Chicago. One can easily cite Delmonico's, which served some of the most exquisite meals in American culinary history, as proof of the quality of the restaurants of the period, but it must be remembered that it was only one restaurant of hundreds in that city.

The original Krystal in Chattanooga, Tennessee, occupied a classic "white box" location in the corner of a central city parking lot. Krystal operates a store at this location to this day. (Krystal Company)

3

Castles and queens

THE WHITE CASTLE SYSTEM exemplified the leading edge of the industry at the end of World War I; Dairy Queen exemplified it twenty years later at the beginning of World War II. This was not a period of great innovation and only minor technological improvements occurred in the industry between 1919 and 1939. What changed was the role that the industry played in daily American life. How it changed was through an elaboration of old themes to create new products that were successfully marketed throughout the nation. The result was the transformation of a minor retail activity into a major part of American life.

The restaurant revolution was not preordained. It was not destined to occur at this time, nor was this the only possible outcome of the social forces that were reshaping American life during this period. American society could easily have developed other paths to meet the needs for an increasingly agglomerated society. Food companies could have developed other solutions for feeding the growing masses. Yet, the revolution did take place, and while this period appears prosaic on the outside, it actually served as the critical bridge between the old way of doing business and the new. The resultant growth was so astounding that even the writers of the 1939 Census of Business commented:

Despite the diversion of nearly 2 billion dollars of consumer purchases into drinking places and liquor stores which did not exist in 1929, sales in restaurants and other eating places were greater in 1939 than in 1929, and the number of such places was 26 percent greater.

The 1920s and 1930s saw the restaurant evolve from a luxury to a necessity. The new outlook was reflected in a variety of structural changes in the industry, and was marked by a lack of general innovation. The chain restaurant began to be transformed from a group of two or three stores under the same management to a complete organism of interchangeable parts which could be and were duplicated by the hundreds. Fast-food evolved from a menu item to a restaurant theme. The drive-in evolved from a curiosity to a significant business form in which the automobile became not only a means of transportation to the dining room, but the dining room itself.

The chain restaurant was one of the most important instruments in creating this new order. Single-city chains were especially common during this period, and most cities had one or more local restaurants with multiple outlets. The Horn & Hardart Automats of Philadelphia and New York City are the best known of these smaller operations, but a wide variety of dining concepts and groups have their origins in the 1920s and 1930s. The importance of chain restaurants, however, should not be overemphasized. Although some of the nation's most famous chains were created during this period, there were only about 2,400 chain restaurants in the nation in 1929 and slightly less

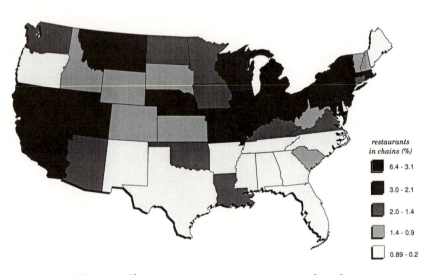

restaurants
in chains (%)

■ 6.4 - 3.1

■ 3.0 - 2.1

■ 2.0 - 1.4

□ 1.4 - 0.9

□ 0.89 - 0.2

Figure 6. Chain restaurants as a percentage of total
restaurants (by state) 1939. (Census of Business)

than 3,000 in 1939 (Fig. 6). More importantly, virtually all of the numerical growth took place among sectional and national chain operations.

The development of Howard Johnson's well exemplifies the evolution of these operations. Johnson started his career in the restaurant business by taking over a struggling news-stand–soda fountain in Wollaston, Massachusetts, with a borrowed $500 in 1925. The soda fountain sold three flavors of commercial ice cream which Johnson soon replaced with his own high-butterfat homemade product. Business boomed and he added hamburgers and hot dogs to the menu of his original store, as well as selling his ice cream at stands around Boston. In 1935 he was approached by a friend with property on Cape Cod about expansion into that area. It was soon clear, however, that Johnson did not have sufficient funds to build the restaurant. So he persuaded his friend to build and operate the new restaurant featuring his products. The franchise concept was successful beyond Johnson's wildest dreams, and he opened 39 more restaurants in 1936, 20 in 1937, 12 in 1938, and 14 in 1939. In 1940 he received the franchise to provide food service to the brand new Pennsylvania turnpike, and by 1941 his empire of more than 150 restaurants stretched from Florida to New England.

Sectional and national chains seemed to be appearing in every part of the nation during this period and included such famous names as A & W Root Beer in Lodi (later Sacramento), California, Bob's Big Boy in Los Angeles, the first Dairy Queen in Kankakee, Illinois, and White Castle, first in Wichita, Kansas, and later in Columbus, Ohio, and Marriott in Washington DC, to name a few. The broad distribution of these operations and their longevity have made them appear more prominent than their actual numbers warrant; in 1939, only about 4 percent of the almost 100,000 restaurants with table service were chain operations.

The geography of the revolution is in many respects its most confounding aspect. Flint, Michigan, with less than a single sit-down restaurant per 1,000 population, had the highest ratio of chain to independent restaurants in the nation for cities over 100,000 in 1929 (Fig. 7). Other leading chain cities included Boston, Buffalo, Utica, Rochester, Pittsburgh, Milwaukee, and Providence. The least chained cities during this period were in the West (noted mostly for spawning chain restaurant concepts today), the American manufacturing belt, and the South. Much of the explanation of this

Figure 7. Chain restaurants as a proportion of all eating places in major cities, 1939 (Census of Business)

pattern must lie in the types of restaurants that were commonly in chains during this period: lunchrooms, cafeterias, and hamburger stands.

Lunchrooms

Lunchroom and the cafeteria operators perceived the advantages of chain operation early and were the truest examples of modern chains at that time. While most lunchrooms and cafeterias during this period were independently operated, some significant chains did develop. These organizations laid the foundation for later chain-store development by demonstrating the importance of synergy and the interchangeability of consumer loyalty by developing multi-store units which appeared to be clones, rather than unique units. Through the maintenance of quality control, these stores were assured a long-standing consumer loyalty, a problem that continually plagued the diners of this period. Though the earlier diners had maintained visual integrity, they were unrelated otherwise, and food quality, cleanliness, and prices varied widely from unit to unit.

A number of large single-city or city-cluster lunchroom chains developed soon after the turn of the century. The largest included John R. Thompson's 104-unit chain in Chicago and surrounding

cities, the Baltimore Dairy Lunch with more than 100 stores, Childs'
Unique Dairy Lunch of New York City with 86 units in 1920, and
Kelsey's Waldorf Lunch, operating 75 units in cities extending from
Boston to Buffalo to Philadelphia.

The growth of the Bickford chain, one of the most dynamic of the
period, well illustrates the fluidity of these chains. The names,
numbers, and ownerships of these lunchroom chains, however, was
in a constant state of flux. The evolution of the Bickford organization,
one of the most dynamic of the period, well illustrates the fluidity of
the management and store associations. Young Bickford first entered
the restaurant industry in about 1902 when Harry Kelsey hired him to
work in the first Waldorf Restaurant in Springfield, Massachusetts.
He was paid $10 a week for working seven twelve-hour days. About
1906 Bickford was hired to manage Waldorf Lunches in Buffalo. He
did so well at this that he was quickly moved by the company, first to
Providence and later to Boston. He soon changed companies,
however, to manage stores for the growing Capitol Lunch System in
New York City. He moved again in 1909 to Washington to manage a
unit of the White House Lunch chain, where he was offered an
opportunity to buy into the business.

Bickford soon acquired two partners and set about building a chain
of lunch counters in Washington. By 1911 they owned six stores, but
on January 1, 1912, Bickford sold out to his partners for $25,000 and
moved to Philadelphia to work as a manager of that city's Waldorf
restaurants. In June 1912 he moved to Boston and invested his money
in the Waldorf system.

In succeeding years Bickford and his various associates assembled
chains of restaurants extending from San Francisco to Boston. They
purchased the Capitol group of five restaurants of New York City
in 1921, the Kinney–Kelley and Hartford Lunch chains in 1924,
and the White Lunch System on the West Coast. Bickford changed
the White Lunch System's name to Foster's and built a West
Coast chain of restaurants ranging in quality from simple family
cafeterias to San Francisco's world famous Cliff House. The company also acquired the Hayes Lunch System of Boston in the same
year, which came to be known as the Hayes–Bickford Lunch System.
His son started a small chain in New York which became a part of
the parent company in 1944. Bickford's again began expanding
in the 1950s with the purchase of M & M Cafeterias in Miami and
Oliver restaurants in Pittsburgh. The company entered industrial

The many sandwich shops of the 1920s and 1930s were often included in census lunchroom statistics. (Special Collections, Georgia State University Library)

food service in 1952. By 1956 Bickford's operated 59 restaurants in New York City, 46 in the San Francisco Bay area, 19 in greater Boston, and a variety of real estate, office buildings, and smaller activities in those cities and elsewhere. Bickford's may have been the most diverse restaurant empire of the period, but it was hardly unique.

Most lunchrooms were independently operated, however, and

chain operations were the exception, rather than the rule. Lunch-rooms were also relatively important only in the South and on the West Coast in the 1920s and 1930s–the least chained regions during this period (Fig. 8). Indeed, relatively speaking, lunchrooms were not a significant element of the general restaurant landscape even in the home cities of the nation's largest lunchroom chains. New York, Boston, Washington, Philadelphia, and Chicago all had fewer than average of this restaurant type, in spite of the presence of the previously mentioned chains.

Figure 8. Lunchrooms as a proportion of all restaurants with table service, 1929 (Census of Business)

Cafeterias

It is somewhat more difficult to obtain a clear image of the evolution of the cafeteria. The tendency for many of these stores to be operated by non-profit organizations or as tied company operations makes their numbers and locations difficult to determine. The largest number of them were operated independently, though we tend to think of them primarily as chain-store operations. Certainly the Childs group in New York was the earliest chain, followed by the Boos Brothers of Los Angeles in 1906. The 1920s was the greatest period of development for these chains, and several of the nation's

Figure 9. Numbers of cafeterias (by city), 1929 (Census of Business)

largest chains—Bishop's Cafeteria's of Waterloo, Iowa, S & W of Charlotte, North Carolina, and Morrison's of Mobile, Alabama—were founded in 1920, following the somewhat earlier Forum chain of Kansas City, Missouri, in 1918. Famous chains notwithstanding, the distribution of cafeterias in 1929 followed the urban hierarchy almost totally (Fig. 9). New York City had 786 cafeterias in that year, followed by Chicago with 195, then Boston, Washington, Detroit, and Philadelphia.

The commercial cafeteria has largely fallen out of favor today and is common only in the South and Midwest. Severl chains developed in the post-war era, most notably Piccadilly of Baton Rouge and Furr's of San Antonio, but only in the heartland of the restaurant's popularity. Many excuses for the national demise of the restaurant form have been given, including the death of inner-city dining and the non-automobile orientation of their operation. However, the growth of the Sunbelt chains and the presence of a Los Angeles cafeteria as one of the nation's top grossing independent restaurants raises serious doubts about those rationalizations.

The cafeteria is still alive and thriving in the South and the Midwest (Fig. 10). The after-church crowds on Sundays and the before-service crowds for Wednesday prayer meetings fill many a southern cafeteria to overflowing. Similarly, the cafeteria still thrives in those areas of the Midwest where the small-town ethic is still alive

Piccadilly and its competitors are increasingly locating new stores on Hamburger Alleys.

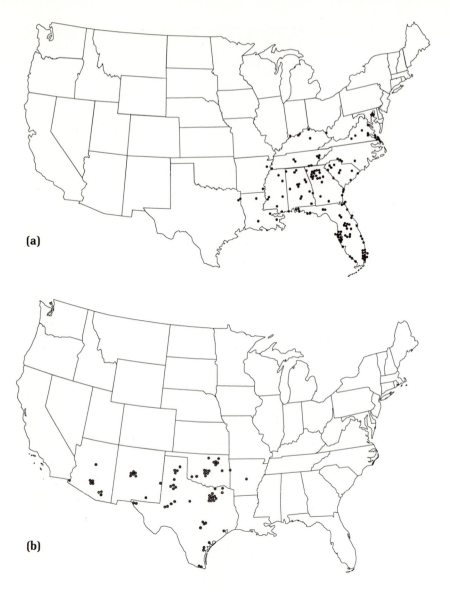

(a)

(b)

Figure 10. Major chain cafeterias, 1978–88.
(a) Morrisons, 1978   (b) Furr's and Bishop's, 1987

(c) Lubys, 1988   (d) Piccadilly, 1978.

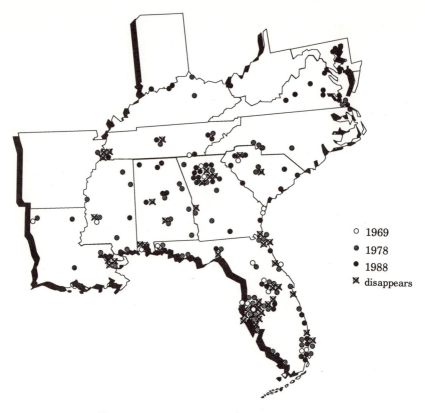

Figure 11. Morrison's cafeterias, 1966–88

and well. These are not institutional places bringing back memories of the army, school dorms, and the factory; rather, they are places specializing in wholesome, traditional body food. Southern and Midwestern cafeterias are making ˊsurprising comebacks today by catering to mature couples. Morrison's, Piccadilly, Furr's, and Forum have all begun successful aggressive expansion campaigns in the past few years (Fig. 11). They are popping up among the McDonalds of the Hamburger Alleys, in malls and their environs, and even in staid residential shopping centers in small towns and large cities alike. The cafeteria's doomsayers may have to wait a while longer, for this venerable institution may yet have a future.

Hamburger stands

The true progenitor of the contemporary fast-food store was probably Walter Anderson of Wichita, Kansas. Anderson opened a diner in a remodeled streetcar in 1916 specializing in hamburgers. This first store was soon joined by two more in 1920. Edgar "Billy" Ingram joined the growing chain in 1921, when Anderson was unable to acquire a lease in his own name on a fourth location. The duo decided to name the new restaurant "White Castle". The new partnership was exceedingly successful and the business expanded rapidly over the next few years.

Surprisingly, the White Castle chain was able to establish a national identity with less than 200 locations located in only a handful of cities (Fig. 12). The chain's distinctive building, along with its "new" hamburger sandwich and consistent quality, seems to have attracted competitors almost as quickly as customers. Beginning with White Tower in Milwaukee in 1926, the competitors appeared across the central South like mushrooms after a storm (Fig. 13). The Louisville-based Little Tavern chain appeared in 1927, to be quickly followed by the White Tavern Shoppes (1929) of Shelbyville, Tennessee, the Toddle Houses in Houston, Krystal in Chattanooga, Dobbs-Hull Houses in Memphis, White Huts in Toledo, and more. Interestingly, the competitors' headquarters were concentrated in a comparatively narrow band across the Midwest as they spread their stores relentlessly toward the East Coast.

The White Tower chain was the most blatant copy of the White Castle concept. This chain expanded rapidly from its Milwaukee base until it ran into the growing White Castle System in Detroit in 1930. The ensuing court battle over copyright infringements and unfair trade practices apparently distracted both companies from keeping up with their fast growing competitors. Both were drained by their lengthy battle, and neither was as dynamic after the court case as it had been previously.

The White Tower chain well illustrates the expansion of a typical chain of this type and the dynamic nature of the industry during this period (Fig. 14). Beginning in Milwaukee, the earliest branches were built in the industrial cities nearest to their home base. The Midwest has always poorly supported the restaurant trade, however, and it soon became clear to management that unit sales and profits increased as they expanded eastward.

Figure 12. White Castle cities, by year established, 1916–50

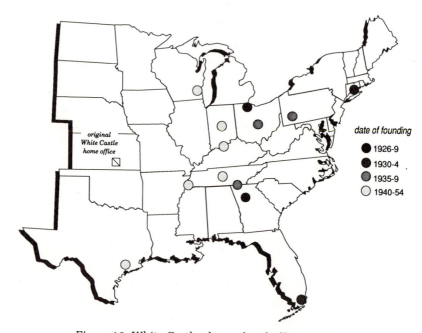

Figure 13. White Castle clones: head offices, 1926–54

date of
founding

● 1926-9
● 1930-4
◉ 1935-9
◎ 1940-50
○ 1951-

Figure 14. White Tower locations, by year established

White Tower

Pittsburgh is a dreary place on a rainy, Sunday morning in spring. The skies are an endless grey, the wetness is impenetrable, the streets bristle with chuck holes, broken pavement, and frost-heaved cobblestones. Suddenly I was greeted by an old friend that I had never met. White Tower! I couldn't believe it. I had read of these mystical places, I had seen pictures of them, and here stood one in full operation. It was like an anachronism amid this world of parking lots and decaying buildings.

Parking in the lot at the corner, I walked back to my treasure. Two ladies of the night guarded the door. They seemed to be resigned to the fact that no one would come along on this quiet Sunday morning, but they looked at me hopefully. Why else would anyone be in this place at this time of day? I smiled and they perked up, and then they slumped back into resignation as I hurried on through the door with a cheerful "Howdy, ma'am."

There were only three customers at the stools along the short bar at this hour. A couple of street people dressed in grimy, olive army fatigues nursed cups of coffee at the end of the counter. It was clear that their coffee was more than a casual drink because they hunched their shoulders protectively when I entered, as if to protect their cups from stray marauders. A lady of indeterminate age and garish dress sat on a stool nearby. She glanced up expectantly, but soon realized that I was just some kind of weird slumming suburbanite and started to stare again into the depths of her empty coffee cup.

A tired waitress ambled over to my end of the counter. It was too early for a "slider," so I ordered coffee.

"That all?" she asked. She was beginning to wonder why this alien had invaded her comfortable surroundings.

"No, give me scrambled eggs too," I added, ignoring my last cholesterol count.

The limpid coffee arrived and I was left to muse in peace. I felt I had stepped into a time warp. The white, enameled steel walls, the 1930ish signs, the grimy grill exuded a sense of simpler times in other places.

"If someone could just figure out how to package this," I thought, "they could make a million. Johnny Rockets, you tepid California clone, watch out! Here comes the real thing." But then, on reflection, maybe the world wasn't ready for the real thing. David Lowenthal suggested many years ago that Americans prefer Walt Disney's New Orleans to the real thing because it is clean, shiny, and safely plastic. Maybe he had a point.

The eggs arrived with a minimum of flourish and I toyed with them for a while. Like the restaurant, they looked like something left over from the 1920s. It was slowly dawning on me why these places were disappearing.

White Towers were often located on leased sites that could be vacated by moving the building with a few weeks' notice. (Library of Congress)

Paying the check and leaving too much tip, I tried to saunter past the sentries into the rain and slush to my car. One had disappeared. Left disappointed, I thought. But as I stepped into the parking lot my suburban naivete was shattered by the sight of a gently swaying pick-up truck parked in the far corner of the lot. Well, maybe there was business on quiet Sunday mornings for some.

White Tower moved its corporate headquarters to Pittsburgh in 1930 to better manage its growing eastern empire; White Castle soon followed by moving from Wichita to Columbus, Ohio. Both companies quickly saw the opportunities in the eastern cities and jumped from their midwestern focus to the Atlantic Coast in the 1930s to establish stores in the major industrial cities. The larger and more aggressive White Tower quickly spread to more cities to control these markets, while White Castle tended to concentrate its efforts in a few cities. Half-hearted attempts to colonize the suburbs in the eastern cities sapped the strength of both companies, as did the continuing court case during the 1930s. World War II had a less negative impact on these companies than on most. Both had established manufacturing divisions to build the white enameled steel panels of their buildings during the 1930s, and while many restaurant chains went bankrupt or simply closed during the war, these companies concentrated on their building materials divisions. Neither was able effectively to cash in on the post-war restaurant boom, however. White Castle remains in Columbus, Ohio, having become virtually an American institution. It remains one of the nation's top fifty chains and continues to seek a place on Hamburger Alley. White Tower, as the Tombrock Corporation, still occupies the same unimposing headquarters building that it purchased in Stamford, Connecticut, in 1940 and has closed virtually all of its White Tower stores.

The White Castle concept was the right restaurant for the right time. The restaurants were oriented to the factory workers traveling on public transportation to inner-city factories. The vast majority of the locations remained in the middle city and did well until the post-war suburban movement created a new dining perspective. Attempts to suburbanize the chain began as early as the mid-1930s in New Jersey and elsewhere. Although some of these remain, the company generally has been unsuccessful in making the transition to an automobile-dominated world.

White Castle still operates many of its early locations in New Jersey, including this suburban store along US 1.

The argument that the "white box" concept had run its course to be replaced by the more modern fast-food chains is unconvincing. The Waffle House chain, founded in 1965, has been quite successful; it has expanded throughout the southeastern United States long after the earlier "white box" stores were supposedly beyond hope. Also it is not clear why these simple low-overhead stores were not suited for life in the suburbs. Identification with the dirty, factory-ridden inner-city, and an inability to design and operate stores that appealed to the automobile-oriented suburbanites, are generally cited as the major factors underlying their decline. These are slick and logical explanations, but they may be too simplistic because the managements of these companies have demonstrated repeatedly that they had both the ability and the interest to compete successfully in the suburban market. White Tower, for example, was an early franchisee of the Burger King Corporation and it successfully operated these automobile-oriented fast-food stores for many years. Similarly, Krystal, one of the many clones of these companies, has operated one of the largest chains of Wendy's franchises, through its associated Po Folks, for many years (Fig. 15).

Krystal began in 1932 when Rody Davenport Jr travelled to Columbus, Ohio, to look over a new restaurant there which had become the talk of the nation. He returned home a few days later convinced that the White Castle concept would work in Chattanooga. Busy with his hosiery manufacturing company, Davenport approached J. Glenn Sherrell, a teller for the First National Bank of Chattanooga, with the deal of a lifetime. Davenport would build the restaurant and make Sherrell a partner if Sherrell would operate the new venture. Sherrell accepted the offer and the company was founded.

The first Krystal was built at the corner of Seventh and Cherry in Chattanooga. Gordon Smith of Chattanooga designed the new restaurant building, which was more than faintly reminiscent of its progenitor in Columbus, Ohio. It was built of white porcelainized metal with a stainless steel interior. It measured only 10 feet by 25 feet and had ten stools, along the lines of its northern counterparts.

Quality was important to the venture from the outset. Davenport developed a creed pledging to provide a spotless store, good food, friendly service, and the lowest prices. The name came from Mrs Davenport. They were driving in the country one Sunday when they passed a home with a crystal ball in the front yard. Upon spying the ball, Mrs Davenport suggested that, since the partners felt cleanliness

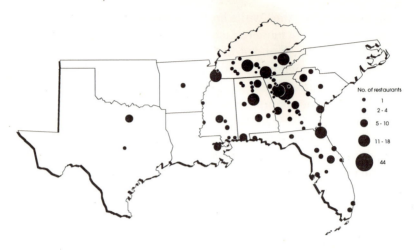

No. of restaurants
- 1
- 2 - 4
- 5 - 10
- 11 - 18
- 44

Figure 15. Krystal Restaurants, 1932–87 Note: Numbers refer to units established, and the total numbers may never have existed simultaneously

was the cornerstone of their business, they ought to name the new enterprise Crystal, as in "clean as a crystal." The spelling was changed to give the name a memory twist, and a crystal ball was incorporated into the restaurant building's design.

The store opened on October 24, 1932, when French Jenkins entered and ordered six "Krystals" and a cup of coffee. The meal cost thirty-five cents. The first Krystal menu was limited to coffee, homemade pies, breakfast, including eggs, toast, and waffles cooked to order, cold drinks, and of course the famous square hamburgers ("Krystals"). Business was astounding, even during the Depression. The second store was opened a few blocks away in February 1933. The third store was built in Atlanta in 1934, and expansion to Nashville followed in 1935.

Today the Krystal Company is one of the largest privately owned restaurant chains in the nation, with 233 stores and 8,000 employees. The company expanded carefully during its first fifty years and has remained in its southern homeland. On the eve of its fiftieth anniversary in 1981, the company began an aggressive expansion program which has pushed it into new markets.

Krystal thus represents a white box chain that has transcended the many problems that have plagued this genre. The company has continued to be successful with its original concept restaurants, has profitably operated a large franchise system founded by one of its successors, and has skillfully launched a new concept chain aimed at a future market.

The star in the west: the drive-in

The instrument of destruction of the "white box" revolution was apparently born in Dallas, Texas, in 1921, the same year that Anderson and Ingram created the White Castle System in nearby Wichita, Kansas. Instantly popular, the drive-in took almost twenty years to achieve its full potential. The first drive-in was opened by J. G. Kirby, a candy and tobacoo wholesaler. It took the form of the Pig Stand, a barbecue place featuring barbecue pork sandwiches on the Dallas–Fort Worth highway in September 1921. The chain was most popular in Texas and adjacent states, although at one point it had a bi-coastal distribution. Kirby did not have the field to himself for long, however, and by 1923 A & W Root Beer had opened its first drive-in location in Sacramento, California. A & W well exemplifies this segment of the industry. The chain was formed in 1919 when Roy Allen bought a walk-up root beer stand in Lodi, California. Three years later he formed a partnership with Frank Wright and the chain was renamed A & W. The company set out on a national franchise campaign, and root beer stands were soon appearing throughout the nation, especially in the Far West.

J. Willard Marriott became a steady customer of the Salt Lake City store of the A & W chain in the summer of 1926 with his future wife Allie. His cousin Sherman had the franchise for Fort Wayne, Indiana, and was quite enthusiastic about the future of this new chain of soft-drink stands. Marriott began researching the Salt Lake store and discovered that it sold an average of 5,000 mugs of nickel root beer on summer days. It grossed $7,500 a month during that period. This was more than sufficient for operators to "retire" during the remainder of the year. By March he had decided to purchase the franchises for Washington DC, Baltimore, and Richmond, Virginia, in partnership with Hugh Colton, for $1,000. The new company's entire capitalization was $6,000, mostly borrowed.

Ignoring the seemingly obvious tourist locations downtown, the two partners sublet an eight-foot frontage portion of a bakery on Fourteenth Street NW, located in a shopping center and surrounded by apartments and residential areas. It was a challenge to set up the required equipment including a 400-foot aluminium cooling coil, carbonating machine, cooling vats for the mugs, nine stools, a counter and storage space for the mugs, root beer concentrate, and washing facilities. When the partners ran into problems assembling their equipment in the cramped space, another franchisee was sent from Terre Haute to assist them.

They opened on May 20, 1927, after distributing 1,300 coupons for free mugs of root beer. The crowds were immense on this day as people sought news about Lindburgh's flight across the Atlantic. Marriott met Lindbergh years later and thanked him for his assistance in getting his restaurant chain started by creating such large street crowds on his first day of business. Within months, the partnership began making arrangements to open a second store on Ninth Street, and the empire was set in motion.

Two points should be noted from this description. First, the export of new restaurant ideas from California is neither new nor confined to simple franchising, as can be seen in the beginnings of the Marriott empire. Similar examples are common. For example, the Pig & Whistle chain began when Harold Hagan, a sign salesman, noticed a restaurant calling itself the Pig & Whistle while visiting Los Angeles in 1924. He was so taken with the concept that he founded a restaurant with the same name upon returning to Allentown, Pennsylvania. Later that year, on a visit to relatives in Atlanta, he established several more locations in that city on a whim. A few months later he received a call from his father, who told him, "You better get on down here. You got a real thing going with these places." The Pig & Whistle chain eventually expanded into Texas and the West, featuring drive-in service and what was to be the traditional hamburger fast-food fare of the future. This bi-coastal movement of ideas was furthered by such trade magazines as *American Restaurant*, which kept the professionals as informed then as they are today about current successful concepts and equipment.

Secondly, the drive-in concept itself was not the key to the significance of what was to take place in the future. Certainly eating in the automobile was a novelty, but, as A & W demonstrated with their curb and walk-up service, other factors contributed to the rise of these places. The older chains, such as White Castle, tended to smell of old grease and to be hot and sticky inside during much of the year.

The ebullience of this period is well mirrored in this photograph of
two Dairy Queen operators in Long Island in the 1950s.
(FSA, Library of Congress)

Furthermore, the new A & Ws, Pig & Whistles, and Dairy Queens
were located not in the inner city to serve people at work, but in the
residential neighborhoods where they were associated with pleasure.
Even Marriott's downtown Hot Shoppes were located in residential
rather than work-related sites. These new stores targeted the discretionary food dollar, not the work dollar. They represented
pleasure, not a necessary evil. This pattern continues today as the
public seemingly resents the institutional cafeteria and sandwich
room, but will go out of its way to consume virtually the same cuisine
offered in an atmosphere associated with pleasure. World War II
found Americans still flocking to little "white boxes" along the road
to fulfill their dining pleasures, but the signs now read Dairy Queen,
not White Castle.

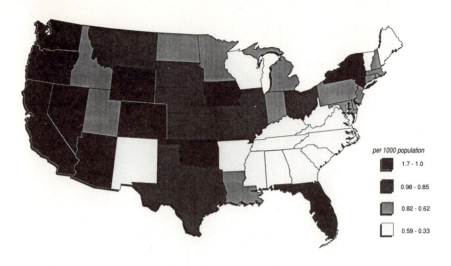

per 1000 population

■ 1.7 - 1.0

■ 0.98 - 0.85

■ 0.82 - 0.62

□ 0.59 - 0.33

Figure 16. Restaurant workers per 1,000 population, 1920 (14th Census of the United States)

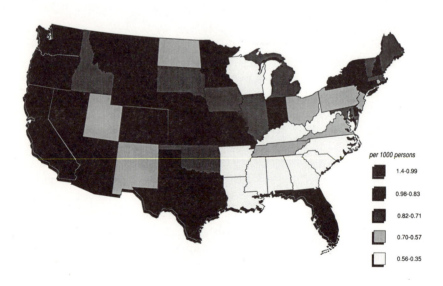

per 1000 persons

■ 1.4-0.99

■ 0.98-0.83

■ 0.82-0.71

■ 0.70-0.57

□ 0.56-0.35

Figure 17. American restaurants per 1,000 persons, 1939 (Census of Business)

Them that has, gets

The 1920s and 1930s may have been a period of phenomenal growth for this industry, in terms of both numbers and imagery, but the relative distribution of restaurants changed very little. The largest concentration of restaurant workers was on the West Coast in 1920, and the largest number of restaurants remained there in 1939 (Figs. 16 & 17). The basis of this pattern is clear: Western distances and proclivity for travel have always meant that Westerners were more likely to be away from home at mealtime than the more tied factory and farmworkers of the East. Western towns also tend to be small, with limited stocks of many retail items. For example, portions of California's Central Valley operated as a dispersed retail center with comparatively sophisticated retail stocks, but these were scattered among several communities. It is also an old western tradition to expect, even to look forward to, traveling to the nearest large city once or twice a year to purchase more exotic items and enjoy the other amenities. These needs also created a greater demand in this region for dining away from home than was typical of other areas.

The regionality of dining out becomes even more clear when cities, rather than states, are examined (Fig. 18). The most intense rest-

Figure 18. Metropolitan restaurants, with table service, 1929
(Census of Business)

aurant presence in 1929 was centered in the nation's most important ports (New York and New Orleans), the Midwestern wholesale/retail centers (Omaha, Oklahoma City, Memphis, and Wichita), and the West Coast. The West stands out regionally as having the highest density of restaurants in the nation, the only exceptions being Salt Lake City, a dominantly Mormon community (which incidentally did have large numbers of lunch counters and drink stands) and Tacoma, a mill town.

The large communities which were least well served at this time were concentrated in the traditional mill town area of the Northeast, especially New England and environs. Fall River, Massachusetts, had less than a half a restaurant per 1,000 people in 1929, while nearby New York City had more than five and a half. Even today, these industrial towns have the fewest sit-down restaurants, the fewest fast-food chain restaurants, and some of the lowest patronage levels of the few restaurants found here. These are meat-and-potato communities with male-dominant households. Home menus tend to be simple and straightforward, oriented toward plain heavy meat dishes, boiled or mashed potatoes, and a minimum of "rabbit" food. Further, the tradition-oriented male breadwinners are little interested in participating in away-from-home dining experiences, much less in grazing at some fabulous salad bar. Eating away from home is done grudgingly and always falls to those places that serve safe food. Beer gardens are safe, as are diners and Italian cafes. Chinese restaurants, McDonald's (until the grandchildren learn to say Ronald McDonald), and salad bars are immediately suspect. The result is a paucity of restaurants even today and little variety among those that do exist.

This regionality of the restaurant distributions changed little during the 1930s. By 1939 the West's high per capita rates had increased, the Midwest rates continued to be mixed depending on the personality of the community, and the Northeast had far fewer restaurants than expected outside of a few suburban communities. It is especially interesting that some of the nation's most famous restaurant chains began in, or migrated toward, the Northeast during this period, including Howard Johnson's from Quincy, Massachusetts, White Tower from Milwaukee to Pittsburgh and thence to Stamford, Connecticut, and Friendly's Ice Cream.

Gourmet restaurants, or even pseudo attempts to create such places, were still beyond the ability of most operators during this period, and few existed beyond a show place or two in the larger regional centers. The explosion of such places had to wait until the development of flash freezing and microwave technology, which allowed the preparation of more complex food items by "chefs" with limited training and experience.

Crowds flocked to the Hamburger Handout and other walk-up hamburger
stands during the 1950s. (Jim Collins, Collins Foods)

4

America transformed

AMERICA COMPLETED THE dramatic transformation from a small-town, family-oriented culture to an individualistic urban–industrial society soon after World War II. The pervasive changes accompanying this transition so altered daily life that the very fabric of the social order was forever altered for virtually all Americans. The nature of almost all basic human drives—from shelter to sex roles and communication to diet—were so transfigured by these changes that any discussion of their causes soon becomes lost in the wealth of conflicting theories. On the other hand, the effects of these changes on the way we arrange our lives have been so far-reaching that they have permeated almost every corner of the landscape. We live differently; we work differently; we have different relationships between the sexes; we eat differently. Our landscape too has been dramatically transformed, and nowhere more than in the rise of the restaurant as a symbol of this new landscape and the society that created it.

French Fries

An old woman in a straight-back chair holding a McDonald's cup. She is surrounded by several bundles of newspapers. She wears thick glasses that distort her eyes to the viewer.

Anna Mae: "If I had one wish in my life, why I'd like to live in McDonald's. Right there in the restaurant
"I like the young people workin' there. Like a team of fine young horses when I was growin' up. All smilin'. Tell you what I really like

though is the plastic. God gave us plastic so that there wouldn't be no stains on his world. See, in the human world of the earth it all gets scratched, stained, tore up, faded down. Loses its shine. All of it does. In time. Well, God he gave us the idea of plastic so we'd know what the everlasting really was. See, if there's plastic then there's surely eternity. It's God's hint.

"You ever watch folks when they come into McDonald's? They always speed up, almost run the last few steps. You see if they don't. Old Dobbin with the barn in sight. They know it's safe there and it ain't safe outside. Now it ain't safe outside and you know it.

". . . McDonald's. You ever see anybody die in a McDonald's? No sir. No way . . . Noooooooooo, you can't die in a McDonald's no matter how hard you try. It's the spices. Seals you safe in this life like it seals in the flavor. Yesssssss, yes!

"I asked Jerrell could I live there. See they close up around ten, and there ain't a thing goin' on in 'em till seven a.m. I'd just sit in those nice swingy chairs and lean forward. Rest my head on those cool, cool, smooth tables, sing me a hymn and sleep like a baby. Jarrell, he said he'd write him a letter up the chain of command and see would they let me. Oh, I got my bid in. Peaceful and clean.

"Sometimes I see it like the last of a movie. You know how they start the picture up real close and then back it off steady and far? Well, that's how I dream it. I'm living in McDonald's and it's real late at night and you see me up close, smiling, and then you see the whole McDonald's from the outside, lit up and friendly . . . I'm part of that light, part of something even bigger, something fixed and shiny . . . like plastic.

"I know. I know. It's just a dream . . . But you got to have a dream. It's our dreams make us what we are."

—BLACKOUT—

Jane Martin, Talking With . . .

Restaurants and the rhythm of American daily life

So much has been written about the American restaurant in the past twenty years that one is soon lost in the swirl of statistics and anecdotes. There are statistics that prove almost anything: the rise of restaurant sales, the changing interrelationships of the various restaurant types, new and renewed cuisines, architectural styles, locational preferences—are all documented endlessly. One is inevitably drawn to think in terms of the fast-food revolution, the franchising explosion, and the rise and fall of the seemingly endless numbers of chains, decors, and cuisines. All of these things are important, but they are not new. The first franchise operation in America was the Singer Sewing Machine Company prior to the Civil War; virtually all fast-food items developed during the late nineteenth century; new cuisines have been an integral part of American life since that first Thanksgiving dinner of Indian fare in the seventeenth century; while revolutionary designs are as old as Thomas Holme's plan of Philadelphia and L'Enfant's plan of Washington DC. One must conclude that these elements obscure rather than illuminate the changes taking place.

The dining experience and its role in the rhythm of daily life is at the center of this apparent cultural chaos. Everything else—the new chains, the new cuisines, the media hype—are the results of this redefinition of the rhythm of family life. The traditional role of the wife, spending her days preparing meals to be consumed when her husband arrives home from work is barely a memory for most Americans under 40 years of age. Eating meals away from home has become so commonplace that children now begin planning their birthday celebration by selecting a restaurant. Several chains, most notably Showtime Pizza and Chuck E. Cheese, were founded virtually to meet this demand. After-daycare birthday parties at McDonald's have become pervasive in suburban America. Almost 90 percent of Americans eat in a restaurant at least once a week, and 40 percent eat in a restaurant every day. Many eat more meals away from home than they do in their own homes.

Of course, these generalizations must be tempered by the significant regional variations in dining patterns that underlie all of these national trends. While the national family budget for eating out has been increasing relentlessly over the past twenty years—from $26.60 to $31.72 per person per week between 1984 and 1988 alone—the amount spent by region varies significantly. Mountain Westerners, for example, spent $28.28 weekly in 1987 whereas New Englanders spent $36.42, almost 30 percent more.

Unfortunately, sales figures are not effective measures of the relative importance of dining in a given community. Per capita sales of restaurants in New York, Chicago, and Los Angeles far exceed those found in smaller cities, but how much of that difference stems from the higher cost of living in the larger cities? Similarly, the numbers of restaurants per person can be misleading because of regional variations in the relative size and volume of the restaurants. The Restaurant Activity Index (RAI), an indexed ratio of restaurant sales to food store sales, was developed by *Restaurant Business* magazine to overcome some of these statistical problems. This index has many advantages over traditional statistics about restaurant activities because it is not unduly affected by the higher incomes of the Northeast and the Far West, or by variations in the cost of living. However, it is strongly influenced by large numbers of visitors in a market, and all of the highest indices are related to such areas. This may actually be an advantage in helping to understand the restaurant in American society, as these areas play an important role in the new American social landscape.

The highest RAI indices in 1987 were to be found in the Far West, the industrial Midwest, Florida, the more affluent suburban areas of the Northeast, and almost all college towns (Fig. 19). Not surprisingly, the highest index occurred in Honolulu with its large tourist trade. The "Redneck Riviera" of the Florida panhandle and the Grand Strand along the North Carolina/South Carolina coast also stand near the top of the list. Panama City, Deston, Fort Walton Beach, and their sister communities along the Florida Gulf Coast are classic examples

Figure 19. Metropolitan area Restaurant Activity Indices, by market, 1987.
(*Restaurant Business*)

The strip in Myrtle Beach, South Carolina, exemplifies the domination of these areas by independent and regional operators.

of these resort communities, which consist largely of endless lines of motels and cottages lined along the dunes on either side of the narrow two-lane road stretching along the shoreline. A favored destination for many southerners and midwesterners seeking inexpensive family vacations, this coast has few elegant resorts, few golf courses, and limited facilities. Although the highway is lined with restaurants, souvenir shops, convenience stores, package stores, and an assortment of entertainment centers ranging from water slides to miniature golf, the facilities for the most part are casual, independent operations. Grocery stores, traditional apparel marts, and other non-tourist-oriented retail facilities are almost non-existent here.

This is the landscape of the independent restaurant. National fast-food units have begun appearing during the past couple of years, but most establishments are locally owned and operated because the short season does not lend itself to the year-round chain mentality. However, these seasonal, independent operators do manage to make fair returns on their investments in spite of their short seasons. For example, Captain Anderson's, the best known seafood restaurant in Panama City, Florida, was the 99th-highest-grossing restaurant in the nation in 1988. It should be noted, moreover, that the restaurant's annual gross sales of just under $5 million were more difficult than it might seem to achieve, as the average ticket of just over $18.00 per person was well below the national average for equivalent restaurants in similar settings. Other centers with high indices include most of the remainder of coastal Florida, southern California, and the remaining larger western cities outside of Utah. College towns almost always have high indices, most notably State College, Pennsylvania (Penn State), Ann Arbor (University of Michigan), Raleigh/Durham, North Carolina (UNC, UNC State, and Duke), and Lawrence, Kansas (Kansas University). Similarly, major convention centers such as Chicago, Miami, and Atlanta have high RAIs, as do some military communities such as Columbus, Georgia, dominated by adjacent Fort Benning.

Surprisingly, the largest regional concentration of cities with high RAI indices is found in the industrial Midwest. Industrial cities traditionally have below-average levels of restaurant dining—the per capita restaurant sales even in the industrial Midwest are not particularly high—making this region's pattern even more intriguing. Certainly, this concentration is not a statistical fluke, as an even greater concentration of high indices was found in the 1977 statistics.

Several factors seem to contribute to this pattern, including the many dual-worker households, the low unemployment picture in 1987, high blue-collar wages, and the many stores serving specialty ethnic items for home consumption which were counted as restaurants in this survey.

The communities that have not participated in the restaurant revolution are those that also have not particpated in the general post-war economic and cultural revolution. The largest single group of such communities are the industrial cities of Pennsylvania, West Virginia, New Jersey, and upstate New York. Several factors appear to contribute to this phenomenon, especially the large population declines characteristic of most of these communities over the past forty years coupled with little or no in-migration from outside of the region.

Western Cafe

Four days of Inner Harbor Baltimore plastic monotony drives me out of my faceless hotel in search of real food and real people. Fells Point soon appears out of the early morning mist, but its yuppie image is too much this quiet morning and I drift on through streets of neat, permastone row houses. Suddenly I am in a neighborhood shopping area, though breakfast opportunities are limited to a Little Tavern and the Western Cafe. The Western appears to be a dinner restaurant, although a small sign in the dusty window proclaiming "Two eggs, hash browns and toast, $2.25" suggests otherwise.

My worst expectations are fulfilled when I step into the darkened restaurant. A mammoth bar stretches down the one side. A barmaid sips coffee at the far end while talking to a customer. Empty red Naugahyde booths fill the remainder of the restaurant. A breakfast place this is not. Desperation and hunger finally drive me inside to a booth.

The scene suddenly changes. New customers begin drifting in almost by magic. A blond waitress somewhat reluctantly parades up from the back with a menu, cutlery, and a cup of coffee. Momentarily flustered by the appearance of a stranger, she blurts, "I brought coffee. I can throw it away if you don't want it."

I assure her that it is all right and she puts it down, along with a garish generic menu. I scan the inside and don't find the advertised special, but decide to order it anyway.

"I'll have two scrambled eggs, please."

She scribbles "2 S" on her pad and looks at me. Confused I look back, and finally break the standoff, "Do I need to make any other decisions?"

"It comes with hash browns and toast."

"That's great," I respond, and she disappears.

The restaurant fills quickly now. Each new customer is greeted by name by customers and waitresses alike. The pace quickens. Madge moves quickly among the booths dispensing coffee.

"Mr Gene like some coffee today?"

"Does Don want coffee?"

A tall, thin, balding customer, obviously in his seventies, breaks the flow by loudly announcing, "I decided to have a good breakfast this morning."

Madge responds laughingly, "You mean you're eating something you're not supposed to have."

"If you only do what you're supposed to . . ."

"Well, if you do just a little," she replies, moving to the next table with his order for eggs on her pad.

My perfect eggs, two aging tomato slices, and mound of hash browns suddenly appear. I know I've struck gold as I take a fork of potatoes and the taste of paprika and onions fills my mouth like heaven. Then the cannon shot of black pepper deep in the spoonful lets me know that the chef is highly tuned to the tastes of his eastern European clientele. I settle in for a relaxed breakfast.

The pace of the restaurant speeds up further with the arrival of a new wave of customers.

"Madge, I thought you were off today," one shouts above the din.

"No, I'm working today and taking off tomorrow. It's my birthday. I'm going to get myself something."

Two men, one tall and thin with a slight look of Ichabod Crane, the other small, balding, with a round Ukrainian face, sit at the end table and immediately launch into a heated discussion. The small man is clearly agitated, and draws Madge into the conversation when she brings his coffee.

"But you haven't seen it yet," Ichabod suddenly shouts.

"We drove by. We don't like it."

Ichabod smiles and shakes his head and finally says, "Who asked you?"

"I don't care," the shorter man responds.

"Your sister just told you she don't like it and you don't like it."

The shorter man shakes his head.

"But you haven't seen it yet," Madge rejoins from another table where she is now pouring coffee.

"I says to her . . ."

"What are you talking about?" two girls in their early forties ask from their back booth next to the table.

"Oh, Mike's niece is buying a new house out . . ."

That immediately sets Mike off again and he jumps up from the table and slides into the next booth, pushing over the dark-haired girl to make room, and launches into his sad tale of woe about his poor sister's girl who is leaving the neighborhood and moving out to the wilderness of suburbia.

Madge sits with Ichabod to keep him company, as he is abandoned with his newly arrived breakfast. He yells again at his previous seat-mate and the two women, "And he hasn't seen it yet."

There are no strangers at the Western Cafe breakfast table. Customers talk, not with the civility of regulars moving through the breakfast assembly line at some suburban yuppie coffee shop, but with the familiarity of lifelong friends. There are few secrets here. The talk is about life and loves and family and yesterday and tomorrow. Everyone already knows about everyone else's warts and blemishes and wounds—and loves them anyway.

Johnstown, Pennsylvania, for example, has the lowest per capita number of restaurants in the nation most years, some of the lowest levels of per capita spending on restaurant dining generally, and very low fast-food consumption levels in particular. Even the casual visitor to Johnstown is quickly struck by the overpowering level of depression, cultural conservatism, lack of external influences, and introverted community atmosphere which underlie these low dining-out statistics. There is little new here. Though well kept, the homes are old and small by national standards. Suburban sub-divisions, so characteristic of similar cities elsewhere in the nation, do not dot the outskirts of this municipality.

This is a strongly eastern and southern European ethnic community with large Orthodox and Roman Catholic churches, grocery stores featuring whole aisles devoted to pasta, dairy cases bulging with piroshkis and kolbasa, and virtually no signs of nationally trendy ethnic food items such as tortillas and bamboo shoots. The local radio station still features polka parties and traditional north-eastern rock.

The restaurant scene is particularly conservative. Few upscale restaurants, a meager supply of national chains, a large selection of pizza parlors (especially take-out and home delivery), even more beer gardens, and the occasional Italian spaghetti house characterize the Johnstown restaurant scene. This basic meat-and-potatoes (actually pasta, piroshki, and pot roast) populace would seem to have little interest in dining away from home and even less concern for culinary exploration. One local resident summed up the situation after being invited to dine in a restaurant one evening by growling, "Why should I pay to eat out when I have perfectly good food right here in my own kitchen?"

Traditional restaurants dominate Appalachian industrial communities like Johnstown, Pennsylvania.

The interior South also largely spends far less than the national average on restaurant fare. Many of these communities still have incomes below national averages and large percentages of their populations living far below the poverty line. The lower ratios found in the Oklahoma/Texas/Louisiana oil patch stem from the impact of the recent oil recession. Noticeably higher ratios were tabulated in the 1977 survey for some of these oil cities. The largely agricultural orientation of the oil patch also contributes to its lower levels of dining out during all economic times for many smaller cities found here. Likewise, it is not surprising that most of the communities of California's Central Valley have similarly low ratios. Chico, Redding, Visalia, and the others are conservative farm towns which tend to be little interested in change.

The corporate revolution

The modern restaurant revolution is often said to have begun in 1954–5 with the founding of the Ray Kroc era of McDonald's. The McDonald brothers' introduction of the walk-up self-service "drive-in" in 1949 caused an immediate sensation in the restaurant industry which echoed across the nation. The large crowds of eager customers created volumes and profits previously unknown in the fast food industry. Initially the bachelor brothers were not interested in expanding their operations. As they put it, why make more money to just will it to some church you never attended?

The brothers willingly handed out their secrets, gave tours of their facilities, and generally assisted competitors. Jim Collins, for example, was building a restaurant for his father-in-law in Los Angeles when one day he was taken to San Bernardino by a friend to see the McDonald's operation. The large crowds amazed him and the operations seen during a grand tour given by the brothers during a slow period were impressive. He hurried home and after a little mental arithmetic scrapped his original plans for the new restaurant. Within months he opened the Hamburger Handout based on the McDonald brothers' model and grossed $420,000 in his first year of operation. He opened a second store in a few years and by 1960 had four Hamburger Handouts in Los Angeles, and was also selling advice to entrepreneurs in other markets. Visiting one of his protégés in San Francisco that year, he discovered that she was serving a new item,

Kentucky Fried Chicken. She insisted that he go to Kentucky and meet Colonel Sanders. Collins purchased a franchise after a three-day visit and added Kentucky Fried Chicken to his Hamburger Handout menu. He bought the southern California rights to the chain in 1962 and quickly began both operating and franchising stores in the region. The Sizzler Family Steakhouse chain was purchased from a friend in 1967. Soon afterwards Collins Foods International became a public company with $8 million revenue the first year. Today Collins Foods operates almost 300 Kentucky Fried Chicken stores in the United States and overseas, owns or franchises more than 600 Sizzler Restaurants in the United States, and operates several other concepts both in the United States and abroad.

The Collins experience was a far from unique result of a visit to the McDonald brothers' operation. Glen Bell, a frequent customer of the brothers' store in San Bernardino, persuaded a home-builder friend to build a clone which opened featuring hamburgers and tacos, rather than just hamburgers. Prosaically, he added his name to the store's feature item and called the new enterprise Taco Bell—now a unit in the PepsiCo restaurant giant. Many other less successful clones, based both on the original McDonald's and their early imitators, also opened during this period. The Chicago-based Bressler Ice Cream Company started the Henry's chain with the assistance of Collins using the Hamburger Handout as its model. Carrol's and Golden Point also helped spread the word in the Midwest before these chains converted their units into other chains.

The pressure to franchise the new concept was intense, and the McDonald brothers reluctantly sold their name and operating concepts to several entrepreneurs during the early 1950s. They were unhappy with this arrangement, however, because it took too much of their time, so they began casting about for a new solution to the problem. Ray Kroc came to San Bernardino in 1954 to discover who was purchasing so many multi-mixers from his restaurant equipment distribution company. As with so many others, it was love at first sight. Flying home to Chicago the next day, Kroc decided to purchase the national franchising rights of the company. He purchased the entire rights to the company a few years later, after lengthy disagreements with the brothers over operations.

The McDonald's story is only a small part of what was taking place during this period. Harland Sanders, a Corbin, Kentucky, motel and restaurant operator, stopped in Salt Lake City to visit his old friend

McDonald's-style walk-up fast-food stores appeared in the 1950s throughout the nation, as seen in this store featuring pit barbecue, hamburgers, hot dogs, milk shakes, and pies in Atlanta, Georgia. (Special Collections, Georgia State University Library)

Pete Harmon on his way to a Christian Church convention in Australia. Harmon was looking for a new menu item for his hamburger restaurant and Sanders treated him to a pot of his pressure "fried" chicken. Harmon was entranced. When the Colonel passed back through Salt Lake on his return, Harmon proudly took him past his restaurant which now prominently advertised "Kentucky Fried Chicken" on a sign outside. Harmon began trying to persuade Sanders to franchise his concept. Sanders eventually acquiesced in 1954. Thus, Kentucky Fried Chicken franchising was born in the same year as McDonald's, and for a time was a larger company.

Interestingly, the third member of today's big-three restaurant corporations also dates its origins to 1954, when David Edgerton became the first franchisee of InstaBurger King company with a franchise for Dade County, Florida. Edgerton soon teamed up with James McLamore. McLamore's impact on the company was immediate as he created the Whopper, redesigned the broiler to make it more efficient, and began opening stores throughout Miami. By 1957 the partners began regionally franchising their revised system under the

This Victoria Station has sat abandoned for more than a decade after the demise of the chain.

Burger King name. In a few years they purchased the national rights to the system and entered the national fast-food race.

Many less important chains were also founded during 1954–5, including the Sonic chain of hamburger drive-ins in Shawnee, Oklahoma, several pizza chains (the most notably being Shakey's), and a couple of taco chains. The presence of so much activity in such varied locations suggests that the overall success of the group was part of a larger mood sweeping the nation, rather than solely the ingenuity of the individual founders.

Clearly, the franchised chain restaurant was one of the most important forces underlying the restaurant during this period. More than 1,000 multi-city restaurant chains had been founded in the United States, ranging in size from the small eight- or ten-unit local fast-food chain to the massive McDonald's Corporation, the largest food service organization in the world. The chain syndrome is such an integral part of food-industry thinking today that many "concept" restaurants are founded for the sole purpose of creating a franchise restaurant chain.

Although the success rate among franchised restaurants far exceeds those of independents, the restaurant business is fraught with hazards for all participants. Virtually every major competitor in the business since the 1950s has made strategic operational errors resulting in major financial problems. The lucky chains – such as Kentucky Fried Chicken, Domino's, and Long John Silver's—have been able to save themselves from the bankruptcy court. The less adroit have ended up alongside Victoria Station, Sambo's, and Burger Chef in the "lost" column.

Few chains actually have national distributions, in spite of their apparent strength and omniscience. This regionality is a function partly of regional dining preferences—e.g. chains specializing in fast food fish are most common in the South Atlantic and Pacific regions where this cuisine is most popular—and partly of the developmental strategies of the corporate owners. Most chains develop a regional base and expand outward from there. Some, however, like Marriott and Howard Johnson's, use the commissary approach to provisioning their stores which restricts their spread. An analysis of the growth of some typical chains well illustrates this point and helps clarify the factors underlying their continuing regionality.

The spread of chains

McDonald's

McDonald's has come to be symbolic of the chain-store food industry for many Americans. The largest food server in the world, the chain serves 96 percent of all Americans annually and almost 8 percent of the entire nation's population every day. Many believe that the fast-food revolution specifically began on a bright December day in 1948 at 6 pm when Arthur C. Bender slid that first bag of hamburgers across the serving shelf to a nine-year-old girl at the octagonal

McDonald's building in San Bernardino, California. While that is debatable, the role of this company in shaping the fast-food revolution is undeniable.

This new enterprise was neither the McDonald brothers first restaurant, nor their first success. They entered the restaurant business in 1937 with a drive-in restaurant in Los Angeles. Moving to San Bernardino in 1940, the brothers successfully operated a drive-in featuring hamburgers, barbecue, and 23 other items for many years. Eventually they decided that the use of car-hops created more problems than they solved. In 1949 they risked everything by shutting down for a few months to completely redesign their store into a self-service restaurant. Initially, sales at this new walk-up restaurant were disappointing, but soon they were attracting the family clientele they sought and the store began to set records.

The first McDonald's looked little like the national chain bearing that name today. The store was a simple white octagonal building with a great overhanging awning to protect the patrons at the window. Their limited menu consisted of 15-cent hamburgers, 19-cent cheeseburgers, milk, coffee, buttermilk, orangeade, root beer, Coke, pies, potato chips, and popcorn from an outside vending machine. French fries and milk shakes were added to the menu later. Patrons were encouraged to "Buy'em by the Bag" in emulation to the "white box" syndrome of White Castle and its clones. The Golden Arches were not even a dream yet. Speedee reigned as the corporate symbol.

The McDonald brothers attracted instant attention with their new restaurant, with a cover story appearing on *American Restaurant Business* in 1952. Seemingly, Ray Kroc was one of the few people in the industry who did not see this article praising the brothers' new design, but he did come out from Chicago in 1954 to see who was ordering so many milk shake machines in this obscure California community. Kroc was instantly impressed, and negotiated a deal whereby he became the national franchise agent for the McDonald's system. He sold his first franchise in Fresno, California, in 1954, though the store didn't actually open until 1955, for a fee of $1,500 and 1.9 percent of the gross sales of the stores. The McDonald brothers sold a franchise for Chicago during the time the negotiations were taking place with the Chicago-based Kroc, who was thus forced to open his pilot store in suburban Des Plaines, Illinois, in April 1955.

The early development of McDonald's was a simple expansion

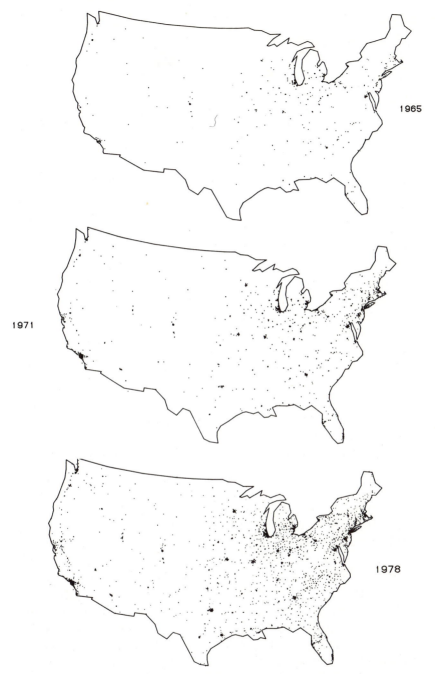

Figure 20. The expansion of McDonald's Restaurants (Unpublished maps by
William Carstenson)

model from the original Chicago and southern California bases (Fig. 20). The California franchisees had quite loose agreements, however, and in frustration Kroc soon concentrated on his midwestern home territory where he could better control his franchisees. The first midwestern franchisee in Waukegan, Illinois, was so successful that Kroc gave copies of their financial statement to almost everyone who spoke to him about the new concept. The company soon sold franchises in Connecticut, Cincinnati, and Dallas to break out of the original expansion-based diffusion model, and at the same time continued to spread through the medium-sized towns of Illinois, Wisconsin, and Michigan.

The pattern of a large city base and expansion into surrounding towns can easily be seen as early as 1965. Washington, Detroit, Cleveland, greater Chicago, Los Angeles, Atlanta, and similar cities are major centers, while few stores appear much removed from them. The pattern increases in intensity through the 1960s, with a national distribution not really appearing until the late 1970s.

In many respects, the McDonalds' story was a re-enactment of the post World War I period of the 1920s. Walter Anderson and Billy Ingram went into business in 1921 with the White Castle System in Wichita, Kansas. Their immediate success led them to begin a rapid expansion into the larger cities nearby. Their success soon spawned numerous local and regional clones, some of which became important in their own right. Finally, the success of these chains spurred unrelated entrepreneurs to create new chains, most notably A & W Root Beer, the Marriott organization, and Howard Johnson's.

Sambo's

Many restaurant concepts utilized the same basic growth philosophy during the 1950s. Sambo's is especially interesting because the company was spectacularly successful in the early years and then suddenly collapsed. Like most failed national chains, the problem was not that there were insufficient interested franchisees, nor that the concept was not nationally viable. Rather, the problems stemmed from internal mismanagement and strategic planning errors as the central office became distracted from its principal operating goals by interests in other businesses.

Sam Battistone Sr had operated Sammy's Grill in Santa Barbara for many years when he met Newell Bohnett, an equipment salesman

McDonald's saved this classic early store (in foreground) to use as a party store at this Portland, Oregon, location. A newer version of the store can be seen in the background.

and designer, in 1957. Believing that times were changing in the restaurant industry, the two entrepreneurs established a beach-front pancake house named after themselves (Sambo's) in June with the motto, "What this country needs is a good 10-cent cup of coffee." Featuring twenty-one types of pancakes, the restaurant was little different from hundreds of similar places being founded during the same period. Bob's Big Boy Drive-Ins were then being converted to coffee shops, and Harold Butler had founded Denny's (née Danny's) in 1954. The California coffee shop genre was well established when these two entered the scene.

Sambo's was far from successful initially, grossing only $90,000 in the first year. The tide turned during the second summer, however, and the lines of waiting customers soon stretched for more than a block on Sunday mornings. Battistone and Bohnett became so enthused about their success that they decided to open a second restaurant in Sacramento. They opened four more in 1959, and by 1963 they had developed a chain of twenty restaurants on the West Coast. The chain had expanded to ninety-two restaurants, 2,500 employees, an enlarged menu, and its first stock exchange offering during 1969. It continued to be driven by expansion during the next few years and eventually came to include more than 700 restaurants in forty states by the late 1970s. Management quickly launched several other restaurant concepts and developed a massive support system to extend their operations.

The fall from grace was even more rapid. Profits suddenly started to decline. Accusations flew as the company desperately tried everything from closing units to changing the name of the surviving stores. In November 1981 the chain filed for bankruptcy and the remaining assets were sold. The problems were legion, but mostly were the same as those of the other fallen chains: an inability to control the rapidly expanding empire, a poor internal division of finances, loss of quality control, and management stress. In contrast, Denny's continued to expand and did not run into its own organizational Waterloo until the late 1980s, when it was sold to a number of owners in rapid succession who are still trying to save what is now the only national coffee shop chain.

Revolution and reaction

The total number of restaurants was therefore not the critical issue in the restaurant explosion during the 1950s; nor were the concepts, nor the entrepreneurs. Rather, people were ready to reassess their dining pleasure if the proper store was available. The change was not instantaneous, by any means. The 127,000 restaurants in 1954, with sales of slightly more than $7 billion, had increased only to about 135,000 in 1967. Sales had more than doubled, however, to more than 414 billion in 1967. The growth rate changed radically during the following twenty years. The total number of restaurants more than doubled by the mid-1980s, and total sales increased by almost 1000 percent to more than $128 billion. The McDonald's Corporation alone had sales of more than $12 billion in 1987, with well over $10 billion taking place in their US stores—more than all restaurants nationwide grossed in 1954.

This incessant discussion about McDonald's and its phenomenal growth should not be construed to imply that chain-store operations were the engine that drove the early transformation of the industry. Large chains were still relatively unimportant during the 1950s. Individual units and small chains did as well as the larger industry giants during this period. Indeed, there were fewer than 18,000 chain eating places in America in 1958 with fewer than 4,000 belonging to chains of more than 100 units. It was the concept, not the corporate organization, that created the momentum during the early period. Things have changed radically today. In 1986 the top 100 chains only accounted for about 76,000 stores; in 1987 they accounted for 28 percent of all restaurants, and for 45.3 percent of total sales.

An interesting countercurrent to this chaining of America shouldn't be overlooked in the marketing hype of the industry. A recent survey of readers by *Consumer Reports* found that the average American sees little difference between the various chain competitors within the same class. While the magazine's respondents gave answers which made it appear that they could and did discriminate between the various chains, the final results spoke otherwise. Essentially, the scores of the top chains by class varied by only a few points. For example, the top-scoring Bob Evans chain received a score of 71 in the family dining category, but Marie Callender Pie Shops were ranked at 70, Shoney's at 68, and Po Folks at 67. In fact, a mere 10

Po Folks' use of distinctive restaurant architecture and signage helps associate the chain with the down-home image it cultivates.

rating points out of 100 separated the top eight family dining houses in the survey.

Critically, one must wonder if respondents were actually discriminating between chains or just voting for their local favorites, as all of the top family dining chains have only regional distributions. One must assume that few respondents had eaten at more than one or two of the actual competitors. Further, the comparison of the relatively elegant West-Coast-based Marie Callender Pie Shops with the down-home atmosphere of the Columbus (Ohio)-based Bob Evans, or the even more country Nashville-based Po Folks, boggles the mind. All of these chains serve family fare, but their interpretations of this food are very different. The Marie Callender upscale decor and extensive menu, featuring a variety of pot pies, pasta salads, steamed vegetables and homemade pies, is a far cry from the food found in either of its near-competitors in this survey. Bob Evans, for example, attracts travelers with its bright red barn facade and plain Midwestern cooking. The aggressively southern Po Folks, using a kraft paper menu featuring Chicken an' Dumplin, Chicken Biskit Pie, Southern Style Catfish, and endless cute homilies such as "We're PO But We're Proud," represents a completely different dining environment from those of the West Coast coffee shops.

The more nearly nationally distributed fast-food chains also had little variations in their scores, although again there appeared to be little brand loyalty among adults. In spite of massive advertising campaigns, the fast-food chains have momentarily saturated their markets. System growth is increasingly coming at the expense of competitors, rather than drawing new customers to the marketplace.

Finally, the increasing dominance of the marketplace by fast-food chains does not mean that all chain-restaurant types are doing well. Growth is clearly concentrated in the fast-food sector among the top 100 chains. Mid-scale chains have been especially weak in recent years, with only a 2 percent sales growth noted between 1981 and 1986. Upscale restaurants have fared even more poorly, losing 1.9 percent in sales during 1985–6 and suffering a 2.5 percent decline in units. It would appear that the restaurant industry is in store for many more adjustments as it attempts to deal with the problems of poor product differentiation, saturated markets, and changing dining habits.

Petridis Hot Dogs of Bayonne, New Jersey.

5

Sprouts and baked beans

THE POST WORLD WAR II restaurant explosion revolutionized not only where we eat, but what we eat as well. America's traditional eating patterns have undergone more change since 1954 (the founding year of McDonald's, Kentucky Fried Chicken, and Burger King) than in the entire previous century (Table 1).

The enthusiastic actuator of this transformation has without question been the fast-food industry. Consumption of foods favored by this industry has risen dramatically during the past thirty years. For example, beef and chicken consumption rose 50 percent between 1960 and 1976. Even more dramatic has been the change in the role of the potato in the American diet. The use of fresh potatoes plummeted to a quarter of its 1910 level during this period, while frozen potato consumption exploded after McDonald's adopted the frozen french fry as the standard for fast-food restaurants. The ingestion of other favorite fast-food ingredients has undergone similar changes over the past thirty years as mozzarella cheese, tomato catsup, pickles, ice milk, and soft drink consumption have all increased dramatically. Simultaneously, the consumption of non-fast-food ingredients (such as flour, fresh potatoes, pork, and many vegetables) has plummeted. The salad bar fad created a virtual panic in the iceberg lettuce and fresh mushroom industries to meet the demand. Carrot and green pepper consumption also increased dramatically during this period, while the demand for non-salad bar vegetables, such as cauliflower and cabbage, has actually declined.

McDonald's alone annually uses 100 million pounds of cheese, 30 million dozen English muffins, 800 million tons of frozen french fried

Table 1 Approximate US daily food consumption

	1910	1950	1976
Total	4.4 lb	4.1 lb	4.0 lb
Beef	2.4 oz	2.2 oz	4.2 oz
Chicken	0.6 oz	0.9 oz	1.9 oz
Fish	0.5 oz	0.5 oz	0.6 oz
Cheese	0.2 oz	0.5 oz	0.9 oz
Whole fresh milk	1.3 cup	1.5 cup	0.9 cup
Frozen Dairy	0.3 tbs	3.0 tbs	4.4 tbs
Flour, cereals	12.9 oz	7.3 oz	6.3 oz
Fresh potatoes	8.7 oz	4.2 oz	2.2 oz
All potatoes	8.7 oz	4.6 oz	5.1 oz
Fresh fruit	5.4 oz	4.7 oz	3.6 oz
Corn syrup	1.0 oz	1.7 oz	6.0 oz
Soft drinks	0.4 oz	3.5 oz	10.8 oz

Source: Center for Science in the Public Interest

potatoes, $700 million worth of chicken, and 600 million pounds of hamburger. It consumes no turkey, no freshwater fish, no green beans, no sweet potatoes, nor, for that matter, a host of other traditional American foods. The impact of this company and its fellow travelers on our diet has become pervasive as the restaurant industry has shifted roles from being the product of our foodways to being a cause of them.

This does not imply that the nation's traditional foodways can be totally discounted in affecting the distribution and success rates of American restaurants. A regional preference for pork and fish in the Southeast, for example, has spawned innumerable Southern barbecue stands and fish camps, while California's Pacific Basin orientation has brought it thousands of Asian restaurants to complement its traditional Western coffee shops and steak houses. Pizza is a national dish today, but in its Northeastern homeland it is the junk food of preference; in the Southwest it remains a virtual oddity. The restaurant industry may have been quite effective at introducing new foods and spreading old favorites to wider audiences, but the nation's traditional dietary patterns still remain important foundations to success and failure.

Ethnic foundations of the American diet

American culture lies across the nation like a lumpy four-layer cake atop a broken plate of unmatched pieces. The plate is made up of the original colonial cultural regions—New England, the Midland, the South, and the Spanish Southwest—intermixed with a few cultural shards of minor regions such as the Hudson Valley Dutch and Mississippi Delta Cajun (Fig. 21). The layers represent time periods and are formed from the great ethnic migrations which swept like waves across the nation. These immigration waves sought out spots of opportunity and passed around the lumps of inopportunity. Each immigration layer was individually flavored as the various regions made their contributions to America at different times. Germans and Irish dominated between the Revolution and the Civil War. The early Industrial Revolution found tens of thousands of Germans and Scandinavians entering in search of better farmlands. The heart of the Industrial Revolution found the political situation in Europe altered and hundreds of thousands of eastern and southern Europeans came in search of a better way of life. The twentieth century saw an attempt to close the doors to in-migration, and few came between 1920 and 1940. Since the end of World War II, that slack period has been more than balanced with hundreds of thousands of Latin Americans, Asians and, in a sense, African–Americans who began leaving their traditional homes in the South in large numbers to spread across the remainder of the nation for the first time.

Internal cultural mutations and technological innovations are also mixed into the great migration layers, with the greatest intensity of change concentrated on the two coasts. The northeastern corridor was the centre of the nation's economic and cultural elite in the beginning, and the impact of these ethnic changes was first strongly felt there. The West Coast has risen as a major center of cultural innovation since the 1960s and more recently has become the center of change in our popular culture, especially since the transfer of the operation centers of the major network television entertainment divisions to that region. Today, cultural change tends to emanate from one side of the nation or the other, jumping immediately to the opposite coast and trickling finally into the interior through the urban hierarchy.

It is amazing that any of the colonial foodways have survived in the

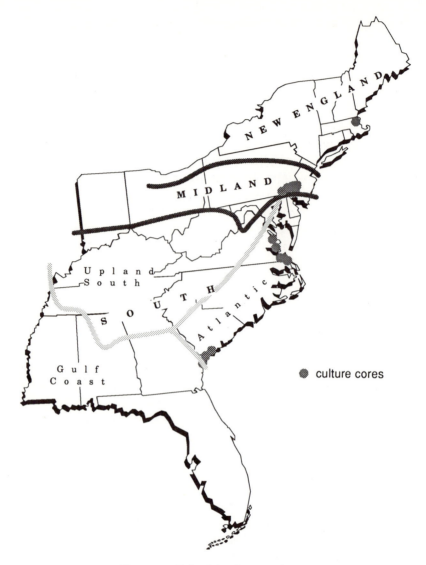

New England

Midland

Upland South

South

Atlantic

Gulf Coast

◉ culture cores

Figure 21. Colonial culture regions

face of the overwhelming impact of the changes that have taken place. For that matter, one must even wonder about the durability of the ethnic layers themselves in the face of the invincible wave of television, national food companies, endless cookbooks, and home magazines, to say nothing of several centuries of intermarriage and cultural intermixing.

Traditional American dietary regions

Colonial America welcomed settlers from a vast array of Old World origins. The four principal settled areas quickly took on distinct regional identities which have more or less continued until today. Smaller areas also developed, but tended to have little external influence. For example, the Dutch character of the Hudson Valley seems to appear as viable as ever in the face of the constant expansion of New York City, yet the impact of this way of life has spread little in three hundred years. Even a casual visit today brings sights of Dutch farmsteads, Dutch Reform churches, and the smells of Dutch foods. One must wonder how such a place could have survived so intact all these years. Indeed, the presence of Dutchness is so strong in some areas that the cynic must wonder how much of this untouched cultural backwater is real and how much has been enhanced to help boost the tourist dollar and local pride. While visible Dutchness is increasing, one must wonder about Dutchmen.

New England

New England was the scene of the first significant continuous settlement on the eastern seaboard beginning at Plimouth Plantation south of Boston in the early seventeenth century. The earliest immigrants came primarily from eastern England, though some had spent many years in the Netherlands. This small group was soon joined by others from throughout the rest of England. Their diet was a combination of traditional English and Indian foods, in all cases dishes with few frills. Wild game, corn, pumpkins and squashes, chickens, and beans were important elements in the initial diet. Much basic food had to be imported from England in the early days.

Cookbooks and travelers' descriptions tell us that stews and pots dominated the cuisine of the region well into the eighteenth century. Game remained important in most rural areas. Wheat bread increased in importance as true baking ovens became more common and the price of wheat declined. Pork and chicken were the first domestic meats to become readily available for domestic use, although by the mid-eighteenth century beef was the most important meat in most areas.

Identifying classic New England fare today is not easy. Clam bakes and lobster huts fulfill our imaginations, and it is doubtful that a single restaurant guide would be complete without telling us of that perfect out-of-the-way place such as Nunan's Lobster Hut in Porpoise Point, Maine. Similarly, Norman Simpson's Berkshire Traveller Press has made the New England Inn an historic shrine, as travel writers list everything from the rambling Red Lion in Stockbridge—around the corner from the Berkshire Travellers' offices—to the small places along the main street in Castine, Maine. But when the dust clears, one must wonder how much of the traditional Yankee fare has survived as a part of the daily local diet and how much survives only as part of the tourist menu.

The Midland

The Midland is easily the most complex of all our initial cultural potpourri. Settled by a diverse mélange of emigrants from a broad spectrum of European sources, this cultural soup soon became a rich stew as English settlers intermixed with the Dutch, the Swedes, the Finns, and the Indians who had preceded them, and were soon joined by large numbers of Germanic (Pennsylvania Dutch), Scotch-Irish, and Welsh immigrants. The mixture was more unique than the final culinary product.

The cultural mythology of this region is so confusing that some redefinition of terms is in order. Traditionally, the term "Middle Atlantic" has included the states of New York, New Jersey, Pennsylvania, and Delaware. Unfortunately, the cultural associations of this area do not match our traditional historic image of the region. For example, upstate New York was settled primarily by New Englanders moving westward after the Industrial Revolution and the Erie Canal conspired to make traditional New England agriculture a poor livelihood. Upstate New York is thus culturally more akin to New England than to the Middle Atlantic.

New York City has always stood alone culturally. The city has never had the vast cultural tributary region which we perceive for other colonial cities. It is difficult to identify a distinctive New York way of life and impossible to see its spread to surrounding areas, almost until the twentieth century. The Hudson Valley continued as a Dutch culture island well into the twentieth century, but represented more of a wall than a cultural spring. Northeastern colonial New Jersey was settled primarily by Dutch and New England settlers and its initial cultural landscape was much like that of New England with bits of Dutch cultural ornaments swirled through for added flavor. Southwestern New Jersey was settled first by Swedes, then by the Dutch, and finally by English Quakers. Elements of these groups mixed into a distinctive medley that gives this cultural landscape a unique cast even today.

The traditional heartland of the cultural Middle Atlantic has always been Pennsylvania and Delaware, as well as parts of Maryland, western New Jersey and northern West Virginia. The mixture of early emigrants included English, Welsh, Scotch–Irish, and Pennsylvania Dutch, but few of these people are quite who they appear to be. The English tended to be from the Welsh border country, with a distinctively different material culture than was typical of those settling in New England. The Scotch–Irish were not Irish at all, rather Presbyterian Lowland Scots who had emigrated to the six northern counties of Ireland and thence to America. Their way of life was distinctively different from the Catholic southern Irish who later came in large numbers. The Pennsylvania Dutch are not Dutch, but rather Germanic peoples primarily from the upper Rhineland who, if the cultural artifact record is accurate, apparently had been moving out of central Europe prior to their move to America. The result was a cultural stew which began to boil and intermingle from the beginning.

The Middle Atlantic diet was distinctive, yet familiar. Game and corn products were featured during early settlement, but the eighteenth-century settlement of this region made it easier for settlers to revert back to their traditional foods. We are told that the most distinctive elements of the Pennsylvania Dutch diet include their breads, their soups (mostly flour and potato), their smoked and other sausages, pork, and, importantly, their combination of sweets and sours. If the potato is king of this pantry, then corn is queen.

Pot cookery is the basis of most medieval European plain-folk cooking and the Pennsylvania Dutch are no different. Beyond chicken, corn, potato, onion, and pepperpot soups, other favorite kettle meals included beef and dumpling, sauerbraten, hasenpfeffer, and stews. Cornmeal mush once was eaten as often as three times a day. Straight or fried, smooth or lumpy, this dish was basic fare for many families.

English Quaker cooking started distinctively in America, but had largely merged with the foodways of the other ethnic groups by the early nineteenth century. Elizabeth Lea's *Domestic Cookery* (1830s) opens with directions for boiling meats, but soon takes on baking, frying, and stews. More interesting are the recipes for sauerkraut, apparently eaten in large quantities by English Quakers, scrapple, bologna sausage, and many other "Dutch" foods. If this picture is an accurate portrayal of Quaker foodways, it appears that ethnocentric fare had been largely replaced by a single regional diet by 1830. Individuals might include some elements of their own ethnocentric history in their standard home menus, but classic ethnocentric dining had been largely replaced—much in the same way that the housing and other ethnic elements of the landscape had been amalgamated by this time.

It's not easy to get a great Pennsylvania Dutch country meal today in tourist Dutch country. The Pennsylvania Dutch are big business and the heartland is more plastic than Teutonic. Better to wander up to the Kutztown Folk Festival—a little cute, but fun—or to the Belleville Market in the Kishcaquillas Valley. A special treat is a visit to the Country Village Restaurant nestled at the western end of this pleasant valley. The outside of this plain restaurant would never stop an Amish-hunting tourist. There are clues, of course, like the frequent clustering of dark and black cars crowded in front of the simple building on a Friday evening. The girth of the departing patrons and their obvious hometown look also help identify the place as a local haunt. A quick look inside quickly gives away the secret. Two long buffet lines of traditional "Dutch" soups, pork and chicken favorites, endless desserts, exquisite homemade pies, sweet and sours to satisfy the most demanding Mennonite patron—the gourmand's heaven has been unearthed, almost like a trip back in time to the Woodward Inn of yesteryear. And the price is set to attract the thrifty local market, not the tourists, who rarely slow in their frantic search for photos of quaint Amish wagons and roadside stands run by undiscovered Amish quilters, bakers, and churners.

The South

The South is the most visible and the most difficult to define of all of the traditional American culture areas. It is visible because so much of the region's day-to-day life has survived the onslaught of modern life. The Southern drawl, Southern food, the importance of religion, country music, blues and gospel, the laid-back lifestyle, Southeastern Conference football, Atlantic Coast Conference basketball, and bass

The Country Village Restaurant in central Pennsylvania serves traditional Pennsylvania Dutch fare with little modern interpretation.

tournaments still dominate daily life here. It is difficult to define because the South has never truly been a single place. At best, one must recognize three Souths: the Atlantic Coast, the Gulf Coast, and the Mountain South.

Cut from the same cloth, these regions are distinctively different. Any self-respecting Southerner can immediately distinguish a Virginian from a South Carolinan, and both those from someone from Alabama, by accent alone. Foodways have similar regional nuances. Brunswick stew is a common dish throughout the entire region, but is made with ham and chicken in Virginia, pork and chicken in the Carolinas, and chicken and pork as one moves toward Texas; lima (butter) beans begin as a major ingredient in the heartland, to be eventually replaced by peas; the North Carolinan potato filler becomes corn meal in the Gulf, and the whole dish eventually becomes tamale pie in west Texas and New Mexico. More than forty distinctive recipes were found in a casual perusal of Southern cookbooks, each the same yet different. Southern barbecue sauces have even more variety and could be the subject of a book in themselves.

Southern barbecue can't properly be eaten in a fancy place. Barbecue pits are becoming more hygienic as health laws force them to screen the pit and move the tables indoors, but the best is still a bit frowsy, even by regional standards. Barbecue pit chain restaurants have been rare until recently and few do well because of the regionality of the fare. It is impossible to select even a "good" barbecue place to meet everyone's needs because of regional variations in pit styles, barbecue sauces, Brunswick stews, and a myriad of other essential ingredients. South Carolina's mustard sauce is so spectacularly different from North Carolina's vinegary version and the Gulf Coast's sweeter sauce that almost no one is going to find all such places palatable.

The classic pits, no matter what recipes they use, have much the same menus. Plates of chopped and sliced pork are the mainstays, usually served with selections from a list including french fries, cole slaw, baked beans, Brunswick stew, and green salad. A slab or two of white bread is mandatory, along with a gallon pitcher of sweetened ice tea. Desserts are unimportant, but if available are cobbler, fried pie, and soft ice cream, or some combination of the above. Barbecue sandwiches are almost the only other item on the menu in a really good pit, though more and more are slipping into full menus.

The Black River Barbecue and Outlet is a carefully designed caricature of the classic, rural, Southern barbecue complete with abandoned Plymouth in the front yard.

Traditional Southern fare still dominates the region, although finding pure dispensaries is becoming more and more difficult. The biscuit is king of the Southern breakfast. Biscuit sandwiches, biscuits swaddled in white sausage gravy, or biscuits, eggs, and spicy Southern sausage are breakfast favorites. Dinner (the noon meal) was the main repast in the old days and the table was filled with the basic fare of the region. Pork and chicken have always been the favorite meats, while game is more important here than elsewhere in the nation. Catfish and other freshwater fish are consumed in large quantities, especially among the African–American population. The distinctive regional vegetable favorites include okra, butter beans, black-eyed peas, yams and sweet potatoes, collard, turnip and other greens, and yellow squash, to name a few. Favored desserts include fruit cobblers and fried pies, yam and sweet potato pies, and banana pudding. Buttermilk is disappearing from restaurant menus as one of the "included" drinks, while sweetened ice tea by the pitcher remains king. Colas are consumed in veritable oceans. It is not by accident that Coca Cola, Pepsi-Cola, Double Cola, and several others were invented here. Traditional rural Southerners often just covered their daytime dinner table with a cloth (or placed the serving dishes in a pie safe), to eat the remnants of the noon meal in the evening.

Cynics would say that no Southern cook need possess more than a frying pan. Everything seems to be fried, including such unlikely candidates as okra and pies. The region's distinctive cooking style is completed with the boiling to oblivion of most vegetables with fatback to create a soggy, greasy mass of indeterminate nutritional value.

Restaurants were few and far between in the old days, mostly clustered around the courthouse square of innumerable county seats. Food was often served family or buffet style in these places, and it is a rare courthouse square that still doesn't support one or more today. Typically, the buffet line will include fried chicken, a stewed dish, and some pork. Catfish are increasingly common as pond-raised catfish catch on, and most will have barbecue on at least one day of the week. Four or five of the region's other favorites will be available daily on a rotating schedule and will include at least one fried vegetable. All meals will include biscuits and corn bread. A separate desert table covered with pies, cobblers, and soft ice cream finish the array. Most importantly, the feast will have a fixed price, probably under $5, though inflation is setting in. Even the "Two Dollar Cafe" in

Darlington, South Carolina, has had to raise its prices above this limit—but it is still less than the regional average.

Cafeterias are a ubiquitous part of the region. The early chains may have been concentrated in the northeastern, midwestern, and far western cities, but the largest chains today are headquartered in the South. Although some are expanding out of their original regional bases toward the West Coast, even the largest chains are essentially regional operations.

The Southwest

The Spanish came in the sixteenth century and founded what New Mexicans like to call the nation's oldest European settlements. The arid climate, combined with the Spanish conquistadors' distaste for farming, soon altered the diet of these new arrivals. The Indian triad of corn, beans, and squash became mainstays as they were intermingled with the Spanish love of beef to create a distinctive diet. The role of beef was further enhanced with the nineteenth century arrival of Anglo ranchers and their even larger herds of beef.

The popular image of a traditional dish of beef, beans, and beer for this region is much nearer the truth than most frontier images. The paucity of Anglo farmers, the distance to traditional distribution centers, and the lack of large Anglo settlements meant the disappearance of many temperate-climate favorites. Beef and beans were plentiful and cheap. Chickens and eggs were available in town and were consumed in quantities when available. The problems of baking yeast breads made corn bread and tortillas common in the poorer localities, although many Hispanic villages had community ovens to bake bread—some of which is still sold under the arcades of Santa Fe and Albuquerque. Tamales, beans, chilies and other stews, and dried and fresh beef were all common mainstays. Tacos, burritos, nachos and most other "Tex-Mex" fast foods are for the most part twentieth-century inventions, although they of course had regional ancestors.

Cajunland: a culinary island

Cajun cuisine entered the national "nouveau" arena several years ago and K. Paul Prudhomme became the cuisine's unofficial spokesman. Once Cajun cuisine mostly meant gumbos, jambalayas, and etouffés made from the fish and fauna of the region, or red beans and rice. Crawfish, oysters, shrimp, frogs, turtles, and a limitless variety of fish, from the humble catfish to the now venerated redfish, were important parts of Cajun dishes. Before the region became chic the ultimate feed was boiled crawfish poured into large metal sinks and eaten with the hands over newspaper, or raw oysters and Jax beer, or shrimp boiled in special rémoulades as only the Cajuns could.

The cuisine has gone chic today with the assistance of K. Paul and Justine Wilson, but one still needs to head into the marshes or the Atchafalaya Swamp for the true fare of the region. The Rainbow Inn, in the heart of the Atchafalaya spillway, once was a favorite stop for hunters and fishermen passing through Pierre Part. Today this venerable Cajun restaurant looks much as it did more than twenty-five years ago when as students we used to be trucked into the area to interview Spanish moss pickers and frog giggers and to chow down on crawfish etoufée, red beans and rice, and endless cans of Jax on those hot, late spring Saturdays. Delmonico's it's not, but then Cajun foods don't properly lend themselves to the Commander's Palace atmosphere of the New Orleans Garden District.

The ethnic layers

This basic cultural plate was forever shattered by the great European migrations of the nineteenth century. The Irish and Germans were the first new large groups to emigrate to America in the first half of the nineteenth century. The often penniless Irish fleeing the famine and British oppression headed to the New World in search of opportunity. Most came to Boston and New York because they were closest and had the lowest fares. The poorest purchased tickets to Halifax and the Canadian Maritimes, and walked southward to the United States to save as much as a third on each ticket. Few had any inclination to head for the booming agricultural frontier in the Midwest and instead they found jobs in the labor-hungry seaports.

Most early Irish arrived with few skills fit for this new world and were forced to accept the most difficult and lowest-paying jobs. Thousands were responsible for building the great public works projects of Boston and New York City, the Erie Canal, and many eastern railroads. Few were miners, though a large Irish community

The Rainbow Inn of Pierre Part, Louisiana, has changed little
over the years.

worked the anthracite coal mines of Lackawanna County, Pennsylvania, and the copper mines of Butte, Montana, the latter thus
being the most Irish community in the nation for a time. However,
these were the exceptions. Most had little incentive to move westward and they remained near Boston and New York. The Irish impact
on taverns and bars was great, but little was added to traditional
American fare except a few ethnic favorites such as corned beef and
cabbage and some potato dishes.

The German immigrants of the nineteenth century, in contrast,
tended to arrive in Philadelphia, New York, and Baltimore, and
then move onward to the Midwest. Indiana, Illinois, and Wisconsin
were important early destinations, while later groups moved onto
the Great Plains. In 1980 the most German counties in the nation
were in the Dakotas, Wisconsin, and Indiana, while Milwaukee,
Cincinnati, Chicago, and St Louis had the largest total Germanic

populations. A strong Germanic cuisine appeared almost immediately in the Midwest. Schlitz, Miller, and Pabst made Milwaukee the center of American brewing for a time, while Oscar Meyer and several other sausage and prepared-meat manufacturers still call that city home. Even today, a tour through many parts of Iowa, Wisconsin, Minnesota, and Indiana yields strong German accents, great German foods—through not necessarily German restaurants—and endless Lutheran churches. "Beer gardens" began appearing in the large eastern cities soon after 1820 and several large ones are recorded for New York City in the 1830s. While German restaurants have never been common, the beer garden and its modern descendants are widespread in most Germanic neighborhoods. Food is an important element in these beer gardens, now often called "taps" in the Midwest, which are not at all the same as bars and saloons; families are welcome at the Ottawa Tap, but never at the Tower Bar.

The second layer began forming after the Civil War and was distinct primarily because of the addition of large numbers of Scandinavians who were responding to railroad advertisements for cheap lands in America. These groups are almost entirely concentrated in the Midwestern states north of Chicago.

The third layer began in the late Industrial Revolution with a significant shift in the ethnic origins of immigrants. The most important groups were the Italians, the Poles, the Russians, and the refugees from the failing Austro-Hungarian empire. Smaller numbers of Greek, Portuguese, and other groups also migrated during the late nineteenth century, but generally they had little impact on the ethnic landscape.

The Poles began arriving in numbers in the 1850s and most moved through the eastern seaboard cities toward the Midwest. Chicago quickly became the largest center of Polish population outside eastern Europe and it remains as such today. Other important centers were Buffalo, Milwaukee, Pittsburgh, New York, and Detroit, where the Poles often worked in the hardest and most difficult occupations, especially steel and heavy engineering. Hamtramck, a large Polish neighborhood in Detroit, was one of the most important sources of auto workers in that city. Polish communities tended to be quite clannish, with little of the outgoing, gregarious community life so characteristic of the Italian communities. Kolbasa, piroshki, stuffed cabbage, borscht, and other Slavic favorites were available in com-

J.T.'s Beer Palace of Scranton, Iowa, is a classic beer garden as seen in this 1930s photograph. (FSA, Library of Congress)

munity stores, but even today these communities have some of the lowest per capita restaurant levels in the nation. Dining out has never been a significant part of their community life.

In contrast, the restaurant is important to the Italians, who began leaving the Italian Piedmont in the 1870s to work as skilled craftsmen in the silk textile industries of the Northeast. They were joined after 1880 by large numbers of unskilled peasants from southern Italy and Sicily, who soon dominated the Italian–American population. New York was the most important port of entry for these later immigrants, and the city soon housed the largest concentration of Italians in America. These later arrivals often lacked the money and inclination to move westward and easily found jobs in the large port cities. Many southern Italians came as contract laborers to work in the textile, apparel, and mining industries. The somewhat earlier-arriving eastern Europeans were favored by many employers for work in the steel mills and heavy engineering industries, and few Italians found work in these core industries of the late nineteenth-century Industrial Revolution. New Castle, Pennsylvania, north of Pittsburgh, stands out as an exception. Village people, the southern Italians soon created neighborhood villages in their new urban environment with the formation of Italian Catholic churches, the establishment of traditional bakeries to create the breads and other baked goods so critical for proper "village" life, and, of course, restaurants. Though farming never appealed to many of these immigrants, truck farming or market gardening was another matter. Established immigrants moved as rapidly as possible to suburban fringes to find land to plant gardens, which often grew into commercial operations. Family is the heart of any Italian village, but food is the center of any gathering. These Italian–American villagers quickly established their cuisine and *ristorantes* as important alternative dining environments.

The Greek immigrants deserve special attention because of their special affinity with the restaurant industry in America. The first Greeks emigrated to New Hampshire and southern New England to work in the shoe and textile industries. Virtually all Greeks entered America through New York, which still houses the largest community. Although large concentrations of Greeks exist, Greek immigrants often settled in smaller isolated communities. Occasionally they worked in the larger factories during this period, notably in Detroit, but most preferred entrepreneurial jobs. It has been said that virtually all candy shops in Chicago in the early twentieth century were Greek-owned, while dry cleaners, shoe-shine stands, grocery stores, and restaurants were other popular work-places. It was estimated in 1950 that a Greek man was thirty times more likely to be a restaurant manager or cook than were the men of other late nineteenth-century ethnic groups. A recent study of diners across the northeastern corridor pointed out that ownership of these all-American establishments was largely confined to Greeks. Greek-owned restaurants, however, rarely served Greek food until recent times. Indeed, one would have been forced to conclude that the hot dog was the national dish of Greece on the basis of the fare offered in most typical Greek-owned restaurants in the past, while the hamburger was a close second. For the most part, these places were the mom-and-pop restaurants of their communities and the cuisine reflected the clientele, rather than the ownership.

The economic migrations of the Industrial Revolution ended with the passage of the Immigration Act in 1921, which severely restricted migration to the United States. The Statue of Liberty now stands in New York harbor as a symbol of the past rather than the future. Ellis Island is a museum commemorating something that will never be repeated, no matter how desperate the need.

The vast majority of the nineteenth-century immigrants became concentrated in the large northeastern and midwestern cities which dominated the Industrial Revolution. Chicago, Pittsburgh, Detroit, Milwaukee, and others happily exploited the strong backs of these immigrants by the thousands, while the South and West had few opportunities and even fewer eastern and southern European emigrants. The result was the development of ethnic ghettos in the industrial cities from which there appeared to be no escape. Looked down upon for the most part by their earlier, better established predecessors, the eastern and southern European immigrants settled into various forms of American village life which prospered until the post World War II era, which forever shattered this status quo.

Today there is nostalgia, much talk, and great veneration for these earlier "better" times, but cultural integration has done its work. A casual visit to the western Pennsylvania coalfields, for example, soon reveals precious little difference between the ways of life of the third-generation Slovak, Ukrainian, Italian and other emigrant children who have intermarried to the point where differentiation is difficult and of little concern. For example, the *Panis' Cookbook* (1977) is dedicated "To the memory of our parents and our Carpatho-

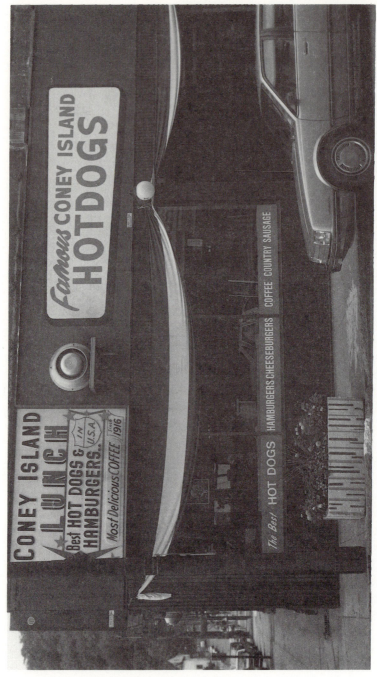

Coney Island Hot Dogs has been operated for more than seventy years by the same Greek family in Johnstown, Pennsylvania.

Russian ancestors who gave us the gift of their heritage . . ." The book was published to preserve the traditional Carpatho-Russian recipes for the next generation, including full menus for Easter and Christmas. All of the basic holiday recipes are here, including paska, kolachi, and bobal'ki. Somewhat unexpectedly, the book also contains recipes for many dishes of other ethnic groups, indicating that these dishes are every bit a part of the contemporary Carpatho-Russian–American diet as the items traditionally associated with their culture. Thus, the entrée section leads with Hungarian goulash and is quickly followed by Swiss steak (not Swiss of course) and lasagna. Other amazing entrées in this section are the quite American Rio Grande pork roast and chicken à la king. Certainly, recipes for holupki, kolbasa, and other ethnic favorites are given, but it is clear that by the 1970s the ethnic stew is well seasoned.

Recent migrations and not so recent foundations

The migration inertia of the inter-war years was broken soon after the end of World War II. Migration within the nation increased rapidly as returning veterans found life back home not quite as they remembered and began moving their families to better lives. California exploded, with an annual migration surplus of half a million persons each year for more than twenty years. Black and white sharecroppers and tenant farmers from the South headed for the better-paying factory jobs in the northern cities. The ethnic purity of the inner-city neighborhoods started cracking as the next generation of eastern and southern European children headed for the suburbs, along with the rest of America.

The African-American migration from the South after 1915, and especially after 1950, is one of the most important cultural readjustments of twentieth-century America. The Civil War had had little real impact upon the distribution of this group: the 92 percent concentration of Blacks in the traditional Southern States in 1860 had dropped only to 89 percent by 1910. Their arrival in northern cities after 1915 had much the same impact on these communities as newly arriving foreign immigrants would have done. The steel and automobile cities were the most important centers of African-American presence during this period. Prejudice, discrimination, and other economic problems for the most part halted African-American migration out of the South between the wars. World War II renewed the demand for cheap labor in the industrial centers. St Louis, Louisville, the Chicago industrial district, Detroit, the Pittsburgh-Cleveland industrial district, and the Northeastern industrial centers received large numbers of African-American immigrants during and after the war as the changing racial climate of the nation made migration easier. African-Americans brought their dietary preferences with them and, while few were able to insert these preferences into the American mainstream, it was soon possible to purchase back-home favorites in their residential and shopping areas. The integration movement of the 1960s made soul food chic, and for a period it became nationally available. The result has been the spread of "Southern" cuisine throughout the larger cities of the nation, although today it is generally available only in Black residential and shopping areas.

The second major post-war migration was by hundreds of thousands of Mexicans streaming across the southern border after the 1960s. Most of the western United States was once a part of Mexico, and small numbers of this group have lived there for centuries, although until recently the vast majority were concentrated in New Mexico. The changing Mexican agricultural economy of the late nineteenth century sent many agricultural workers northward across the border. The demand for cheap labor in the Far West, coupled with the end of Asian in-migration in the 1880s, created a strong market for their services, both in agriculture and in the construction of railroad and irrigation projects. The pace has quickened even more in recent years as the economic differentials between the two nations has increased. The distribution of Mexican settlement has also changed, as California increased its national percentage of resident Mexicans from 41 percent in 1970 to 52 percent in 1980, not counting the large numbers of illegal and uncounted residents—possibly as much as 30 percent of the total. A large Mexican-American community began to develop in Chicago after 1910 because of the large numbers of these people employed by the railroads. Their residential neighborhoods have expanded rapidly in recent years, and today Chicago is the largest center of Mexican-Americans outside the Sunbelt. Barrio life is much like that within any unassimilated American ghetto, and innumerable restaurants have developed to serve traditional foods. The origins of the Mexican cuisine revolution in the Far West are not clear, but probably date from the nineteenth century. Many Mexicans worked as cooks and domestics, and most Western Anglos were familiar with Mexican cuisine in the past. The cuisine began gaining wider acceptability during the late 1950s and by the 1970s had become standard regional fare for all cultures. It is only now entering many parts of the eastern United States.

Chinese migration to America was concentrated during two periods. The earliest group began arriving in the 1850s to work the gold mines in California and later to build many of the western railroads. A strong anti-Asiatic movement developed after labor shortages declined and unemployment increased in the Far West in the 1880s. Many Chinese were literally driven from their fields, their jobs, and their homes by angry mobs. Congress passed legislation in 1882, severely restricting the in-migration of Orientals until 1943. Only slightly more than 100,000 Chinese lived in the United States during the 1880s, and that number declined throughout the nineteenth century as some returned to China and the remainder, unable to bring wives to this country, generally remained unmarried and without children. The impact of these surviving Chinese far outweighs their numbers, however. While many Chinese in the West returned to San Francisco, Sacramento, and Portland after 1880, small numbers of isolated Chinese families remained in the mining and railroad communities of the region where they often operated laundries and restaurants. A few Chinese laundries and restaurants were also found in the eastern United States, including such unlikely communities as Des Moines, Iowa, and Providence, Rhode Island.

The second period of Chinese migration to the United States began about 1965 and has centered primarily upon the nation's larger metropolitan areas, especially San Francisco, New York, and Los Angeles. New York City's 60,000 foreign-born Chinese represent the greatest concentration of recent immigrants in the nation, although the San Francisco Bay area still has the highest total Chinese population. Large numbers of these migrants did not come from the Peoples Republic of China; many are ethnic Chinese who left Southeast Asia, Hong Kong, and Taiwan because of the unsettled political futures of those places.

These recent migrations have brought many changes to the structure of Chinese settlement in this country. Most of the nation's traditional Chinatowns, for example, have not grown because of the increased numbers of immigrants. Many of the new arrivals have chosen to live in suburban neighborhoods and the older, largely residential Chinatowns have tended to become primarily shopping areas. The pattern of Chinese restaurants has changed as well. Most were originally concentrated in their community's Chinatowns. Today they are scattered throughout the nation's metropolitan areas and now commonly appear even in smaller cities. In the past Chinese restaurant fare usually consisted of Cantonese cuisine, as the majority of nineteneth-century Chinese immigrants were from a small area of southern China near Canton. Most Americans came to believe that this food was typical of that nation as a whole. Nowadays the variety of Chinese fare that is available is amazing, and most larger communities offer the major regional cuisines—especially Cantonese, Hunan, Dim Sum, Mandarin, Szechuan, and Mongolian.

The contemporary American cuisine

The standard American cuisine of the 1990s is quite different from that of the original settlers. The great migrations, the acculturalization process, and the food technology explosion have brought exotic new foods to virtually all communities at low cost. The classic American meal—steak, baked potato with butter, and green salad followed by apple pie à la mode—probably never existed as a national standard outside some cultural chauvinist's imagination.

An overview of the standard American diet within the context of its regional variations is valuable in understanding the changing restaurant landscape. Americans generally eat larger quantities of meat than almost any other nation. More flesh is consumed per person than in any nation outside such great meat-producing nations as Argentina and Australia. Beef has been increasing in relative importance and today is the dominant meat. A trend toward "white" meats began on the West Coast in the 1970s and is currently diffusing through the urban hierarchy; fish, chicken, and turkey now are increasing in popularity with turkey being especially important on the West Coast. Pork consumption is declining nationally, although it remains popular regionally. Americans also consume more green vegetables, more soft drinks, more sugared products, more exotic fruit, and more coffee than any other nation on earth.

Regional foodways still dominate most areas, in spite of the many changes that have taken place in the nineteenth and twentieth centuries (Table 2). The northeastern United States sustained the largest influx of nineteenth-century European migrants and this has given the cuisine of the region the most "ethnic" cast of any in the nation. Veal, lamb, fish, pastas, bakery products (rolls, pies, cakes, pastries), yogurt, tea, coleslaw, olives, and pears are consumed in larger quantities than that typical for the nation as a whole. These items speak strongly of the Italian, Slavic, and other eastern European traditions in the region. The bakery is far more important to these commuities than to the nation as a whole, as it is not practical to produce many favorite items at home and mass production bakeries are unable to do these products justice.

The Midwest was initially settled by migrants from the eastern seaboard and large numbers of immigrants from Germany and Scandinavia. Other ethnic groups came in large numbers later on, but tended to concentrate in the cities. The result is a distinctive cuisine in which the foods of the urban dwellers are often quite different from those found in the rural areas. The rural Midwest dines on its twentieth-century interpretation of the Middle Atlantic cuisine. Pork and corn products play an inordinately important role. Greens of any kind are less common. Germanic settlement areas, such as much of Wisconsin, consume large quantities of potatoes, beer, and other starchy favorites. A recent survey by the Center for Disease Control found Wisconsin to have the largest percentage of overweight persons in the nation.

Few foods stand out, as seen in Table 2 for the Northeast, suggesting that the diet of the Midwest is far closer to the national norm than most. Doughnuts, sweet rolls, and hot cereals are consumed in greater amounts than the national norm, but otherwise breakfast is little different. Lunch continues as a large meal, with a strong preference for pork, beef, and potatoes. Otherwise the dietary pattern is unusually usual.

Southern cuisine remains the most distinctive and least changed from its historical origins of any set of regional foodways in the nation. The USDA statistics show an extraordinary consumption of cornmeal, white flour (for home baking of biscuits and pies), tea (sweetened, cold), colas, beans, sausage, and a variety of other traditional favorites. These preferences are translated into menus that are little different from those described for the nineteenth century. Biscuits with sausage or egg and grits for breakfast; a large hot dinner featuring either pork or chicken and three vegetables (including at

Table 2 Selected regional food consumer purchase patterns, 1978
(Percentages of consumer expenditure above or below the national average)

Food	N. East	N. Cent.	South	West
Veal	37	−12	−16	−9
Lamb	25	−11	−18	5
Yogurt	18	−9	−14	5
Pears	18	−4	−15	—
Pies, tarts, turnovers	15	−6	−5	−5
Non-cola soft drinks	15	−2	−9	−4
Pkg. coleslaw	15	—	−6	−9
Fresh fruit juice	14	−6	−6	−3
Butter	13	3	−12	−4
Fresh/frozen fish	13	−6	−5	−3
Rolls, muffins	12	−1	−6	−6
Pasta noodles	11	1	−10	−1
Tea leaves	11	−10	7	−8
Cigars	11	—	−7	−4
Cake	11	−2	−6	−4
Rice	10	−14	3	1
Pork roast	9	4	−8	−5
Luncheon meats	6	4	−5	−5
Buttermilk	−16	16	−7	7
Potato chips	−5	9	−3	−1
Sweet rolls, coffee cake	6	7	−11	−1
Ground beef	−5	6	−2	−1
Chuck roast	−5	6	−2	−10
Fruit drink powder	−4	6	−3	1
Oat cereal	2	6	−3	1
Fruit soft drink	−1	6	−9	4
Doughnuts	4	5	−7	−3
Frozen potatoes (fries)	—	5	−2	−4
Cornmeal	−14	−13	39	−12
White flour	−11	−3	20	−6
Other tobacco (chew)	−7	−1	13	−5
Fresh pork & ham	−6	—	8	−3
Canned stew & entrees	−8	−1	8	1
Whole chicken	2	−5	7	−4
Canned/dry beans	−4	−2	7	−6
Cola	−1	—	7	−6
Sausage	−1	2	6	−7
Other non-alc. bev.	−3	−6	−7	16
Other frozen juice	−2	1	−10	10
Apple juice/cider	8	−10	−7	8
Breakfast away home	−1	—	−6	7
Other bakery products	6	−3	−9	7
Dried fruit	−2	1	−7	7
Non-white bread	7	−1	−12	6
Other fresh fruit	6	−2	−10	6
Canned fish (not tuna/salmon)	2	−4	−4	5

Source: Fabien, Linden and Helen Axel (eds.), Consumer Expenditure Patterns (New York: The Conference Board, 1978).

least two of the following: peas, greens, okra, pole beans, squash), corn bread, and iced tea; followed by a similar supper. Ethnic foods are rare, salad bars are coming, pizza is common only in the cities.

The Far West is an extremely complex environment and few would attempt to consider it a single place. There has been little change in the dietary patterns of the Intermontaine in the past twenty years, beyond the introduction of the standard fast foods and a growing tendency to eat out. The West Coast and its interior satellites, however, represent a very different world.

California is considered the center of culinary innovation for the nation today. Many restaurant owners and entrepreneurs make annual treks to this Mecca to find out what is "hot" and what is not in the restaurant game. The West Coast is a multi-personality, restless, driven community desperately searching for an unidentified nirvana. The trends, contradictory as the region, simultaneously spawn markets for new, exotic ethnic cuisines, new health food regimes, and a return to nouveau diner food. Vegetables are often consumed raw or cooked so lightly that they are raw by the standards of other regions. This is the land of ground turkey in supermarkets, but rarely in restaurants. Sausalito, California, has declared itself a cholesterol-free zone, along with already being nuclear- and pesticide-free.

The West Coast has always been a restless milieu. Where else could Hangtown Fry (oysters and eggs) have been invented? The pattern continues. The rise of regional cuisines owes much to the West Coast as these diners willingly adopted Tex-Mex, Cajun, "diner", Sante Fe, and now "northwestern" cuisines. K. Paul may have created modern Cajun cooking, but it was largely Californians, California media, and California restaurant chains which adopted, adapted, and sold it to the nation. The result is a parade of chefs and owners visiting the Fog City Diner and its brethren in search of new concepts in order to be avant garde back home in Indiana.

The Edison (New Jersey) Diner along US 1 is typical of the contemporary
version of that venerable restaurant form.

6

Cornucopia becomes smorgasbord

GEOGRAPHY AND HISTORY have long conspired to make it virtually impossible for a restaurant chain to become truly national. McDonald's is the most viable contender for this title with its 8,000 stores in the United States, but even it falls short. One may drive all day in the South, the desert West, and southern Great Plains without spotting a McDonald's, except at an interstate interchange or in the largest communities along the way.

Many restaurant chains boast of stores in forty or more states. However, outside of their home areas, few are able to venture beyond the largest freeway interchanges and cities. Pizza Hut, Domino's, Dairy Queen, and Kentucky Fried Chicken, among others, are also nearing national status, though they have not attained it yet. Regional foodways and the organizational problems of maintaining a far-flung empire remain formidable obstacles to a truly national distribution for any single company.

Denny's coffee shop chain well illustrates the problems of the national restaurant chain. Denny's operates almost 1,200 restaurants in forty-three states, although its market penetration is far from uniform (Fig. 22). Found practically everywhere in its home territory, it has a ragged distribution elsewhere. The company uses a combination of freeway interchange and middle-income, high-volume corridor locations in most of the West, with additional stores near the center of smaller communities where the retail core remains viable. Its eastern stores have far more restrictive site preferences and are almost entirely relegated to high-volume interchanges of major interstate highways.

The company has met the challenge of servicing a national clientele by developing a menu featuring standardized national foods with a few regional specialties added to create the illusion of a local restaurant. The "national" menu includes the basic pancake and egg breakfast items, a variety of sandwiches, steaks, shrimp, chicken, spaghetti and meatballs, liver, and fish. Over this, a real attempt has been made to develop an effective set of regional menus tuned to its ten marketing areas (Table 3 & Fig. 23).

Denny's has been proud of its role in developing this menu, which does represent a significant attempt to meet a variety of regional needs. A dissection of the menu, however, also helps us understand why chains find it so difficult to succeed on a national scale. The company's perception of the regionality of America is certainly a

Denny's architectural style has undergone many changes from this early model in Orange County, California.

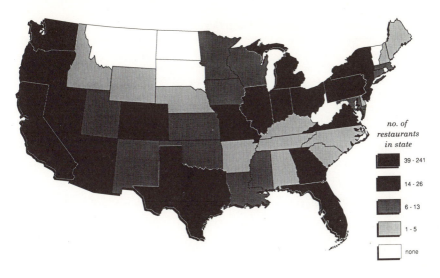

no. of
restaurants
in state

39 - 241

14 - 26

6 - 13

1 - 5

Figure 22. Market penetration of Denny's restaurants, by state, 1986

Californian's eye view of the world. Far Western areas are carefully
segregated, while the interpretation of the South, Northeast, and New
England may charitably be called imaginative. The borders of the
South extend well beyond the normally accepted cultural boundaries
of that region. The extension of Megalopolis into western Pennsylvania is dubious. The depiction of the Midwest isn't much better.
In defense of the company, however, the Midwest is probably
impossible to define because of its inherent schizophrenia created by
compartmentalized industrial cities and culturally traditional hinter-
lands. All in all, the delineation of the marketing regions is adequate,
if somewhat debatable.

The development of regional specialties to make the far-flung
units appear to be in touch with local trends represents an interesting combination of shrewd intelligence and dumb mistakes. Biscuits
were added for a regional touch in some areas, but a frozen product
is served which would bring tears to the eyes of any Southern
grandmother. Hash browns are a mandatory breakfast item in most of
the nation, but the company now serves the deep-fried product
which is offensive to almost everyone who frequents coffee shops.
Indeed, their menu planning generally seems to be oblivious to the
regional variations of food *preparation* found in the United States.
There is no apparent recognition that "good" fried chicken,
spaghetti, or even biscuits in the South are quite different from

Table 3   Regional items in Denny's Restaurants, 1984

Market areas	1	2	3	4	5	6	7	8	9	10
Bagels and cheese	×							×	×	×
White fish	×								×	×
Protein Pleaser	×							×		
Davy Jones (fish sand.)	×	×	×	×	×	×	×		×	×
Catfish dinner		×								
Fiesta fare			×							
Slender steak			×	×	×	×	×		×	×
Chili size				×	×	×				
Mushroom burger				×				×		
Hot beef sandwich				×	×	×		×	×	
Fish in a basket								×		
Hot turkey sandwich									×	×
Dinner Italiano									×	×
Burger Italiano									×	×
Boston scrod										×

Source: Roseann Bye, "North American Foodways as Viewed by the Food Industry," *North American Culture,* 2 (1985), 40.

"good" fried chicken, spaghetti, and biscuits in the Great Plains, and both of these are different from what is served in Megalopolis— where, incidentally, the biscuit is so alien that Denny's frozen version might well be mistaken for a hockey puck. The menu developers seem to have entirely overlooked this aspect of regional foodways.

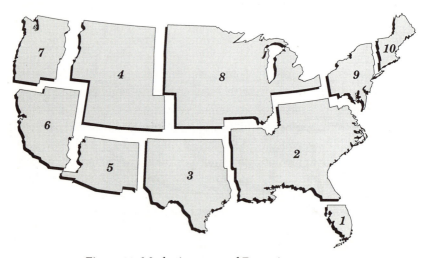

Figure 23. Marketing areas of Denny's restaurants

There has been a recognition by Denny's that their regional offerings have been inadequate and plans have been made to expand the regional fare, including new Mexican and fish items in the Southwest and Pacific Coast states. Their perception of a solution to the problem simultaneously demonstrates the problem, as they attempt to "fix" the western menu without realizing that their most pressing problems are in their eastern stores. Interestingly, it has been contended that one of McDonald's strength's in meeting problems has been the power invested in the regional advertising and franchisee associations in coercing the company to make changes to meet their particular needs.

The rise and fall of a restaurant chain

The mechanics of maintaining thousands of restaurant units throughout the nation also works strongly against the potential success of national chain operations. Few companies have been able to maintain McDonald's strict control, and failure has befallen many. The 1960s was the greatest period of expansion in American restaurant history, and many chains set off franchising frenzies in order to establish national identities. The most aggressive quickly set about selling franchises for entire states or cities, while even the careful were often swept up in the excitement of the moment and expanded more rapidly than was practicable. The problem is so endemic to the industry that one author titled his history of the fast-food industry *The Endless Shakeout*.

A classic example of the problems associated with rapid national expansion is seen in the Burger Chef chain. David Edgerton and James McLamore of Burger King were frustrated from the beginning with the unreliability of the original Instabroiler that was the key to their attempt to separate their product from the crowd of hamburger chains. In 1954 McLamore redesigned the machine and the partners approached General Equipment Company of Indianapolis to manufacture their revamped automatic broilers. General Equipment had been manufacturing the Sani-Serve soft ice cream and Sani-Shake milk shake machines almost from the beginning of the fast-food revolution. The new broiler design was so successful that General Equipment decided to use it to establish their own Burger Chef chain in 1957 which, they hoped, would in turn spur sales of their restaurant equipment.

General Equipment had both the financial backing and the equipment expertise to foster rapid growth of their new entry into the fast hamburger field. Burger Chef was soon expanding more rapidly than Burger King itself and the race to catch McDonald's had started. By 1968 Burger Chef had only some dozens of stores fewer than McDonald's, and it appeared that McDonald's domination of the fast-food industry would be challenged. The fast growing chain had also caught the attention of General Foods, which wanted to enter the fast-food industry to gain the high margins already being obtained by its traditional competitors (Pillsbury's Burger King; Ralston Purina's Jack in the Box; etc.). Burger Chef was sold to General Foods in 1968, and within three years it was clear that the chain's remarkable expansion program had collapsed. Burger Chef was eventually sold to the Hardee's System and most of its units were incorporated into that chain.

Two explanations are generally offered to explain the rapid demise of the Burger Chef chain. Jack Roshman, the company's largest franchisee and co-founder of the Ponderosa chain, has argued that it was the very synergy created by General Equipment's manufacturing about three-quarters of each unit's equipment, while also operating the chain, that spelled disaster. He suggested that the company spent too much of the available research and development money on designing new equipment, rather than on improving the management of the fast expanding chain. In contrast, John Love, an industry analyst and author, has argued that the end was brought about by the General Foods managers who believed that too much money was being spent on the acquisition of new sites. They apparently were also upset that some field men were earning more money than the front office managers. The field staff was fired and the company began relying on local real estate promoters, who were more interested in selling sites than in making the company profitable. Operational inefficiencies and poor site selection together seem to explain the failure of most of the chains that had fizzled.

Restaurants and regions

The regionality of traditional dinning patterns also plays an important role in making true national chains difficult. A seafood house in Tampa serves quite different fare from that of a seafood house in

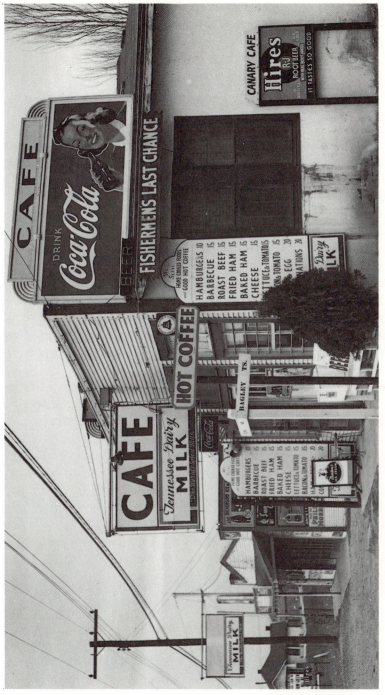

This 1942 photograph of the Fisherman's Last Chance, near Dallas, shows the classic, independent grill before the fast-food revolution. (FSA, Library of Congress)

Seattle. The food served at a Santa Barbara coffee shop is amazingly different from what is found in a similar establishment in New Hampshire. A diner is a cafe is a grill simply does not apply when we get down to comparing New Jersey's Edison Diner to California's Hoyt's Cafe to Atlanta's Majestic Grill.

General restaurants

The coffee shop–grill–cafe remains the most common restaurant type nationally, though the fast-food restaurant is closing the gap quickly. The general restaurant is most important in the declining industrial cities of the Northeast and least important on the dynamic Pacific Coast.

Even the most isolated and traditional mom-and-pop cafe has been forced to make changes in the face of the corporate steamroller. Although independent mom-and-pop operations still dominate the restaurant scene in most communities except on the West Coast, the future is clear. Chain coffee shops are increasing their market share each year. The fast-food companies will continue to expand their menus to increase average ticket amounts and broaden their appeal to our aging population. The future of the independent greasy spoon is bleak.

Howard Johnson's and Friendly's were once synonymous with the concept of the chain coffee shop. These early companies generally were unable to make the transition to the contemporary scene. Howard Johnson's has suffered repeated financial setbacks in recent years. Friendly's has been passed among several owners in search of success. Today western and southern companies dominate the coffee shop chain market, most notably Denny's of La Mirada, California, the largest coffee shop chain; Shoney's, based in Nashville, Tennessee; and the Village Inn and Baker's Square chains, operated by VICORP of Denver. Every region and most cities have local chains with aspirations, but few have the potential for national distribution.

Chain coffee shops expectedly dominate sales in the South, the Southwest, and the West Coast, where mom-and-pop operations are relatively unimportant. In contrast, the industrial Northeast tends still to be dominated by small, independent, traditional shops. Regional coffee shop chains are expanding rapidly in the Southeast largely because most residents in that area perceive that a hot meal is not composed of a cheeseburger and french fries. Shoney's and the

Kettle chains are the most notable representatives of the full-service chains in the Southeast. Several recent mergers and acquisitions, especially within the Tennessee Restaurant group have begun to challenge the validity of this statement, with the creation of some new mega-chains of coffee shops. The dominant cafeteria chains are also concentrated in the Sunbelt (Fig 10).

The mini-coffee shop is a southern phenomenon which is a post-war interpretation of the original White Castle concept. White Castle remains the forty-first-largest chain in the nation, but has changed little from its original design. It remains more a fast-food outlet than a general restaurant. Like the original White Castles, these new restaurants stress twenty-four-hour operations, breakfast at all hours, and selected sandwiches. The Waffle House also advertises itself as the largest purveyor of T-bone steaks in the world.

Waffle House is a privately held, well-managed, aggressive chain headquartered in suburban Atlanta. Started in the 1960s by some ex-employees of the Huddle House chain, the new company literally set up shop down the street from its progenitor and both still remain headquartered only a few miles apart. Its current rapid expansion out of its original regional base is especially interesting because its growth raises serious questions about the commonly accepted rationalization that the White Tower and White Castle chains declined because of changing national tastes (Fig. 24). Little different from the "white box" concept in locational strategy and menu, this very private chain represents a strong denial of that often-quoted

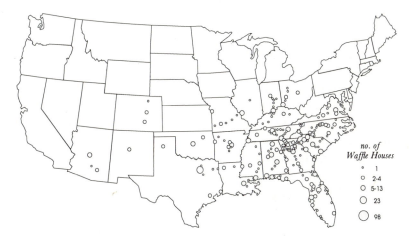

no. of
Waffle Houses

· 1
○ 2-4
○ 5-13
◯ 23
◯ 98

Figure 24. Distribution of Waffle Houses, 1988

The simple, clean design of the Waffle House is a strong force in its success.

belief that the "white boxes" died because of changing tastes. The Waffle House may not appeal to the entire population, but to many it is virtually a home away from home.

It has been said that much of the small-town Northeast has its eyes firmly fixed upon the rear view mirror. Stepping into many general restaurants of this region is like stepping into the past. Even the chain coffee shops of the Northeast hark back; Elby's, Perkin's, Park n' Eat, and others radiate a sense of the past, rather than the future. The independent diner/cafe thus remains king of the Northeast. The diner menu is little different from that offered by the chains, especially the Waffle Houses, but the atmosphere and management are entirely different. Aging, almost certainly well-worn, the typical southern New England diner serves a full breakfast at prices that would drive the chains into Chapter 11 bankruptcy, with a personality that could never be duplicated in plastic. The diner still dominates, though often it has taken on a new permastone exterior and a plastic paneling with Styrofoam wood-trim interior. Apart from the charm emanating from the diner building itself, there is actually little difference in character between the cafe and the diner of this region.

Kenny's Kitchen

Kenny's Kitchen squats along a southern New England road like an out-of-phase gray battleship camouflaged to look like a mountain chalet. The tired red neon sign blinks out "K ny's itchen" on a tired pole that has been brushed by too many eighteen-wheelers. The parking lot, crowded with cars with local license plates, tells the stranger all he needs to know.

Pushing through the varnished double vestibule doors, the crowded tables and steamy atmosphere take your breath away. The flash of the chef presiding over his giant hot grill affirms the initial hopes. The restaurant's decor is simple 1950s-modern. A grill along one wall, a worn green formica counter with red Naugahyde stools across the back, and about twenty unmatched tables form the heart of the restaurant. The large hand-lettered sign taped to the back of the cash register announcing "We will be closed from Aug. 10–21 for vacation" confirms Kenny's unshakable place in the community. The remainder of the decor consists of a large yellow and orange lithographed oil painting of some vaguely European place, a shotgun blast of scribbled signs on the back of place mats advertising the specials of the day—"S O S $1.49," "Fresh Fruit Bowl 75¢"—and, of course, the ever popular, hilariously laughing man shouting "You wanted it when?!!"

Kenny stands behind the counter as king of his domain. About thirty-five, his now outmoded ducktail haircut, open, starched, once-white, shirt—sleeves rolled up to display a variety of tattoos—complete this image of an aging impresario, which began with the glimpse of a battered red Mazda RX-7 parked out back. The grill is loaded. Ten sunny-side up eggs line the front of it. The back edge is piled with bacon ready to be shoveled onto plates in an instant. One whole side is piled with crispy, paprika-orange, chunky hash browns. Kenny rules his domain with a quick, easy efficiency born of many years of practice.

Alice is the true star of the show. Tall, dark, and slender, she controls the twenty tables like the captain of the ship, sending little Alice, her daughter–helper, scuttling across the room with a wave of her hand to clean tables, fill coffee cups, and serve customers.

Little Alice handles the couples. Big Alice handles the men. Her half-open blouse flutters as she swoops down on the new arrivals with mugs of steaming coffee, their spoons tinkling as they poke out of the cups. A flash of the broad expanse of the plain which is her chest, a smile, and she flies off to another table to smile again, pour, and move on in a continuous rhythm. Taking orders, refilling coffee cups, dropping off filled platters of eggs, hash browns, and bacon, she is the picture of economy of motion. The men barely look up before their cups are filled. She is everywhere, yet always at the center.

This is a place where men meet for breakfast before going out to their jobs, husbands and wives share a moment before heading off in separate directions for work, and families tarry on a Saturday morning. The customers are in animated conversation. There are no solitary eaters here.

Little Alice, wearing an old-fashioned green waitress outfit with its stiffly ironed white apron, is surely her mother's daughter. She lacks experience, but vainly copies her mom's action anyway. Little Alice bats her eyes, she slinks, the men smile indulgently. She has learned the rules of the game, but lacks that charismatic sensuality that makes Alice the star of the show. There is a confrontation off in the future sometime, but this morning it's just two hard-working waitresses slinging eggs and filling coffee cups in a symphonic ballet.

"No, we're out of the fresh fruit this morning, honey. How about some french toast?" She scribbles the order furiously and is gone as if by telekinesis.

The food arrives almost before the coffee cream is poured and the menu stuck behind the napkin holder. The egg yolks are a little runny, the white toast greasy from two much liquid margarine splashed across it, the jelly forgotten. The crisp brown-red hash browns are heaven! The meal's shortcomings are soon lost in their goodness. A glance upward and Alice is back with the coffee pot, even though little Alice is working just a table away. Grape-jelly packets are produced from thin air without a word as she surveys the table and is gone.

Big Alice barely shows her motions as she slides through the tables, pouring coffee on her way to the cash register. Taking a customer's bill, she counts the money, flashes a quick smile at the customer, and moves back down the counter. The king reaches out and gives her a pat on the rear as a new round begins with three new customers coming through the door.

"Three coffees? Find a table anywhere."

The beer garden/tap tends to be the small-town midwestern expression of this phenomenon, and often the only restaurant in smaller communities. The menu tends to be more restricted than those of larger communities where more traditional cafes and doughnut shops typically service the breakfast trade. The beer garden is disappearing from many smaller communities today. Rural depopulation and economic stagnation have become a way of life throughout much of the Corn and Dairy Belts. Thousands of villages and their restaurants, taps, bowling alleys, and grocery stores are slowly dying as the clientele disappears. The further loss of the all-important youth market, which tends to prefer the fast-food emporiums appearing on the edge of town, makes the future of these places appear bleak.

Pancake houses also have a strongly regional distribution. The International House of Pancakes is the largest chain, but despite an international distribution the company is a significant element of the restaurant landscape only on the West Coast. The other large pancake house chains are also most important on the Pacific Coast, except for Perkin's Pancake Houses in the Northeast. Pancake houses are virtually unknown in the South, Megalopolis, and New England. The Waffle House chain does not particularly highlight its namesake menu item, nor does it serve pancakes.

The doughnut shop is an important element of the breakfast trade in many parts of the nation. Dunkin' Donuts was founded in Quincy, Massachusetts, in 1950 to capitalize on this important New England breakfast tradition, and is the largest of these chains. Mister Donut, founded three years later by Dunkin' Donuts founder William Rosenberg's brother-in-law, was initially located in nearby Revere, Massachusetts, but is now based in Minneapolis to tap the all-important Midwestern doughnut market more easily. The doughnut shop is the place to find the breakfast crowd in much of the northern Midwest.

Doughnuts are also an important element of the breakfast scene on the Pacific Coast. Winchell's is the largest West Coast doughnut chain. Long owned by Denny's Coffee Shops in Los Angeles, the chain is concentrated in southern California, though it is found throughout the Southwest and Pacific Coast. Doughnuts are not a popular breakfast item in the South, and doughnut shops catering to the breakfast crowd are comparatively rare. Krispy Kreme, the largest southern chain, is mainly restricted to the region's largest cities, where non-Southerners also tend to be concentrated.

Independent specialty restaurants

The specialty restaurant is the epitome of the American restaurant business and it may take on many guises as it attempts to attract its generally fickle clientele. Much research has been carried out and few

The restaurant life of small-town Wisconsin hasn't been altered much by the fast-food revolution.

answers arrived at in search of the perfect formula for success in this market concept. There appears to be little significance to the distributon of top-grossing independent restaurants pattern in terms of cuisines, concepts, or locations (Fig. 25). The top-grossing restaurant in America in 1988 was the Hilltop Steak House of Saugus, Massachusetts, with total sales of $47 million. Saugus is an unlikely location for the nation's top restaurant, yet the Hilltop is consistently one of the 100 top-grossing restaurants in the nation. Most of the other members of this elite group are perennials as well, although ten to twenty new restaurants join the group each year.

The distribution of top-grossing independent restaurants does not match the nation's population distribution; the pattern is tied more to tradition, economic power, and recreation. New York City—actually Manhattan—supports the largest concentration, as one might expect. Chicago follows quite naturally as the second most important center. The factors controlling the distribution of the remainder of the nation's top-grossing independent restaurants is less obvious. South Florida's appearance as the third largest focus is clearly caused by intense recreational activity in the region, and indeed it would have been even more important if the Disney and other "corporate"— though not chain in the traditional view—restaurants had been included in the survey. However, the concentration of volume restaurants at Megalopolis sites outside of New York City and Boston is surprising, and also unexpected is the poor showing of western

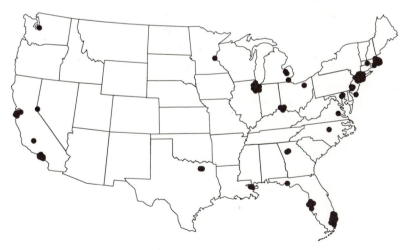

Figure 25. The top 100 independent restaurants in America, 1989

cities. In fact, it is astounding that the center of contemporary restaurant innovation, California, has so few restaurants on this list.

National trends in fine dining cuisine are little different than those demonstrated for the nation's top-grossing independent restaurants, though generally the food is less sophisticated. Steak and seafood restaurants are the most common fine dining outlets and they are found in virtually all communities. Flash freezing and the drive toward "lighter" meals has made seafood available almost everywhere today. While the interior West generally steers clear of fish (disregarding the not-so-local trout), specialty restaurants featuring beef and steak are common there.

The South is possibly the largest center of fish consumption in the nation. In coastal areas large quantities of local shrimp, oysters, and ocean fish are served, while in the interior there is a tendency toward freshwater fish. The "fish camp" restaurant is an almost ubiquitous tradition in the Carolinas. Pond-raised catfish are increasingly common in the South, and both production and consumption are quickly spreading outward from the early center in the Mississippi Delta. Indeed, catfish have been spotted on menus as far north as Iowa and as far west as western Oklahoma. Southerners prefer pork and chicken generally, and throughout much of the small-town South the specialty restaurant of choice is the barbecue pit.

The Northeast hosts two types of non-ethnic specialty restaurants. The most typical is the independent roadside dinner house or "nightclub." These places offer a far broader menu than similar establishments in the West. Pork chops, spring chicken, and at least two Italian dishes are absolutely essential. Even outright steak houses in the Northeast tend to have more non-steak choices than their Western counterparts. Roadhouses, night clubs, and similar places tend to be more common in Megalopolis than in the more staid Corn Belt, especially in the smaller communities.

The country inn is also undergoing a resurgence of popularity in the Northeast and is now a relatively important form of independent restaurant. Most of these places provide limited lodging and larger numbers of meals for adventuresome treks from nearby cities. Many serve basic home cooking, but some produce exquisite meals, as seen in John McPhee's equally exquisite description in *For Equal Weight* of his favorite, but unnamed, inn in suburban New York City.

Chain specialty restaurants

Norman Brinker and his wife Maureen, "Little Mo", Connelly Brinker went to the movies one night in 1965, and the chain specialty restaurant was never the same again. The movie was *Tom Jones*, the idea was the development of a specialty restaurant capturing the experiences of the tavern scenes in the movie, and the product was Steak & Ale. Brinker had been a regional vice-president of the Jack in the Box chain until two years previously, when he had resigned, moved to Dallas, and purchased a cafe which he named Brink's. The new venture had been less than successful. Hard work and long hours had not brought the returns that Brinker sought.

The first Steak & Ale opened its doors in Dallas in 1966. A sense of intimacy was instilled in the restaurant by creating a series of small dining rooms with fireplaces. The simple menu—five cuts of steak, corn on the cob, baked potato, and mushrooms—was written on a cleaver. The restaurant was an instant success with a first-year gross revenue of $400,000.

The second Steak & Ale opened in Dallas in 1967 and was even more successful. Rapid expansion followed, and by 1976 the chain grossed $100 million in its 100 stores. Brinker realized that there were inadequate financial resources to cover the entire country and began considering taking the company public. In the fall of that year the Pillsbury Company, already the owner of Burger King and the Poppin' Fresh Pie Shops, offered $100 million for the company, and Brinker took their offer.

The chain now had the resources to expand even more rapidly in terms of both what they served and how many cities they could cover. By 1980 the Steak & Ale menu had become the "standard" menu of the genre, with four steaks, three cuts of prime rib, lobster, crab, chicken, and various of combinations of the above. The company also began experimenting with a host of alternative concepts to capture a larger share of the market, including the Jolly Ox and Bennigan's.

Competition was fierce during this period. Challengers appeared everywhere. The older Chuck's Steak House and Cork and Cleaver were soon joined by Victoria Station, Stuart Anderson's, and many others. The market began to reach saturation, and the ever-restless public started searching for new dining experiences. The cholesterol scare and the parallel decline in beef consumption generally have been blamed for bringing these chains to their knees, but that is too simplistic an explanation. Although steak consumption did decline during this period, it is doubtful that the typical middle-income target market was significantly concerned with this issue. Certainly a major consideration for this group was growing boredom with an aging concept.

The result has been the rise of whole genre of total-concept restaurants. These restaurants take sharp aim at the soul food concept of dining and create total environments to give the consumer sense of place. Excluding such obvious total-concept venues as Epcot Center and the various Rouse & Company entertainment zones, the Specialty Restaurant Corporation of southern California has created some of the finest examples of this genre. Baby Doe's Matchless Mine is the recreation of the surface equipment and paraphernalia of the Matchless silver mine of Leadville, Colorado, in the 1880s. The food is rather ordinary for a restaurant of this type, but this is of little concern to diners who come for the ambience.

Ethnic restaurants

The first ethnic restaurant in America featured French cuisine and was located in either New York or Philadelphia in the late eighteenth century. A veritable explosion of "non-American" cooking has been available to the American public since that time. A recent study of Pennsylvania discovered a total of 126 different ethnic cuisines being served in the restaurants of that state. The array of choices is amazing and the total numbers astounding.

Ethnic restaurants have been increasing in relative importance throughout the twentieth century. There were almost 80,000 persons for every ethnic cuisine in Philadelphia in 1920; by 1930 the number had shrunk to about 40,000; while today there is an ethnic restaurant for about every 7,000. The total numbers have also increased dramatically, with 23 being tabulated for 1920, 50 for 1930, and 253 in 1980. It must further be assumed that these numbers represent a serious undercount of some Italian and other European cuisine restaurants located in neighborhoods where such ethnic cuisine is considered normal fare.

The rapid expansion of these restaurants has meant that it is almost impossible to keep an accurate count of their growth. Ethnic restaurants in ethnic neighborhoods often operate in such a netherworld existence that their arrivals and departures go unnoted. Veritable

Baby Doe's Matchless Mine makes a strong statement to passing motorists from its strategic location overlooking the perimeter expressway and scenic beauty of the Chattahoochee River in Marietta, Georgia.

tons of ethnic foods are also sold by street vendors, from sidewalk stands, and through other ephemeral outlets.

Ethnic restaurants tend to be either exclusively oriented toward providing food to the local, ethnic, neighborhood people, or targeted as specialty outlets for the larger general market. These are quite different kinds of places, and the foods served in each are quite dissimilar. A *local* ethnic restaurant serves home cooking, with few of the flourishes and extra touches one expects from a restaurant targeted at the specialty market. The cuisine of a local ethnic restaurant has made few changes to satisfy the American palate. The ingredients and flavors of these meals are often only marginally acceptable to middle-class American tastes and typically are either very bland or amazingly spiced. "Atmosphere" is nonexistent. The finest Chinese meal I ever had, for example, was in a nondescript, basement cafe in San Francisco's Chinatown with a friend who once lived in the neighborhood. No menu, no silverware, no English— exquisite food.

The distribution of home-style ethnic restaurants is directly related to the distribution of the various ethnic groups. Mexicans and Mexican restaurants are concentrated primarily in the southwestern United States, with minor centers increasing outside the region, especially in Chicago and Atlanta; Vietnamese, Korean, and Japanese neighborhoods and restaurants are concentrated in southern California; Cuban and Central American ones are most common in southern Florida.

Ethnic restaurants targeted for the general market have a very different distribution. Ethnic food is a progressive innovation in our society and the concept is diffusing from only a few centers. Asian restaurants are spreading principally from southern California. New York has a large and recently established Chinese community and is the center of innovation in the eastern United States. Dallas and San Antonio have become aggressive centers of Mexican food innovation nationally. European foods generally are spreading out of East Coast cities.

The recent explosion of Asian immigration to America has been accompanied by a parallel expansion of Asian restaurants in the top fifty cities. Chinese restaurants have become almost ubiquitous as our rapidly increasing Chinese population has tended to concentrate in the metropolitan centers. In spite of the federal government's attempts to redistribute them, large numbers of Vietnamese and other Southeast Asian migrants have become concentrated in southern

California. Koreans also have clustered in a few cities, though not necessarily in California. Japanese immigrants are the most concentrated of all Asian groups, as are Japanese restaurants.

The end product of this process is the development of distinctive regional patterns for the availability of ethnic food. While all of the nation's twenty-five largest cities offer at least fifty ethnic cuisines, those nearer the West Coast tend to have more Asian and Latin American restaurants, the Southwestern cities have more Mexican and Latin American outlets, and the Northeastern cities the largest percentages of those serving European cuisine, especially the current darling of the industry, regional Italian fare.

Chinese, Mexican, and Italian restaurants have virtually national distributions today. Mexican restaurants were the first to attempt national franchise development, with the San Antonio-based El Chico chain and Frank Carney's Chi Chi's based in Louisville. Both have had their difficulties, but have introduced these cuisines to many new areas. General Mills recently began expanding its Italian Garden chain nationally, while the Sbarro chain is also among the top growth chains in the nation. No national Chinese chains have emerged at this time and none is expected soon. Restaurant development is a classic outlet for the strong Chinese entrepreneurial spirit, and it is quite difficult for corporate chain operations to compete effectively with these family operated, low-overhead operations.

Fast foods

"Fast food" is one of those terms everyone understands, but it is difficult to define. John Mariani's authoritative *Dictionary of American Food and Drink* tells us that fast food is

> food dispensed quickly at inexpensive restaurants where only a few items are sold, often precooked or prepackaged. These items include hamburgers, hot dogs, french fries, pizza, milk shakes, soda, and ice cream. As an adjective, the term was traced to 1969, although as a noun it must precede that date by a few years . . . Today the term fast food is often synonymous with junk food [another indefinable term which is also understood by everyone], which also appeared in the 1960s and 1970s but which includes store-bought items . . . considered to have little nutritional value or to contain "empty calories."

This is a rather horrifying description of the food that has come to dominate the image of restaurant dining for many Americans.

The fast-food revolution has been one of the most dynamic in the nation, and some argue that this type of restaurant is the most important in the nation (depending upon how one defines fast food, of course). However defined, fast food is king within its suburban realm, though its territorial imperative is now bringing it into the traditional commercial core(s) of the larger cities as well. The image of hamburger alleys housing one of each of the major national fast-food chains has become as much a part of the stereotypical view of American suburban life as Little League baseball and tract homes. Little could be further from the truth. Michael Roark's pioneering examination of American fast-food restaurants demonstrates that the nation's regional dietary preferences play an important role in the distribution of these chains. Some external factors also play a role in the number and type of fast-food stores found at a particular location. Virtually all fast-food units have been built during the past thirty years. Sunbelt communities thus tend to have many chain fast-food

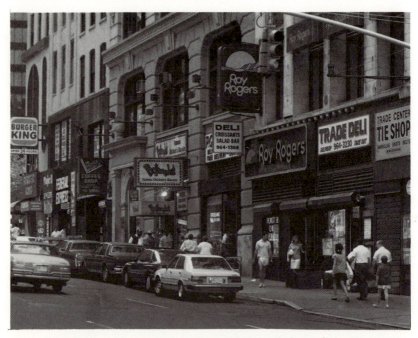

Manhattan has become a target of fast-food chains bringing suburban dining to downtown.

stores, whereas inner-city areas, most of the Northeast, and much of the small-town Midwest tends to be little affected by them.

The number of fast-food stores in a community is also controlled by its accessibility to the interstate highway system. Long-distance highway travel has increasingly become concentrated on fewer routes as the interstate system was completed. Today virtually all long-distance travel is confined to these few arteries. Food and lodging chains have capitalized on this concentration of movement by building units at those freeway interchanges that they believe are likely meal or overnight layover locations. Otherwise unlikely locations have often sprouted chain stores and accommodations as a result. These freeway sites generally have little to do with the surrounding communities, though adjacent communities start reaching out toward the freeway. McDonald's was the leading devotee of this strategy—it was once common to find the Golden Arches shining through the dark as the only sign of habitation in large areas of the Southeast and Far West. Many competitors have adopted a similar policy.

The tastes and preferences of the surrounding region are not important in the development of these interchange sites. It is of little concern to these companies if the local residents do or do not eat hamburgers, chicken, or Mexican fast food, as the mix of services is targeted to the likes and dislikes of the traveling public as a whole. In many ways these travelers' accommodation communities are somewhat reminiscent of the nineteenth-century railroads that often bypassed existing towns to then have a station and other accommodation suddenly blossoming on the prairie.

Finally, a great disparity exists between the number, type, and fare of fast-food stores found in suburban and inner-city residential areas. Inner-city residential areas generally have few fast-food stores because of the limited growth that has taken place in these areas over the past thirty years. Local and regional chains tend to predominate in these environments as well, as the larger national chains do not perceive inner-city residential areas as having the income potential to support their higher-overhead operations. In contrast, suburban areas tend to be dominated by the larger national chains. National chains prefer suburban locations because of the younger demographic profiles, the generally higher per capita incomes, and their inherent growth potential. Add to this the increased likelihood that suburban residents will have come from outside the local metropolitan area, and the need for a national, rather than regional, mixture of fast-food stores is clear. Suburban Atlanta's north Fulton County, for example, is largely inhabited by non-Southern, white, well-educated, upper middle-class residents who eat out frequently. The medley of fast-food emporiums is oriented toward hamburgers, Mexican, roast-beef and other national trends, not regional ones. The mix of fine dining is so tuned to national tastes that one must literally leave the area to find a good-quality, regional dining experience. The same pattern is repeated in suburban Dallas, Denver, and similar cities.

Individual fast-food cuisines are also unevenly distributed. Hamburgers are strongest in the Great Plains, the Intermontaine West, the Far West, and growth areas of the South. They are weakest in the industrial Northeast and portions of the Midwest. Chicken is strongest in the South and Southwest (Fig. 26). The Pacific Northwest and South are the two largest fish consuming regions in the nation, and not unexpectedly, they also are the centers of fast-fish consumption.

Pizza is king throughout most of the strongly southern and eastern European immigrant communities of the Northeast and Midwest. Chain pizza operations, however, tend to be relatively weak in the Northeast, where most communities are dominated by independent operators. Almost all of the major pizza chains were founded in the Midwest and they remain strong in these areas even today. However, Frank Carney, the founder of Pizza Hut, has contended that he did

Figure 26. Distribution of Church's Fried Chicken houses, 1987

more to assist Great Plains and Midwestern mom-and-pop pizza parlors than anyone in America. He pointed out that, soon after Pizza Hut moved units into small midwestern communities where pizza was unknown, they were joined by lower-overhead mom-and-pop parlors. The larger Pizza Hut chain took much of the financial brunt of introducing the new food; the independent operators reaped many of the benefits.

A little perspective

Traditional foodways have continued to have a surprisingly strong impact upon the expansion of restaurant chains and cuisines in spite of the changing cultural milieu of the nation and the attempts of individual companies to create national distributions. There have been many changes in these patterns, but when we look at the total distributions some clear regional restaurant patterns emerge.

The Stockman's Bar, open for Sunday breakfast in eastern Oregon.

7

The patchwork quilt

THE NATION'S TRADITIONAL dietary regions have undergone a significant transformation during the past century. In spite of these massive alterations, however, the original foodways of the nation's past have remained the foundations of the present. The result has been the evolution of a set of complex new dietary regions that clearly emanate from the old, but have their own character as well. Dining away from home has become so commonplace in contemporary society that we might also recognize a set of restaurant regions that complement, but in many cases are substantially different from, the dietary preference patterns that exist.

America may be seen as a land composed of six major and several minor restaurant regions (Fig. 27). *Dinerland* is found along the Northeastern seaboard and is most closely associated with the "Megalopolis"—the urbanized area stretching from Boston to Washington. *Taverntown* is largely confined to the Corn and Dairy Belt agricultural regions. The *Barbecue Pit* is the cultural South, but not necessarily confined to the eleven Confederate states. Western America, for most of the nation's history, stood as a singular place. However, the rise of the Sunbelt as a growth region, the influx of hundreds of thousands of legal and illegal Mexican migrants, and almost as many Asians, along the Pacific Coast, has forever altered that unity. The still largely traditional northern section of the West will be called the *Beefhouse*. The much-changed Southwest has been dubbed the *Taco Stand*, a misnomer which attempts to call attention to the large number of immigrants who now inhabit this region. Finally, *Chain Alley*, a new discontinuous urban region composed of

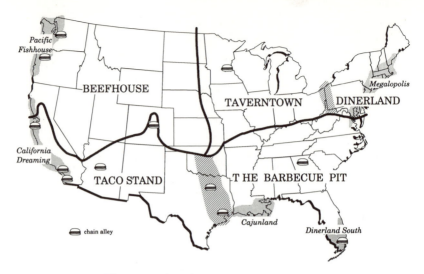

Figure 27. American restaurant regions

the increasingly dominant twentieth-century growth cities, must be recognized. Regional traditions and old ways of doing things have been almost completely submerged in Chain Alley by a demographic avalanche of rootless folk who have been wrenched from their birthplaces to spend their days commuting across a constantly changing milieu.

Dinerland

Dinerland, the oldest restaurant in the United States, historically has occupied the cultural and economic heart of the nation. The term "Megalopolis"—that urbanized band of cities stretching from Portland, Maine, to Richmond, Virginia—has been used to define the core area of Dinerland, but the restaurant region extends much further north and west than the urban region. The first licensed establishment selling food was founded in Dinerland. The nation's finest restaurants are found here as a matter of course. The city with the lowest per capita rate of restaurants and restaurant sales is also found here.

The most distinctive restaurant of the region is the diner: born, raised, and now buried here. The most characteristic restaurant of the contemporary landscape, however, is the neighborhood pizza parlor, with more than half of the population eating in pizza parlors at least once a month. National chains have found it tough going to compete against the local independent operators outside of the suburban areas in Dinerland. For example, only three of the 56 pizza parlors in Johnstown, Pennsylvania are owned by national chains, while one or two additional stores belong to local and regional chains. This still is the land of the independent entrepreneur (Table 4).

Subs are also consumed here in vast quantities. Several regional chains have been expanding rapidly into burgeoning national networks in recent years and these are common in many suburban areas. A Philly steak made in South Philadelphia, however, can not be replicated on some plastic, franchise assembly line. A meatball sub at Filletti's in Baltimore is a work of art. Submarine chain stores may sell Philly steaks and meatball subs, but a truly great sandwich is more than the sum of its parts. Great ones must be created from the perfect ingredients by the deft hands of generations of tradition with

The Pizza & 6 Pack is typical of the many independent pizza parlors
of the Northeast.

Table 4 Dinerland restaurants, 1985/8 (%)

Type	Concord	Camden	Providence	Johnstown	Pittsburgh	Ave.
General	26	19	29	28	27	26
Cafeteria						
Barbecue			1	1	1	1
Fast food	7	16	14	9	17	13
Hamburger	5	6	6	4	6	5
Mexican		2	1	2	1	1
Other*		5	5		6	3
Ethnic	16	25	19	10	15	17
Italian	6	9	9	8	9	8
Chinese	4	10	6	1	3	5
Mexican	3	1	1	1		1
American	24	17	19	19	15	19
Pizza	20	19	10	27	19	20
Sandwich	7	4	9	7	7	7

Source: Field survey, 1985 (Providence and Pittsburgh); telephone directories, 1988 (Concord, New Hampshire, Camden, New Jersey, and Johnstown, Pennsylvania)

*Includes hot dog, roast beef, and less common fast-food stores not listed, but excludes chicken and fish stores.

the perfect sub buns. The perfect sub bun requires the perfect Italian bakery, which may be the hardest thing of all to find.

Statistically, Dinerland has more fine dining restaurants than any other region. This statistic is misleading, however, as the regional average is raised deceptively by the heavy concentrations of fine dining in the entertainment and convention zones of New York and other regional large cities. The existence of rural inns featuring exquisite cuisine is also associated with the presence of these cities; and their growth in recent years has further significantly raised the total numbers of fine dining establishments. Fine dining is far from ubiquitous here, however. Blue-collar and poor urban residents, as well as rural and small-town folks, do little fine dining, and such places are rare in vast tracts of the region.

Italian is the ethnic food of choice in Dinerland. This is the home of the best and most famous Italian restaurants in the nation. Italian villages with grocers, vegetable sellers, bakeries, eateries, and the other necessities of the proper Italian life began appearing in the 1880s. The village *ristorantes* achieved great popularity and soon attracted outside seekers of exotic fare. Several New York restaurant

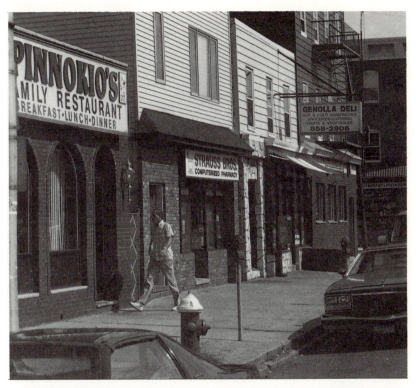

Pinnokio's Family Restaurant in Bayonne, New Jersey's Italian village
serves more ethnic cuisine than most Italian restaurants in other regions.

owners adapted the Neapolitan pie to American tastes in the 1890s,
and dining in these areas became even more popular.

These *ristorantes* provided an inexpensive, attractive, spicy alternative to the dull cuisine of the day. Visits to the nearest Italian
neighborhood soon became an attractive dining alternative for
seekers of new soul food experiences. Italian cuisine remained
largely concentrated in the villages until World War II. After the war,
the suburbanizing ethnic neighborhoods carried their cuisines out of
the inner cities and into the surrounding areas. More often than not,
elegant Italian dining is now found snuggled into a faceless store-
front shopping center of suburbia. Italian food has become such an
integral part of American cuisine that pizza and spaghetti play a
strong role in the nation's lowest common culinary denominator, the
school lunch program.

Chinese food is increasing rapidly in popularity in Dinerland.
Chinese restaurants are found in virtually all towns of even moderate

size. The low cost of Chinese dining, coupled with its long Americanization process and the large numbers of Americans with Far Eastern military service, has made this cuisine not nearly as "foreign" as it once was. This region is second only to the West Coast in Chinese dining.

Home-style cooking remains popular, and the diners, cafes, and "family restaurants" are exceeded in numbers only by the fast-food stores. Almost two-thirds of the population visit a family restaurant every month. Actually, large numbers of people breakfast daily in these leftovers of another era. Dining is simple, the cost is low, the atmosphere homey. Breakfast out has become an especially popular meal for dual-working households which find the expense of breakfasting away from home to be less than the inconvenience of food preparation and cleanup. Lunch remains popular as well.

Small-town life in Wisconsin still clusters around Main Street, the tavern, the cafe, and the bowling alley.

Table 5 Taverntown restaurants, 1988 (%)

Type	Dinerland	F Wayne	Sioux City	Ave.	Casper
General	26	26	30	29	31
Cafeteria		2	2	1	1
Barbecue	1				1
Fast food	13	26	22	24	20
Hamburger	5	11	11	11	9
Mexican	1	2	4	3	2
Other*	3	7	6	6	3
Ethnic	17	13	10	12	15
Italian	8	3	1	2	1
Chinese	5	2	4	3	7
Mexican	1	5	5	5	6
American	19	14	13	14	19
Pizza	20	19	22	21	12
Sandwich	7	2	3	3	3

Source: Telephone directories of indicated communities, 1988
　*Includes hot dog, roast beef, and less common fast-food stores not listed, but excludes chicken and fish stores.

Taverntown

Taverntown is a complex mosaic of traditional agrarian life and immigrant urban landscapes. The early nineteenth-century migrations from the East Coast laid down a set of traditional Dinerland dietary and dining habits throughout Taverntown. The late nineteenth-century migrations of Germanic, Slavic, Italian, Scandinavian, Polish, and other peoples brought distinctive new ways of life which were concentrated almost entirely in larger cities. The Midwest attracted more Germans, Scandinavians, Poles, and other Eastern European groups than did the East Coast, giving it a distinctive texture. Taverntown is thus much like Dinerland, yet it retains its own unique quality.

Taverntown has a split personality in several ways. The number of restaurants north of a line connecting Detroit and Sioux City generally is less than average (with some notable exceptions), while south of the line averages are higher. Fast-food market shares are consistently lower than average above the line as well. Pizza parlors are noticeably less common than in Dinerland, yet this is the home of most of the nation's largest pizza chains including Pizza Hut,

Dominos, Godfathers, Little Caesar's, and Mazzio's. The region has average to below-average hamburger sales, yet probably is the home of the invention of this delicacy (White Castle) and of the fast-food hamburger revolution (McDonald's). Virtually all ethnic foods are consumed in smaller quantities here than elsewhere, and the region has one of the most complex ethnic histories in the nation. It is truly a paradoxical place.

The family restaurant is still the favorite dining-out place for Midwesterners in most small cities and towns (Table 5). The tap, beer garden, or other alcoholic purveying establishment is the most common version of this restaurant in Germanic settlement areas, which is practically everywhere. The food itself, however, tends to be largely mainstream American with a few regional favorites. Thus, the differences between Dinerland and Taverntown are more of style than content, as can be seen in the contrasts between Kenny's Kitchen and the Norske Nook.

Norske Nook

US 10 wends through the hills of central Wisconsin to connect Green Bay and River Falls on the Mississippi. Osseo is about half way. The town isn't actually on US 10 anymore; the main road has been rerouted and the town bypassed, just as it has been bypassed by the interstate and, for that matter, largely by life itself.

The town does try. The community has erected billboards on the highway and on the interstate telling the world that it is a special place. Unfortunately Osseo is in the wrong place. A few hours from Milwaukee and about the same to Minneapolis, it is too close for through-travelers to stop for the night, too far for big-city residents to come for a visit. The signs are dutifully read by the hurrying travelers, but rather than the flash of brake lights one usually hears:

"Let's push on, Helen, it's only two hours to Madison and we can find a nice motel there."

"Its too far for dinner, dear. I just hate the long drive home after."

"Oh mom, it's sooo booooring."

A sign at the edge of the town trumpets the Norske Nook as one of the nation's top ten restaurants. A top restaurant in a village of 1,481 souls? This is enough to intrigue even the most jaded traveler. Off we go toward the main street lights twinkling in the distance.

The main street of Osseo harkens back to an old Western movie set with false-fronted buildings lined up and old-timey signs hanging out. There are too many restaurants, too many craft shops, and too many places selling antiques for such a small place to be real. Big Al's Collectables in the center of all this advertises that its stock is constantly changing. The Norske Nook, across the street, looks just like those places that provided us with lunch and breakfast earlier in the day in Minnesota. It is a most unlikely place for one of America's top ten restaurants.

A great, revolving, gleaming, stainless, refrigerated pie case topped with a toy house and "Norske" dolls leaps out as one enters the vestibule door. The pies are remarkable. Great mountains of gleaming meringue crown giant pudding pies. Golden-crusted fruit pies bulge to bursting point. Pies cooked by someone who really loves them. The pie sirens call out to Jason to tarry awhile on this strange island. A reconnaissance becomes an Odyssey.

The pie case and a low counter take up most of the main dining room. A second dining room lies to the left with a magnificent folk-art view of a fjord. Two de rigueur Wisconsin prints also adorn the walls. The larger is of two small boys in overalls with arms in pockets with the caption "You been farming long?" The smaller is of a boy and girl bottle-feeding a Holstein heifer. Plastic pots and plastic flowers finish off the decor, except for a sign on the back of the cash register advertising "Colonel's Rides and Amusements coming soon."

Two robust, young waitresses wearing vaguely Scandinavian uniforms of red-print skirts, bouncy, white blouses, and frilly aprons bustle about the tables serving customers. An empty table covered with the same red-and-white check in oilcloth beckons from the corner. Atop the table is a red card featuring an oval photo of Helen Myhre, Queen of Pies, holding one of her finest creations. The card lists the pies and includes a "Recipe for a Good Day," stressing unselfishness, patience, industry, kindness, smiles, and a loving heart. How could you go wrong in such a place?

The menu lists all your Midwestern favorites. Steak, ground round, hamburger steak, pork chops, fried chicken, haddock, Walleye Pike, jumbo shrimp, and those all-time favorites hot roast beef and pork sandwiches with mashed potatoes. Not too much Norwegian fare here, one thinks. Maybe the special. No, the waitress tells us that the special is French dip sandwich for $3.25. Well, the stop was for pie anyway, but the choice is impossible. Rhubarb calls out, a delicacy unknown in the South. Mincemeat brings memories of autumns past, with the aunts gathering to make venison mincemeat. Sour-cream raisin sounds intriguing. Coconut cream brings pleasant memories of time spent at a California duck-hunting club. Butterscotch brings back dinner at six o'clock while growing up. The choice is impossible. Damn the waistline, let's order two and skip the entrée.

Youth baseball must be over, as the restaurant begins filling with families about the time the pies arrive. A young couple arrive with five children ranging from seven to one-and-a-half. There must be a twin in there somewhere, though it's not obvious. The well-behaved group swarms around the next table, getting comfortable. Mom looks around to see if everyone is ready.

"Girls, time to do the menu."

Dad starts reading the menu aloud to his brood.
Suddenly, one of the littlest ones shouts out, "I'll have a chicken salad."

Much of rural Taverntown has experienced population decline throughout the twentieth century. Small towns in Iowa, much of the Dakotas, parts of Wisconsin, and elsewhere saw their highest populations before World War I. Some communities were able to stave off decay until after World War II, but growth outside of the exurban fringe is rare. A recent visit to one small city in Iowa found pleasant small homes on the market for $30,000 or less going unsold. Out-migration, school consolidation, the rising failure rate of farms, and the restructuring of traditional manufacturing industries have tended to discourage national chain expansion into the smaller and mid-sized communities. Hundreds of local and small restaurant chains still dot the region. Many small towns have no chain fast-food restaurants at all. The seeds of change are sown in the rising numbers of national chain stores along the edges of these communities, though crisis remains in the future.

The largest cities exhibit many of the qualities characteristic of similar places in Dinerland. Hamburger Alleys are becoming more important along the fringes, as the expressway networks increasingly dominate internal movement within the city. Small independent cafes are finding it harder and harder to survive in the face of customer defections to the better-financed national chains. Change is coming.

Sioux City, Iowa, is typical of so many of these communities. The continuing balance between family restaurants, pizza parlors, and fast-food stands clearly indicates the strength of traditional foodways in the community. The design and architecture of the restaurant units tend to reflect tradition rather than change. But change does lie at the edge of town. The numbers of fast-food places are growing rapidly with about half featuring hamburgers, followed by fast Mexican and hot dogs in popularity. There are also more Mexican table-service restaurants than any other kind of ethnic food. Chinese food is the second most popular ethnic cuisine, while only two Italian places—the most popular ethnic cuisine farther east—were noted. French, Japanese, Mongolian, Indian, and the other nouveau-chic ethnic cuisines are nowhere to be found. The better restaurants feature a mixture of steak, seafood, and other traditional Midwestern favorites.

The Barbecue Pit

Southern life has always been centered around the farm, the family, and the church. Town has always been viewed as slightly evil, or at least a place to be visited rather than lived in. Poverty, rural isolation, and a traditional lifestyle stressing family life and the homeplace have made dining out a foreign concept. Wednesday hot-dish suppers at prayer meeting, annual church homecomings on the grounds, family reunions, (Confederate) Memorial Day cemetery gatherings, and other family celebrations—all amply fulfilled the need for dietary variety.

The restaurant was the product of the city and the Industrial Revolution and little influence of either was felt in most areas until after World War II. Most county seats supported a restaurant or two, but these were busy mainly on Saturdays and during court sessions. These were simple accommodations for a simple society with few resources and little reason to stray from home. Further, most restaurants that did exist featured "home cooking" which was little different from food eaten at home. Even as late as 1930, only eighty restaurants were found in Columbia, Greenville, and Charleston, South Carolina, combined. Virtually all of these were basic grills; there were only three ethnic restaurants in those cities, no drive-ins, and two barbecues.

Even today, a community like Columbus, Mississippi, has few restaurants. Specialty restaurants for the most part consist of barbecue pits and fish camps, including April's Country Catfish and Bass River Fish Camp. A McDonald's out on the highway leads the fast-food pack. Most are local or regional chains. Sandwiches are an often-forgotten Southern tradition. Columbus's closeness to New Orleans is well reflected in the presence of several places selling Po Boys (Table 6).

Pizza Hut has arrived in Columbus. Its coming in many ways signals the beginning of the end of regional isolation. The story is familiar in the Midwest and now in the South. Pizza Hut brings its revolutionary cuisine into communities where only tradition can be found. Typically, the youth are the first to try the new cuisine and then they persuade their parents to come for some special occasion. Pizza soon becomes a part of the community's culinary weekly menu. The Pizza Hut unit begins to show a profit. Independent operators with lower overheads enter the market, which expands further. Mexican, especially Taco Bell (also owned by PepsiCo), and Chinese restaurant entrepreneurs often decide to take the risk and enter the market. Traditional food then begins to disappear.

The family buffet may be the most distinctive of all Southern restaurant traditions. If a town has a single restaurant, it will serve lunch and breakfast buffet or cafeteria-style and will probably close in the afternoon. The L & K Cafeteria of Gainesville, Georgia, with "Over 25 Years of Great Southern Cooking" is a classic example of a Southern small-town cafeteria. A new menu is printed every week and each day features five entrées. Fried chicken, steak and gravy, and ocean perch are on the list every day. The two changing entrées revolve through regional favorites, including catfish, chicken pie, meat loaf, "Southern" spaghetti, and, of course, roast beef on Sunday. Side dishes include mac and cheese, field pees, rice and gravy,

Table 6 Barbecue Pit restaurants, 1984 (%)

Type	Florence	Atlanta	Columbus	Lafayette	Ave.	Pompano Beach
General	30	25	25	25	26	16
Cafeteria	2	2		2	1	2
Barbecue	3	4	6	2	4	
Fast food	30	21	22	27	25	16
Hamburger	12	8	13	8	10	12
Mexican		2		4	1	2
Chicken	6	4	9	8	7	2
Other*	3	3		7	3	2
Ethnic	6	16	6	7	9	26
Italian	2	2		1	1	8
Chinese	4	5	6	4	5	8
Mexican		4		1	1	2
American	20	16	25	23	21	19
Pizza	9	10	6	13	10	16
Sandwich	5	12	16	5	10	7

Source: Field survey for Atlanta; telephone directories for Florence, South Carolina, Pompano Beach, Florida, Columbus, Mississippi, and Lafayette, Louisiana

*Includes hot dog, roast beef, and less common fast-food stores not listed, but excludes fish stores.

squash casserole, fired okra, sweet potatoes, turnip greens and more. The L & K and its menu is litte different from a thousand others in a thousand other small Southern towns.

Cajunland

You can feel the change as you speed across the line into Cajun country out of the Anglo (read redneck) pineywoods of southern Louisiana. The landscape's not much different today. Jim Walters builds homes most every place. The franchise chain store is most every place. The music on the radio is mainly western swing and country. You don't even get your thick, dark roast coffee in a Syracuse China demitasse at Beaudreux's Cafe any more.

But you can still tell when you cross the line. The pace of life in Cajunland is much the same as in the past. Of course, it's harder to find people who speak only Cajun these days. Dugout pirogues don't glide along the bayous much either. New roads and new houses, and DEA drug enforcement balloons, regulations, and money, have changed all those things. The Texas oil people and the tourists and the progress have managed to change the look, but not the feel. They still sell dried shrimp in the bars around Thibidoux. Randol's Restaurant in Lafayette still advertises "Good food, good music, where the young & the old let the good times roll."

"Let the good times roll" is as close to an ethnic motto as one can find for Cajunland. The French *joie de vivre* has always been very much a part of Cajun life and it remains, though not like it was. Ideals are changing. Justine Wilson is now a celebrity. Zydeco gets written up in *Time* and the *Smithsonian Magazine* and receives ovations at the Chicago Blues Festival. Cajun country has been discovered. Cajun culture is something to be revered, enjoyed—and, unfortunately, something that increasingly must be taught.

Cajunland isn't numbers. Statistically, the restaurants of Lafayette, Louisiana, are not that much different than those of Florence, South Carolina. Fast-food stores are the most common restaurants; ethnic food (excluding Cajun cuisine) is almost non-existent. Local cafes and national chains are everywhere. A few cafeterias and barbecues dot the town. What is different is the food and the feel. Oysters, shrimp, crab, snapper, frog legs, and po boys fill the menus to overflowing. My finest jambalaya ever was in a dingy little place just across the bridge in Morgan City. This little bar didn't advertise Cajun

In southern Louisiana even fast-food stands must bow to "Cajun power."

cuisine. It didn't tout Cajun specialities. But the owner talked with the right Cajun lilt and probably learned to cook on his mama's knee. He wouldn't even have known how to start making Southern biscuits and gravy. But the jambalaya and etoufée—that was something else. Cajun is a lifestyle—a lilt, a unique way of living, dancing, and eating. The Cajuns have never worried much about being counted.

Dinerland South

Dinerland South never has really been a part of the South. The place was almost empty, avoided by the Sawgrass people of northern Florida, until this century. But Flagler and the other developers saw an opportunity. South Florida has never been the same since. Once the winter playground of the northern rich, it became the winter resort for all Megalopolis and the rest of the Rust Belt. Now it is home too. The 1960s brought Cuban refugees. The 1970s and 1980s brought more Cubans and Haitians, and other Caribbean folk and South Americans as well. It is no longer truly Dinerland South; it's a mixture of New York and Chicago and Havana and Port-au-Prince and even Osseo, Wisconsin. And it's no longer just the very rich at West Palm Beach and Boca Raton, but also the land of little Havanas and retired villagers pinching pennies, trying to survive inflation on fixed incomes.

The region is a potpourri of traditions, cuisines, and ways of life. The place is cultural chaos wherever one turns, with clashing traditions lying cheek by jowl along almost every street. The obvious of course abounds. Italian *ristorantes* and sushi bars and island retreats and the Boston Pizza Company line the retail strips. Where else could one find a Chinese restaurant advertising the "Best Steak in Town"? Where but here could one find a restaurant specializing in "Florida"blackened seafood and Austrian specialties? Where else are restaurants featuring German home-cooking, New York deli foods, Cuban black bean soup, and jerk chicken side by side? If it can be said that Los Angeles is fifty towns in search of a city, then it can also be said that South Florida is fifty cultures in search of a way of life.

The Beefhouse

"I'm in love with him and I feel fine." The deep bluesy voice of the Sweethearts of the Rodeo pulsates through the white hot heat of a July afternoon. The stone-faced Dew Drop Inn looks cool, the Olympia sign in red and blue beckons. The thought of a hamburger, a cold Olie, and one more for the road sends a chill clear through the body as you step down from the dust-covered pick-up parked almost in the shade of the cottonwoods along the edge of the building. The crunch of the gravel, the even more searing heat of full sun, and finally the moist cool that can only be brought by a "swamp" cooler. The music shifts to Waylon Jennings as you find a booth and settle in. The regulars lean back on their chairs around the tables, talking about the price of alfalfa and cattle futures. An old boozer sits at the ancient bar, nursing a beer as an excuse to stay out of the searing heat. Marie, the waitress, bustles about pouring coffee between moving the steady progression of sandwiches and platters from the kitchen in the back. So little has changed that it's almost like you had never left.

Movies have portrayed the American West for generations as the land of beef, beans, and beer. Things aren't that much different. Beef remains as the meat of choice. Beans have been pretty much replaced these days by salads and big Idaho bakers. Beer and bourbon remain popular—those sissy wines and white liquors are mostly for the transplanted Californians.

The restaurant landscape is pretty simple here, like most other things. The general family restaurant serving breakfast, lunch, and dinner is king (Table 7). The cuisine is basic American. Hold the exotic, the sauces, and the fancy cooking. Mexican specialties increasingly appear on these "American" menus as the owners or cooks are increasingly of Mexican descent. Good home cooking away from home is the order of the day.

Fast food is growing, but mostly out on the edge of town. Hamburgers and tacos dominate; there's not much need for anything else. Distances are great and traditions firmly held. The big Eastern chains are coming—there's no way to stop them. The old standbys still remain too, holding their own much better than in most places. The Davids who live here have fought a series of Goliaths their whole lives, and old local traditions are hard to put by for the likes of Hardee's, Wendy's, and Burger King. A & W Root Beer, Sonic, Arctic Circle, Taco John's, and even independents somehow seem more attractive than those fancy Eastern places. Fast food seems to be a little scruffier here, but then most everything does to Eastern eyes.

Specialty dining means beef. Pure steak houses have never been abundant, but they have always been important. Dining out on the town usually means going to a place that advertises "Steak, Chicken and Select Seafood" or "Steaks, Fish and Southwestern Specialties," or some combination of these. The fish is fresh (frozen), the steaks local, the Southwestern specialties fiery. Barbecue is ever popular, but Southerners beware! The meat is beef. Pork means baby back ribs, not melt-in-your mouth chopped pork with heavenly sauce.

One of the great surprises to first-time visitors is the paucity of Mexican restaurants. Discrimination against Mexican–Americans

Table 7 Beefhouse restaurants, 1985–8 (%)

Type	Casper	Bremerton	Portland	Ave.	Taco Stand
General	31	24	19	24	28
Caf./buffet	1	1		1	2
Barbecue	1	1	1	1	4
Fast food	20	19	20	20	31
Hamburger	9	12	10	10	15
Mexican	2	3	3	3	7
Chicken	4	2	3	3	1
Other*	3	1	4	3	4
Ethnic	15	25	21	20	18
Italian	1	3	3	2	3
Chinese	7	8	10	8	5
Mexican	6	6	4	5	8
American	19	18	21	20	10
Seafood	1	10	4	5	
Pizza	12	12	10	11	9
Sand./Deli.	3	3	8	5	4

Source: Portland, Oregon, data gained from field survey, 1985; Bremerton, Washington, and Casper, Wyoming from telephone directories 1988

*Includes hot dog, roast beef, and other less common fast-food stores not listed, but excludes fish stores.

has tended to make it difficult for them to become financially established in order to develop fine-dining restaurants. More often than not, the first Mexican restaurants in many communities were started by Greeks and others, who blazed the cuisine's way toward acceptability. Real Mexican food is still comparatively rare. For example, the Sinaloa Mexican Restaurant in one western community indicates that it has been serving genuine Mexican food since 1948. The restaurant advertises "Full course Mexican dinners are served daily, including enchiladas, tacos tamales and a 'Merchant's Lunch.'" Cabrito is rare outside of the barrio or pure Hispanic community.

Thousands of Chinese workers were hired by the railroads in the 1860s and afterwards to build tracks throughout the West; Chinese section-gangs also often maintained them later. The Anti-Asiatic Leagues, and the associated persecution, that swept the West Coast in the late nineteenth century never found all of the isolated Chinese families. Small numbers remain scattered in railroad towns throughout the Far West. Chinese laundries and Chinese–American restaur-

Regional and local drive-in chains, such as Arctic Circle, still thrive in much of the West. (Robert Pillsbury)

ants have always been a part of the western landscape, and for many years they provided the only ethnic food sold in much of the Beefhouse. The rising popularity of Chinese foods, coupled with the increasing flood of People's Republic and Hong Kong immigrants as the leases for Hong Kong near completion, has been felt throughout the western United States, and even more so in western Canada. "Chinese–American Food" signs are slowly coming down to be replaced by ones advertising Mandarin, Hunan, and Dim Sum cuisine.

Pacific Fishhouse

The Pacific Fishhouse is increasingly distinctive from the Beefhouse, yet remains a part of it. Salmon, crab, quahogs, and oysters abound in the Pacific Northwest, and each year fish entrées and fish houses

The classic Pacific Fishhouse seafood restaurant features fresh local fare in a minimalist nautical setting. (Robert Pillsbury)

increase in importance. A "nouvelle Northwest" cuisine is developing, based largely on the natural bounty of the region. Originally California-inspired, early Northwest cuisine reflected the region's domination by its southern neighbor. Its more recent slide out of California's shadow to find its own distinctive personality is even more evident in the region's current nouvelle cuisine. The regionally based Skippers (Fast) -Seafood, the Original Pancake House, and Robin's Gourmet Burgers and Spirits well reflect the refreshing originality that has evolved here.

Fish is at the heart of this regional cuisine. Cheap and plentiful salmon, crab, halibut, oysters, and clams make this a seafood chef's dream. Local cool-weather fruits and vegetables also are a part of this increasingly popular cuisine which is producing some of the most original new foods and restaurants in the nation today. The region also supports far more Asiatic restaurants than the remainder of the Beefhouse. Japanese cuisine has become especially popular in recent years. The small Filipino and Indian populations are also beginning to leave their marks as their somewhat more exotic cuisines become increasingly visible.

Taco Stand

The West was once one. Today it is many. The arrival of millions from the East, and more recently hundreds of thousands from Mexico, has given the Southwest a new look. The days of quiet isolation, low population densities, and ranching are gone. Growth has brought with it the normal problems: change, new ways of doing business, and too many people for too few resources. Add to this too little water for too many people, and the picture is complete.

There have always been Hispanics here; indeed, the Hispanics predate the Anglos. In the past, however, the Hispanic communities were isolated and few of their people traveled outside that limited world. The Southwest traditionally has been dominated economically and politically by the great Anglo ranches which commingled little with their Hispanic neighbors.

The traditional center of Hispanic settlement was along the Rio Grande Valley. Later migrations moved the largest centers of Mexican settlement first to Texas and in recent years to southern California. Few Mexicans ventured far north of the border before the 1960s, except as temporary farmworkers who left little mark. Changing laws, the farm labor movement, and ever-increasing numbers have served to distribute these people throughout the region. There are few communities without some Mexican–Americans; they are dominant in many.

Tex-Mex, and increasingly true Mexican, food is appearing throughout the region today to replace the traditional diet of beef, beans, and beer still dominant to the north. Santa Fe style cooking is one of the hottest new cuisines in the nation and is spreading like wildfire out of southern California. (Remember, in the West all things must first go to Los Angeles before they can spread to the remainder of the region.) The revolution is sweeping the nation, yet as always tradition remains strong even in the hotbed of change.

Table 8 Taco Stand restaurants, 1984/8 (%)

Type	Beefhouse	Okla. City	Clovis	Bakersfld	Ave.	Orange Co.
General	24	28	28	27	28	13
Cafeteria	1	3	1	1	2	
Barbecue	1	5	3	3	4	
Fast food	20	34	30	29	31	22
Hamburger	10	11	17	16	15	10
Mexican	3	8	8	6	7	6
Other*	3	4	4	3	4	3
Ethnic	15	12	17	25	18	31
Italian	1	2	4	3	3	3
Chinese	7	5	4	7	5	8
Mexican	5	4	9	11	8	10
American	19	10	10	10	10	14
Pizza	12	9	11	7	9	13
Sand./Deli.	3	7	4	2	4	7

Source: Oklahoma City, Oklahome field gathered in 1984; southern Orange County, California field gathered in 1987; Clovis/Portales, New Mexico and Bakersfield, California based on telephone directory analysis for 1988

*Includes hot dog, roast beef, and less common fast-food stores not listed, but excludes chicken and fish stores.

Clovis, New Mexico, is typical of many of the communities of the traditional Southwest. The mix of restaurants is little different than that found in Casper, Wyoming. The restaurants are about evenly split between family, fast-food, and ethnic/American specialty. Pizza is mostly for the tourist trade. Deli's are unknown, the lone, chain sub

Beef and other traditional cuisine still reigns supreme in the Southwest, in spite of the rise of Tex-Mex cooking.

shop is in a Hamburger Alley serving the transient outside world (Table 8).

Hamburger Alleys are very much a part of the West. The interstate highway system has largely taken the place of the railroad as the small town's link to the outside world. Local entrepreneurs have reached out to these lifelines skirting their communities to build service centers at the interchanges, which through time have grown into Hamburger Alleys leading back into town—much the way that earlier Western towns reached out to newly built railroad depots on the edge of town. The hamburger is king of the western strip and accounts for more than half of the fast-food stores. Taco stands and roast beef and coffee shops are also present in large numbers.

California Dreaming

It is a cliché to speak of California as the incubator of the new American culture. Actually, California is many things. It is a place in search of a past that never existed. Genealogical societies are as strong there as anywhere. Old-line Californians proudly join the Native Sons of the Golden West and other groups to validate their birthright. Millions are spent to save and maintain the San Francisco cable cars. Once charming Mendocino on the north coast is revered as a hidden haven from the masses, while simultaneously serving as a handy set for *Murder She Wrote*. California is also the home of the Crystal Cathedral, the Valley girl, the Beach Boys, and the Hell's Angels.

What has this all to do with restaurants? Much. The California mystique is unique. It is a place where thousands of individuals can believe in the ideals of the John Birch Society while sun-drying fruit and installing solar hot water units in their homes. The restaurants of California mirror this ambivalence. Restless, searching for roots and for the Holy Grail, they appear in all guises and disguises.

It's not easy to be the self-appointed harbinger of the future. Tens of thousands of restaurant critics, owners, and chefs duly make their pilgrimages each year to California to sample the future and search for truth. Unfortunately, there is no Mullah to ritualistically indicate the proper path. The result is a strange combination of tradition and innovation, of new looks, old looks, and pseudo-looks.

If California is the future, then the future of the restaurant business will be a world of chains, concept restaurants, and Hamburger Alleys. The future will see the final demise of the independent grill and a

The lack of vegetation and wider spaces always makes many Western Hamburger Alleys, like this one in Phoenix, Arizona, look a little desolate to outsiders.

renaissance of the chain specialty coffee shop. Hamburger Alleys, leisure zones, and retail foci will become the dominant restaurant locations. Food courts will appear not only in malls, but also in aging gutted downtown office buildings, in created leisure spaces, and even in newly built warehouses in office parks and other places where people congregate. The array of ethnic cuisines will explode into a kaleidoscope beyond belief. All foods will become lighter, fresher, less cooked, less processed, and more packaged. Decors will become more, yet less. Natural is the way you prepare your food, not your building.

Studio Inn

The Studio Inn is a study in California casual dining. It has been carefully sited along the old coastal highway at the crest of a hill. No one can drive through the village without looking at it for a moment or two as they pass. The building itself is California contemporary cinder block with a stucco covering and low-slung roof. The decorator has overcome this architectural paucity by adopting the leading edge of the new-decor wave: he's painted the building white, with a brilliantly lit green awning—nothing garish, mind you, just well lit. The interior greets the first-time visitor with a bar, signalling that this is an important place and that waits are normal. This Sunday evening at dusk is different, however, and it is busy, but not crowded.

The dining rooms are muted contemporary art deco with an off-white covering most everywhere. A turquoise accent on some screens, a lighter shade covering the booths and table tops, break the potential starkness. The blond oak chairs and scrubbed blond staff breaks up the otherwise spare design. Spare, not stark, that's the ticket.

The menu is classic California fine-dining. Lots of fresh-grilled fish, apparently flown in each day from the ends of the world. Monkfish and Norwegian salmon and quahogs and fish so exotic, their names are both strange and unpronounceable. Chicken and oriental dishes and Santa Fe favorites dot the menu. Whatever happened to a good old prime rib or New York strip steak? No room here for such plebeian things; we must save room for the stir-fried chicken and Bok Choi and sun-dried tomatoes and fresh apricots and pinon nuts. Finding a familiar favorite here seems out of the question, but what the heck, this is California . . .

The crowd on a Sunday evening is largely aging upper–middle-class suburbanites who fit the Beamers and Mercedes in the parking lot. Most dress very casually, trying to look laid back in their Ralph Lauren outfits. A few men wear jackets. This is California, don't ask about ties. Certainly no tank tops, sandals, or bushy-bushy hair here.

The couples look very suave. The men sit with open shirts and gold necklaces and loosely wave their fingers while they talk of great finance and big times. The women are animated as they speak of more important things—the new tennis pro, the trip to Hawaii last week, and, of course, real estate deals. Is there anyone in California who doesn't talk about real estate deals? No wonder prices spiral upward so fast.

The salad arrives almost too quickly, with little wait and less flair. It is composed of two large chunks of lettuce. Apparently knives are compulsory for lettuce destruction here. The salad is completed by a few pieces of cabbage and a crushed-looking cucumber which peeks out from under the lettuce. The dressing is from a bottle, but a nice, natural bottle. At least it's not on the table tonight.

The lemon chicken is pure California fare. Two pieces of charbroiled chicken breast with a touch of lemon sauce. At least it's cooked. The "steamed" carrots, zucchini, and yellow squash almost didn't make it to the stove, but they are good raw. Pure, natural rice pilaf without any of those harmful chemicals lies at the side of the plate. One hopes that Uncle Ben doesn't use those nasty chemicals, because he most certainly made the rice. A large limb of parsley for color hides the fact that the plate is almost empty.

The staff work hard at keeping me healthy. My empty coffee cup remains empty to save me from consuming too much caffeine. My water glass remains empty to keep me from consuming too much lemon peel. The check almost never comes, to keep my blood pressure under control about the prices. And Sally, my ever-smiling, tow-headed waitress, with the ever so vacant smile, comes by every once in a while, to save me from considering consuming anything that my mother wouldn't approve of.

Six hours in California, and I already feel right at home.

Chain Alley

Atlanta, Dallas–Fort Worth, Denver, Minneapolis, Houston, Portland, Phoenix, Seattle, San Diego, the East Bay, and Miami have much in common. This group of "twentieth-century" cities has for the most part risen from obscurity since World War II to become leading national centers. Brash, arrogant, exploding with little regard for the past or the present, the future is all that counts for them. They represent their regions economically and often politically; culturally, they represent the new America.

This is the home of the corporate gypsy, the small-town person who left home in search of a different way of life, and of America's footloose populace. They find succor in this fluid society because no one is an outsider. The lifetime friendships and alliances that dominate small-town and established city-neighborhood life don't exist here. Everyone is starting anew together.

Certainly southern drawls can still be found in Atlanta, and twangs in Houston and Dallas, but much of the resident population over thirty was born elsewhere. The residents of these cities may call themselves Texans or Californians or Southerners, but this culture is learned, not a part of their personal history. Their friends and peers are as likely to be in another twentieth-century city as their own. Probably in five years they will be found in a new twentieth century city, just as five years ago they lived in another "home town." That deep regional conservatism, characteristic of the old way of life, is only a vague memory.

Growth is the byword of Chain Alley. Most of those places have been built since 1950. Post-modern patterns dominate their retail and residential scenes. The chain concept dominates the restaurant landscape, and even those that are independent adapt the chain look to their operations. Success breeds an almost instantaneous amoebic reaction, as entrepreneurs have accepted the concept that success and numbers are synonymous. Thousands of restaurants are established for the simple purpose of being purchased as franchise models by the large food companies. The traditional concept that a chef might start a restaurant just to have kitchen freedom is foreign. If one restaurant is good, then three are better.

Twentieth-century cities are composed of more than Hamburger Alleys and regional malls. They are also the conscious redevelopment of older neighborhoods and upscale neighborhoods and racially mixed neighborhoods and entertainment zones and specialty shopping zones. The concept that change is good and that time is short permeates their thought processes. This expressway is done; it's time to start planning its expansion. This mall is complete; how can we expand it? This subdivision is starting to fill; now on to Phase II. Little just "happens" in these places; development is plotted, planned, and accepted in the belief that success can be achieved only through change. The needs of individuals, of the environment, and of tradition are sublimated for the needs of the community. Lord save the poor souls that lie in front of the bulldozers or climb the trees to slow progress for the "common" good.

New York City's Time Square.

8

"Parts is parts"

(Wendy's Corporation, 1980s)

―――――――――

THE CITY IS ECONOMICALLY and socially stratified as never before. The American dream of a rose-covered split-level home in suburbia with two cars in the garage, coupled with the corporatization of the retailing, financial, and home construction industries, has created a new kind of homogeneous heterogeneity in America's urban areas. The city has always been divided by social and economic forces into distinct neighborhoods; today that stratification has virtually become a fetish. Zoning codes, regional planning, development covenants, walled housing developments, the increasing roles of regional shopping centers, the rise of large development companies, and a myriad of other trends have all favored an increasing homogeneity of the neighborhoods.

Simultaneously, there has been a consolidation of retail activities into narrowly defined clusters. The corner grocery, the isolated local service station, and the neighborhood church on a side street have virtually disappeared from our suburban residential neighborhood image. They don't fit. They don't meet community design standards. They create traffic hazards. Move them down to the commercial strip. Keep them fenced next to someone else's home. Economies of travel have always favored clustering, but today even low-threshold services are no longer welcome in isolated locations. Suburban dwellers have long believed that services must be clustered for control, and increasingly, so does the city as a whole. The automobile has almost always been given the credit for this process, but, to quote Pogo, "We have met the enemy and he is us." The automobile has made this change possible, but it has occurred because we want residential streets unsullied by traffic, street action, or garish commercialism. We have made our wish come true and in the process have created a seemingly endless series of homogeneous residential zones tied together with strip commercial developments and, of course, incredible congestion.

Clustering has also created a new environmental setting for retailers that inevitably enhances the advantages of the haves, while making it increasingly difficult for the have-nots to enter the marketplace. Rental rates and the demands of proper signage, decor, and image are much higher in the shopping centers on major thoroughfares than in isolated locations. Competition is greater. Entry costs for the independent have escalated. Failure rates of under-financed entrepreneurs have risen. Investors have become less willing to deal with independents because of this rising failure rate. The faceless corporate domination of the marketplace is clearly furthered by the process.

Increased capitalization costs have also forced an even greater degree of homogenization of activities. Shopholders and developers demand a consistency of neighbor activities to project the proper image and protect their investments. A classic example of this attitude is seen in the case of the Cinco de Mayo Mexican Restaurant located in the Four Worlds Financial Center in New York City. In 1989 the restaurant filed suit against Olympia & York developers of this multi-use complex, for breach of contract. Cinco de Mayo alleged that their agreement to the lease had been predicated on the premise that a high-priced Chinese restaurant and a European-style dessert cafe with first-class decor would be their neighbors in the project. They contended that the Chinese restaurant was moderately priced and that the cafe was actually a fast-food restaurant serving fare that was "low-end and in poor taste."

The demand for clustering thus comes not only from zoning officials, developers, and financial underwriters, but also from the retailers and their corporate godfathers. Clustering brings continuity and security. It also effectively underwrites the end of the independent entrepreneur trying to promote a truly new concept with little or no financial backing in a key retail area—in a sense, it brings an end to independent imaginative innovation.

Restaurant clusters

Restaurants have almost absolutely adopted the cluster locational strategy today (Fig. 28). Less than 5 percent of the restaurants of the typical city are found outside of retail clusters, and the completely isolated restaurant has all but disappeared from the scene. Further, it

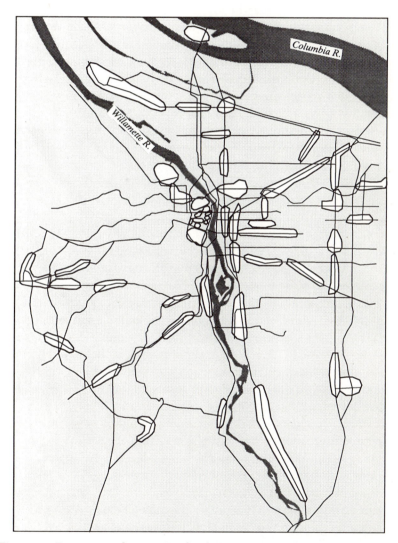

Figure 28. Restaurant clusters, Portland, Oregon. Note the concentration of small clusters in the pedestrian-oriented central business district

may be noted that restaurants are not found in all retail clusters; rather, they are concentrated in select locations which characteristically have attracted at least two competitors as well. The distribution of restaurants thus appears to be tied to a group of relatively easily defined economic, social, and geographic factors. This trend would seem to make prediction of their presence or absence comparatively simple. The high attrition rate, however, suggests that these locational constraints may be more complex than they appear.

Even a cursory examination of the locations of several types of restaurants within a typical city easily demonstrates the impact of the basic locational constraints upon the distribution of these activities (Fig. 29). For example, pizza restaurants in Atlanta are strongly concentrated in middle-income white neighborhoods, especially in newer, suburban areas. The heaviest concentrations are found along the suburban apartment corridors, notably in the northeastern section of the city. Pizza is not as common in the less affluent south side, with the lowest concentrations found in the poorest, Black, residential neighborhoods of the south–central section of the city. The northwest sector inside the perimeter highway, which includes some of the most affluent neighborhoods in the city, also has fewer than expected pizza shops. Pizza clearly is not an important element of the diet of either the rich or the poor of Atlanta.

Ethnic food is highly concentrated in the city within a few zones. The largest cluster is just inside the perimeter highway in the northeast corner (along upper Buford Highway) in a residential zone containing thousands of newly arrived immigrants. Large numbers of Chinese, Korean, Japanese, Indian, Mexican, and other ethnic restaurants operate in this area, generally serving their own ethnic communities the most authentic ethnic food in the city. Ethnic restaurants are also concentrated in the midtown section, just north of downtown, which has long been home to many of the city's less conventional residents. These restaurants are operated both by ethnic and non-ethnic owners. The city's first Ethiopian restaurant, as well as many other less likely cuisines, was located in a gentrifying neighborhood just to the east of midtown known as Virginia Highlands. My favorite ethnic restaurant, now gone the way of most who dare to be different, was located on the edge of this community and offered a combination of home-style Japanese and traditional Southern cuisine. Smaller numbers of ethnic restaurants are found elsewhere, usually in response to specific stimuli. The city's continental

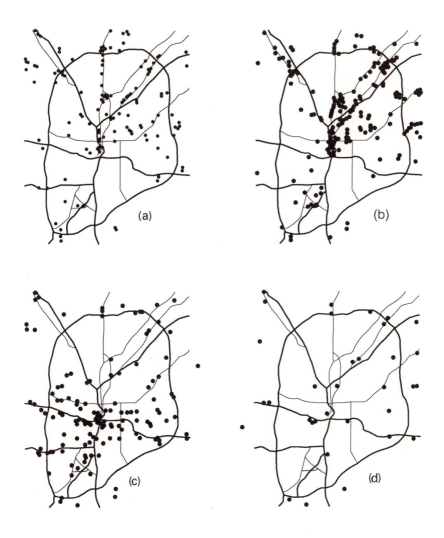

Figure 29. The distribution of pizza (a), ethnic (b), fast-chicken (c),
and fast-fish (d) restaurants in Atlanta, Georgia, in the early 1980s

and French restaurants are largely concentrated in the affluent
Buckhead and Dunwoody neighborhoods. Chinese restaurants often
are included in the major Hamburger Alleys, especially in middle-
income apartment corridors and Black, lower-middle-income areas.

The distribution of fast-chicken restaurants is confusing because of
the differing locational strategies used by various chains. Some

fast-chicken companies prefer to locate in reference to the strongest fast-food alleys of suburbia. Kentucky Fried Chicken, for example, is concentrated largely in these generic alleys, with little concern for the demographic character of the potential market. In contrast, Church's, Popeye's, and several small chains prefer to use a demographic locational approach and to concentrate in what they perceive are the neighborhoods of their largest potential consumers. These companies are rarely found along the large suburban fast-food alleys and are almost entirely concentrated in Black and/or low-income neighborhoods. Fast-fish restaurants have a distribution similar to that of fast-chicken stores. Like Kentucky Fried Chicken, Long John Silver's and Captain D's tend to be found in most Hamburger Alleys. Like Church's, which incidentally heavily advertises the availability of catfish fillets, Yasin's and some others tend to locate almost entirely in reference to the Black market.

Locational foundations of restaurant clusters

Five elements appear to strongly shape the location, character, and structure of restaurant clusters: demographic characteristics, consumer intent, accessibility, regional effects, and temporal effects. No one of these totally dominates the process of creating locational environments and their clusters, nor can any be ignored in understanding the forces shaping the creation of what constitutes either a good or bad locational environment.

Demographic characteristics

Demographic analysis of the perceived market area of a projected restaurant site is the most commonly used locational aid for the placement of new restaurants today. There is an almost universal recognition by retail planners that the economic, social, and ethnic characteristics of the area surrounding a site dictates what will do well and what will die. Indeed, virtually all shopping areas are developed today with specific target markets in mind. Stores are designed, leases signed, advertising created, and stocks ordered on the basis of the presumed target market of a particular center.

Demographic marketing analysis is also felt within the operational strategies of individual units. Retail stocks and strategies are tuned to fit the perceived target market. We have all visited different units of the same department store chain and discovered that stocks of merchandise may be radically different in different sections of the same city. A local department store serving an affluent white neighborhood might have a large section devoted to pastel-colored designer dresses; its downtown store in a lower-income neighborhood might stress lower-priced skirts and blouses; the same company's store in a suburban Black neighborhood might carry designer dresses, but stress different designers and carry items of brighter colors to enhance the darker skin tones found in that market area. This is basic marketing.

The mix of restaurants in the food courts of the malls serving these various demographic environments is also different. Fast-food chains favoring malls, such as Chic-fil-A and McDonald's, would probably be found in each of the malls in the above example. The mall food court servicing the affluent market, however, would fill the remainder of its stalls with more specialized fare and typically would include Hovan's (gourmet gyros), Le Panier (a French bakery), possibly a sushi bar, and maybe even a Pizzeria Uno (Chicago-style pizza). A Black-oriented food court would be more likely to fill the remainder of its non-standardized stalls with one or more chicken retailers, a barbecue place, a fast-Chinese stall, a sandwich shop or two, and possibly even a "soul" food store. The low-income shopping mall would have the fewest choices and might not even have a food court.

Demographics would dictate that the Hamburger Alley in front of each suburban mall would also contain different kinds of stores. The affluent neighborhood strip may not have a McDonald's, Burger King, and a Wendy's; one or more of those stores might well be replaced by a Fuddrucker's or a Chili's serving gourmet burgers. A Le Peep might appear to serve the breakfast market, rather than a Waffle House or a Perkin's Pancakes. A Bennigan's, an Applebee's, and several local chains with outside terrace seating might appear for the late-afternoon relaxing crowd. A Steak & Ale, or an independent dinner house or two, might appear on the strip to provide relaxed evening dining. In contrast, the Black neighborhood would have mostly independent restaurants, even in those affluent Black neighborhoods well able to support all of the restaurants listed for the affluent White strip. The Black neighborhood generally would have more establishments stressing fish and chicken. A more conservative subculture in reference to cuisine generally, the Black strip probably would have more places serving full meals than on the white strip. Among ethnic foods, there would be more Chinese, Mexican, and African restaurants, and fewer serving European and Japanese cuisine. And finally, the entire look of each strip—if (and that's a big "if") each strip is controlled by developers tuned to their market—will be quite different.

Market demographics suggests that the potential range of target markets is infinite. There are Black, Chinese, yuppie, gay, geriatric, and hundreds of other shopping zones potentially present in any city. Each has its own character potential. Some of these constraints are cultural, some economic, and others entirely the product of geographic considerations. The potential for differentiation is limitless.

Consumer intent

Consumer intent also affects the structure of a retail zone. Why is the shopper visiting the area? Some clusters cater to the shopper who attempts to minimize costs or has little discretionary income. Outlet and discount shopping malls are the most obvious examples of this form. Recreational shopping is also an important element of consumer behavior. Recreational shopping may mean browsing in the local mall in dress, shoe, and specialty shops. It may mean traveling to an area where shopping, dining, and entertainment are intermixed. One does not go to Quincy Market in Boston and Harbor Place in Baltimore ostensibly to shop, but rather to wander about looking at interesting goods, to purchase fun food, to watch other people, to relax, and to feel good.

Since restaurant shopping almost always involves a single-site purchase, consumer intent takes on a somewhat different meaning within this context. There are two basic "intents" of eating out. One may dine away from home either because it is inconvenient to do otherwise, or for the pleasure of the event. The first is a necessity, the second a discretionary purchase. Simply put, one eats out either to fuel the body—thus consuming body food—or to feed the soul, thus consuming soul food.

Most restaurants specialize in fulfilling only one of these goals. Fast-food stores are the ultimate body food emporiums. Also included in this category are most family restaurants, most sandwich shops and delicatessens, and many pizza parlors. Consumers come to these establishments primarily because they are hungry. They wish to fuel their bodies as conveniently as possible. McDonald's, Kentucky Fried Chicken, and Pizza Hut do little more than provide the body with food so that one can continue the day's activities. The increasing significance of body food largely reflects the changing nature of American daily life. There is little time to sit and dawdle over lunch in contemporary society. The phenomenal initial success of hamburgers and other fast foods in the 1920s, and McDonald's-style fast-food emporiums in the 1950s, largely reflects the increasing pace of American life. Many of us eat three, four, or more meals a week in the automobile or at our desks as we attempt to keep the pace.

Body food must fulfill several requirements. It must be served relatively soon after the order is placed. Generally it cannot have the potential to create a mess on one's clothing while being consumed. It must have a taste that will not offend. As a result, it is not surprising that McDonald's sells more hamburgers than Wendy's, even though Wendy's hamburgers are judged superior to McDonald's in virtually every consumer taste test. Consumers perceive that they must wait longer at Wendy's single cash register line, that the individual preparation time of their food is longer, and that the "juicy" burger has more potential for disaster. At the very least, it is extremely difficult to eat a Wendy's hamburger while driving, because of its propensity to come apart in one's hands.

Table-service body food has somewhat more latitude in style, but must still be prepared quickly and arrive at the customer's table within minutes of the placement of the order. A recent survey of schoolchildren discovered that pizza was the favorite school lunch food of 30 percent of those queried. Yet pizza parlors traditionally have not been able to attract large lunch crowds because of the delays in food preparation. Pizza Hut confronted this problem by guaranteeing that their newly designed personal pan pizzas would be served in a few minutes, or the next one would be free. If it could persuade all consumers to believe that this offer was legitimate, it would do even better. It's not that people didn't like pizza, rather that the food just does not meet the basic time precepts of lunchtime body food.

Soul food, in contrast, is little concerned with time and much concerned with content. Soul food generally means fine dining and the careful selection of a restaurant to assist in the creation of a particular mood. One might select an inn with a crackling fire and a cozy dining room to arouse feelings of romance. One might travel to an Italian village *ristorante* to enjoy a sense of the old country. One might go to an ostentatious continental food emporium on one of the city's most splendid streets to impress a client, or friends, or some- times even oneself. Under these conditions the quality of the food is less important than the atmosphere and the service. If the food is just adequate but the mood is exquisite and the service impeccable, it will go down in one's memory as great food, great times, and a place to cherish. In contrast, if the food is great but the atmosphere and service are less adequate, the restaurant will go down in one's memory as a place not to visit again.

Dining mood is created in a thousand ways. Locational atmosphere is especially important. Consider two identical Italian restaurants, each with all the proper elements including red and white check tablecloths, a waiter with a touch of accent, a bottle of slightly tart Chianti, fabulous antipasto, steaming garlic bread, exquisite fettuc- cine Alfredo, and dark steaming cappuccino to complete the meal. Place this restaurant on a quiet side-street in the heart of an Italian village. Imagine parking the car and strolling down the street crowded with walkers looking in shop windows, loaves of bread under their arms, the sounds of foreign voices, and a foreign "bustle." Pass the bakery with the smell of fresh-baking bread coming through the basement grate, and finally step into the cool, dark restaurant to be met by a smiling Italian maitre d' who greets you like a long-lost brother, though this is your first visit. Next, imagine going to the restaurant's twin, located in a faceless, suburban shopping center. The parking lot is full of empty beer bottles and debris from a nearby hamburger place. You leap aside from a hurtling teenager in his hopped-up Camaro with stereo blaring. Surviving the parking lot, you arrive at the restaurant to try several faceless glass doors covered with red curtains, each with signs demanding that you seek yet another entrance down the glass front. Finally, you enter to be greeted by an imperious sign demanding that you wait to be served and are eventually confronted with a vacantly smiling blond "hostess" saying: "Good evening guys. Come this way. Michelle will be your waitress tonight. The special tonight is baked lasagna."

The body food and soul food dichotomy plays a critical role in the restaurant location process, and may well partially explain the high fatality rate among contemporary restaurants in the face of extensive demographic research. Whereas the significance of demographics cannot be denied in relation to the establishment of appropriate restaurant location, the differences in the needs associated with consumer intent mean that body food locational considerations are entirely different from those associated with soul food purchases. Body food sales are frequently impulse purchases. The selection first requires that the restaurant enter one's consciousness. Body food restaurants generally make the least impact upon our memory; hence it is extremely important that these places be located among their competitors—competitive linkages, as they are called. All kinds of activities establish competitive linkages, most notably automobile dealerships, ladies' apparel shops, and shoe stores.

Traditional demographic analysis of standard gravity-model-based trade areas is clearly called for in the determination of the location of most body food restaurants. A simple survey to determine the socioeconomic characteristics of typical consumers and the distance they are willing to travel to purchase the service offered, an analysis of the social and economic characteristics of the potential locational sites, and an overlay of accessibility patterns allow the intrepid market analyst easily to demonstrate the best site for the establishment of a new facility.

Soul food restaurants, in contrast, are generally selected before the consumer leaves home. Plans and reservations are frequently made days in advance. Consequently soul food restaurant trade areas take on far different forms from those typical of body food restaurants. Distance-based trade area analyses simply have no relevance to the appropriate placement of these establishments. Though different, the factors underlying the locational needs of soul food restaurants are no less compelling.

Consumers mentally subdivide the city into attractive areas, uncomfortable areas, and large zones of *terra incognita*. The designation of these areas may or may not be based on fact, but tend to be held by large numbers of people. Rivers, lakes, oceans, and hills with views are all considered positive environments. Beautiful residential areas with gracefully aging retail shopping areas also bring a sense of positive nostalgia to most of us. Sparkling new office or hotel towers with magnificent views across the city do so as well. Negative environmental triggers include such concerns as apparent cleanliness, the presence of large numbers of people exhibiting aberrant behavior, and areas of perceived high risk.

The problem is that no city has more than a handful of potentially positive soul food environments. Entrepreneurs who wish to capitalize on these environments must cluster in them. As a result, restaurants line the cliffs overlooking Pittsburgh and stand cheek by jowl along San Francisco's Fishermen's Wharf. The agglomeration of soul food restaurants, however, is not necessarily negative. Consumers often perceive change as good. If the view of the lake was beautiful but the experience negative, one simply selects a different restaurant at the old location on the next visit.

The limited number of soul food environments, coupled with the broad appeal of the images created by these sites, makes it appear that soul food restaurants could draw from an entire metropolitan area. While this does sometimes occur, it often is not the case. All consumer demographic profiles have implicit sets of environments that create discomfort for the individuals within them. Many inner-city residents perceive suburbia to be a hell on earth to be avoided at all costs. Many suburbanites see the central city as dirty and dangerous. Mainstream residents frequently perceive the larger ethnic ghettos of their cities to be crime-ridden centers of drug addiction. Conversely, many of the individuals living in these ghetto areas feel uncomfortable in affluent areas and avoid them whenever possible. As a result, one cannot automatically assume that locational synergy will take place whenever the locational environments and the soul food demands match. Take the example of a popular, upscale, gourmet restaurant featuring northern Italian cuisine in one of our larger cities. The restaurant typically draws clientele from all sectors of the city, especially the elite suburban areas, some inner-city gentrifying neighborhoods, and, of course, the adjacent older, affluent section. Learning that they are going to lose their lease, the restaurant proprietors complete a demographic analysis of their clientele. They decide to temporarily open a second location in a suburban, gentrifying, engulfed village near one of the largest concentrations of their current clientele. The new restaurant is a financial disaster. A closer examination of the original consumer base from the perspective of consumer intent indicated that both the middle-city affluent clients and the inner-city gentrifying neighborhood clients perceived the new suburban site to be located just short of the moon. They indicated that they were unwilling to travel to the far suburbs even for this superb restaurant and that they would and could find alternatives to meet their needs near the original site. Simultaneously, the original suburban clientele continued visiting the old site and avoided the new location; they perceived the romantic journey into the heart of the city as an adventure that was an important part of the total dining experience at that restaurant. Furthermore, they indicated that the prices at the new unit were excessive. While the prices were the same at both locations, it was evident that they perceived higher prices as a characteristic of the inner-city area, an expected part of the mystique of that part of the city. The same prices in a restaurant down the street from their homes were gouging.

Accessibility

The significance of accessibility, both in determining the appropriate location for a restaurant and in its role in the formation of clusters, is self-evident. What is not self-evident is what constitutes good or bad accessibility. Traffic flows are not always good indicators, even in the instance of body food restaurants which are almost entirely tied to them. White Tower was concerned with this problem as early as the 1920s, when it discovered that stores located on the inbound side of the street did greater business than those on the outbound side of the street leading to distant residential areas. Further, one must be concerned more about where the passing cars are going than with the total number passing each day. Automobiles passing a site outside mealtimes don't count because the passengers probably don't want to eat. Automobiles far from either the starting or ending point of the journey are less important as most drivers are unwilling to break a short journey for this purpose. Further, drivers tend to be unwilling to cross traffic to reach a restaurant if congestion reaches intolerable proportions. Some chains have begun combating this problem by building stores almost across from each other along busy traffic corridors.

Soul food accessibility is not based on a traffic count. Soul food consumers operate on nearly a frictionless surface—that is, distance is comparatively unimportant—*if* the trip is interesting and does not take them through a negatively perceived environment. Harold's Barbecue in Atlanta is located between the federal prison and the General Motors Lakewood plant in the center of a large, racially mixed, lower-income neighborhood. This location is perceived to be highly accessible during daylight hours and at lunchtime the restaurant parking lot is crowded with both neighborhood cars and those of suburban businessmen. The food is really quite good and the moderate drive from downtown offices tolerable. Dinnertime is another matter; the parking lot is mostly empty and automobiles from outside the neighborhood nonexistent. At night this neighborhood is perceived as unsafe, and the frictionless surface magically becomes impassable.

Regional effects

The regionality of restaurant preferences plays an important role in shaping the constituent elements of restaurant clusters. A middle-city shopping center in Dinerland has few chain stores and even fewer Mexican, Japanese, and Korean restaurants. Dinerland fast-food strips stress subs, delis, pizza, and local stores. A similar shopping strip in the Barbecue Pit has some chain stores with more emphasis on full meals than fast food. There would be more hamburger and chicken fast food, and increasingly, a Subway or Blimpie sandwich shop, but not an independent sub shop. The Taco Stand version would have many Mexican and somewhat more Asian restaurants, with little continental food. Fast food would stress chicken and hamburgers, and the sub is virtually unknown. In the California Dreaming subregion the numbers of Asian restaurants would explode, including fast food, along with natural food, fish, and chicken, while beef would be far less important. Chain coffee shops would almost totally replace the independent grill. Chain Alley locations would be largely the same throughout the nation, as they are all largely inhabited by the footloose generation of Americans with few regional characteristics.

Temporal effects

Patterns also change through time. The "proper" cluster associations for one time will not necessarily be appropriate at another time. An even larger temporal consideration is the delay effect associated with the spread of restaurant innovations. Innovations spread more like a breaking ocean wave than a bolt of lightning. Once a wave starts ashore, it keeps coming, even though another has formed behind it. In restaurants this simply means that, while Los Angeles is experimenting with exotic Far Eastern cuisines, Portland, Oregon, is treating the previous wave of Santa Fe cooking as if it had been just invented for them, and nearby smaller Salem, Oregon, is excitedly discovering the Cajun wave that came before that, and, finally, tiny Wren, Oregon, is still waiting for its first chain hamburger stand.

Most innovations spread today in what is called a hierarchical pattern. They tend to be introduced first in the largest cities like New York or Los Angeles and then to spread to smaller and smaller cities and finally to the surrounding rural areas. The result is a wave-like distribution of innovations, which means that restaurant clusters that are already considered passé in the largest cities are a novelty in medium-sized cities, and are still regarded as alien and unnatural in the smallest ones.

The acceptance of innovations within each of these metropolitan areas is far from uniform. Typically, the dynamic suburban neighborhoods are full of change, while innovations arrive slowly in the stable inner-city areas. Similarly, affluent neighborhoods see more innovations than poor neighborhoods. Ultimately this brings us to Johnstown, Pennsylvania, where dining in a low-income inner-city neighborhood today is much like a not unpleasant journey back into the 1940s.

Restaurant cluster types

Fourteen different types of restaurant clusters within three general environments can be identified within the contemporary American city. While it is possible for clusters typical of the middle city to be found in suburbia, and certainly for fast-food alleys to be found outside the suburban fringe, the inherent characteristics of the three general environments largely dictates the kinds of restaurants and their attendant clusters.

Central-city restaurant clusters

The growth of commercial activity in the central business district promoted the development of the first discrete activity zones and associated restaurant clusters as early as the beginning of the nineteenth century. Today the typical central business district restaurant cluster stresses large numbers of low-priced restaurants offering traditional fare. Individual activity zones then further shape the selection to meet the demographics of their respective personnel. For example, office zones support large numbers of general grills, sandwich shops, and a few less expensive specialty restaurants, as well as the ever-popular office-building cafeteria. Secretaries and other clerical staff are traditionally poorly paid and the largest demand is for economical opportunities. Financial districts reflect the higher wages of many of their workers, with larger numbers of sit-down restaurants than pure office areas, as well as more specialty restaurants for business lunches. These sections also tend to have larger numbers of "adult entertainment" places, which serve more alcohol than food, but are not truly bars. The large number of stores catering to the take-out and delivery trades reflects the fact that frequently those workers have to work through lunch and cannot dine out.

Fast-food chains have been entering the central business district in large numbers during the past ten years. New York has had a most dramatic increase of these with the conversion of many Horn & Hardart, Marriott, and other restaurant chain sites into pure fast-food locations. Traditional fast food was long thought to be poorly adapted to this environment because it lacked a sense of variety. Office workers forced to select from the same limited number of fast-food restaurants five days a week tend to become bored with the similar fare, but the financial realities of eating at more expensive establishments daily have made fast food increasingly palatable.

The urban food court is becoming a common central-city approach to soften the fast food variety problem. Central-city food courts initially began appearing as a part of the multi-use mega-structures that were popular in many cities during the 1960s. These developments often failed, but demonstrated that the placement of multiple, fast-food outlets in courts, much in the same manner as those found in suburban malls, was an effective way to circumvent the ennui generally accompanying fast food consumption in the central city. More innovative developers then determined that it was possible to gut a low-rise office block to create space for a downtown pedestrian court complete with cute boutiques and a great variety of mix-and-match fast-food fare. The ultimate expression of these courts may be in underground Montreal, where food courts, along with traditional shopping outlets, have been established in the sub-surface passageways connecting the buildings from the Metro system.

Fast-food courts are being created more recently by establishing the pedestrian equivalent of Hamburger Alleys with a dozen or more specialty fast-food stores located virtually side by side near a natural congregation point on a low-traffic side-street of the central city. Street vendors often are encouraged in these environments, to further incrase the variety of fare available to pedestrians and the sense of

Yamhill Market is a very successful food court in the central business district of Portland, Oregon.

street activity. All three of these central business district food court concepts have been very effective in overcoming the problem of fast-food boredom. The true courts are especially busy when weather is poor; the street courts thrive in the fall and spring when there is a nearby park or plaza to attract diners seeking fresh air.

The hotel/convention zone also creates a distinctive restaurant landscape. Hotel coffee shops and restaurants satisfy a large percentage of the demand for breakfast and lunch as conventioneers and business travelers rarely have time to explore outside of their hotels for places to eat. There are few fast-food, sandwich and general restaurants in the area as a result. The numbers of fine dining places catering to the "client" entertainment industry, however, is large. A city's best steak house is usually found near here and not surprisingly both the Ruth's Chris and Morton's steak house chains often locate in these environments. Exotic and ostentatious restaurants cluster nearby, or within a short taxi ride, for the same reasons. In recent years some hotel chains have revived the dining-room wars of the late nineteenth century. The Ritz–Carlton hotel chain, for example, routinely attempts to develop the finest formal dining room in its city as a marketing tool which provokes retaliatory action by its competitors.

The popularity of artificial entertainment districts located in the central business area has grown since the success of Ghirradelli Square in San Francisco and Quincy Market in Boston. These seemingly diverse collections of restaurants, boutiques, and entertainment places exhibit an appalling level of uniformity. A gaggle of "unique" fast-food stores dominate the restaurant scene, while overpriced, cute, theme restaurants and night clubs complete the selection. Food is less important than the expression of a sense of New Orleans or Quincy Market or the Harbor in these places, and it shows.

Middle-city restaurant clusters

The middle city is that vast section of the city lying between the suburbs and the inner city, which has virtually been forgotten in the rush to the suburbs. The area is neither new enough to be attractive to the suburbanites, nor sufficiently old to be attractive for renovation. Retailing is confined primarily to aging neighborhood shopping areas. There is little new in the middle city, though as time passes it becomes increasingly attractive to suburbanites facing the choice of driving too far to work or redefining their housing goals. The houses are old, the store buildings are old, the thinking is old.

The classic middle-city restaurant cluster consists of traditional restaurants serving food consistent with the regionality of the city. This is the land of the traditional mom-and-pop independent grill, the aging specialty restaurant oriented to regional rather than national images, and a handful of independent and local chain

A classic aging middle-city shopping strip in Pittsburgh, Pennsylvania.

fast-food stores. It also largely predates the fast-food hamburger. Hot dog, sandwich, and "general" fast-food stores are far more likely to be found in this environment than anywhere else in the city. There are few chain restaurants and few "new" restaurants.

Gentrifying neighborhoods have quite distinctive restaurant orientation, and most of these areas are located in the inner sections of the middle city. Growth is selective in these environments, and proper development is largely prescribed both in terms of the kinds of homes that should be recycled and the proper kinds of stores that should be encouraged. Chain stores are antithetic to this social environment. The rejection of suburbanite values is an important part of the community ethos. Indeed, T-shirts and bumper stickers defiantly crying "Die Yuppie Scum" were recently noted in one of the less subordinate of these places.

The restaurant atmosphere is in keeping with the general tenor of the neighborhood. The neighborhood cafe is the most common type. Eschewing plastic, these eclectic places often feature what we might call "New York Times Cookbook" cuisine, favouring the dishes and cooking style popularized by Craig Claiborne's well-written books. These residents are concerned about what is happening to the world around them. Natural food stores, cooperatives, and proper restaurants are an important part of their self-image. Ethnic foods are popular as well, especially European cuisine on the East Coast and Asian cuisine on the West Coast. If a city has a single Ethiopian, Bulgarian, West African, or Peruvian restaurant, it will be located here. "Home cooking" is in; corporate, commissary, plastic, mass-produced food is out. Fast-food restaurants are antithetic to this lifestyle and few are found. Local fast-food chains, mostly founded and unrefurbished since the 1950s, are welcome; aging, pre-war greasy spoons are well patronzied. It is far easier to find a New York-style delicatessen or a bistro than a hamburger in this self-conscious environment.

There are two styles of ethnic neighborhoods in most growth cities today and both tend to be located in the middle city. The older of the two has been present at least since World War I and looks the part. Traditional Chinatowns have Chinese-style accents upon their buildings, frequent splashes of red, green, and gold architectural trim, many traditional street merchants, many small shops, and a distinctive aroma. Mexican neighborhoods typically have more stucco buildings. Portuguese, Jewish, and Greek neighborhoods generally have

The ethnicity of this Portuguese–American shopping street in New Bedford, Massachusetts, can be quickly identified by its unique assemblage of retail activities.

Pittsburgh's Squirrel Hill is a classic Jewish shopping neighborhood.

undergone fewer structural changes than most other older ethnic neighborhoods, but the kinds of stores and street exchanges leave little doubt as to the street's ethnicity. Providence, Rhode Island, goes the extra few steps in its glorification of these traditional ethnic neighborhoods by painting the street center lines with the national colors of the resident group.

Newer immigrant neighborhoods lack the generations of ethnic modification of their neighborhoods and look little different from traditional Anglo neighborhoods of the same age and region, except for their signage. Suburban Los Angeles, with its virtual invasion of "new" immigrants from Southeast Asia and Latin America, for example, stands as a classic laboratory of these environments. Some Asian neighborhoods here have become so ethnic that English subtitles do not appear on shop signs, "English spoken" signs are seen in some windows, and Oriental ideographic subtitles even appear on some traffic signs. While some structural changes appear on a few commercial buildings, the majority of the landscape could easily be generic Anglo, if the signs and people were removed.

The restaurant patterns of these two types of ethnic areas are quite different. Both stress traditional ethnic cuisine; however, the older, traditional zone has fewer chain stores. The food of the older area will tend to be more Americanized, and resident ethnic restaurants dominate the scene. The few independent grills in these neighborhoods often serve more ethnic food than some ethnic restaurants in other parts of the city. In contrast, new ethnic-zone ethnic restaurants offer food that is little Americanized and more diverse in type and preparation. Their food is little modified for the classic American palate. Paradoxically these areas also support more national, chain, fast-food restaurants, especially those specializing in familiar dietary items, even if they are not prepared in the traditional manner. Thus, the new area will be simultaneously more foreign, yet, because of the newness of the American experience, more amenable to Americanization.

Black neighborhoods are the most widely spread "ethnic" neighborhoods in the United States and the dietary preferences of this group are clearly mirrored in the restaurants that cluster here. Table service restaurants dominate, usually serving general fare, although traditional Southern foods, often called "soul" food, tend to prevail on the menus. Chicken, fish, and pork are the most common meats, while a variety of vegetables favored by Southerners are de rigueur as

This southeast Asian neighborhood in Orange County, California, has taken on little of the look of its cultural heritage, except for its **signage**.

A right-turn-only sign at the **exit of a southeast** Asian shopping center in Orange County, California.

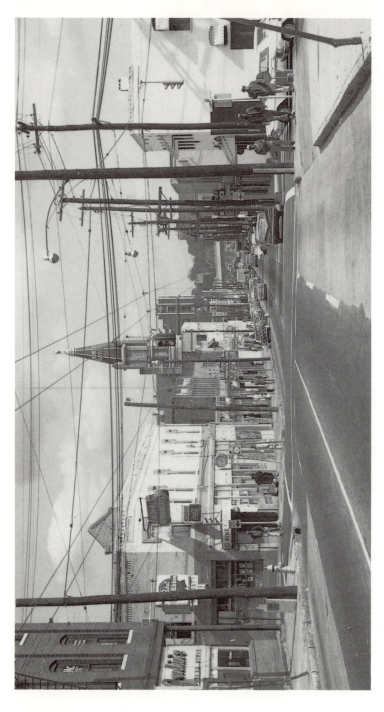

Atlanta's Sweet Auburn once was a thriving inner-city Black shopping street featuring Jenkin's Steak House (foreground), the Royal Peacock Jazz club (middle), and the Auburn Rib Shack (back), as well as the Ebeneezer Baptist Church. (Special Collections, Georgia State University Library)

well. Steak houses are surprisingly common; rib houses are ubiquitous. Chinese food has been growing rapidly in popularity for some
time, and Mexican cuisine, with its liberal use of peppers, is
especially attractive to this group and is now beginning to become
popular. These neighborhoods were passed over by the major fast-
food chain restaurants for the most part, though some individual
companies specializing in chicken and fish have been very successful.

Upscale shopping and residential areas often are found in the
aging, exclusive, residential areas of the middle city. Chic, trendy,
and camp are the adjectives that best fit the restaurants associated
with these areas. It is acceptable for chain stores to appear, but only
those that project the proper image. A McDonald's, a Wendy's, and
two or three other traditional fast-food stores may be found here, but
the parking lots are more likely to be filled with the tired Toyotas and
Chevys of the service people in the neighborhood than the BMWs and
Mercedes Benzes of the residents. Fast food is not acceptable to this
zone's residents. If a hamburger must be consumed it will come from
Chili's, Fuddruckers, and other chains invented to fulfill up-market
junk food needs. Bistros, concept grills, and sidewalk cafes take the
place of the mom-and-pop restaurants. A host of specialty fine-dining
restaurants take care of the problem of dinner. The truly affluent, of
course, have chefs at home and rarely patronize any of these places,
unless they are exercising the universal human need for junk food, or
if it is not convenient to dine at home.

Customers come from throughout the city to visit the elite dining
district. The irresistible attraction of the city's finest food, chic
restaurants, atmosphere, and cachet make it one of the most alluring
dining areas in the city. The crush is such that locals often shun the
best known places for the more attractively priced and less popular
ones. A secondary consideration is that many residents moved to the
area in search of a sense of community. These small neighborhood
places exploit this market by making a point of knowing their
customers and making them feel at home. While sounding simple
enough, the dynamics underlying the creation of this homey feeling
are more complex than they seem, and many die a slow death when
they lose the magic.

This affluent shopping and residential area supports more than two dozen trendy sidewalk cafes, roof and deck singles bars, and contemporary watering holes that quickly fill with thousands of young adults drinking beer and eating munchies while crowds watch on warm evenings.

Suburban restaurant clusters

Suburbia projects an image very different from the world inside the perimeter highway, and the restaurant and retail zones are quite different from those of the older sections of the city. This world was designed for a transient, automobile-oriented society in which the consumer must be snared while passing at 50 miles per hour. Strip developments are as old as cities. Boarding house rows and tavern strips appeared in almost every colonial city as early as the late eighteenth century, but never with the pervasiveness seen in today's society.

The contemporary image of the Hamburger Alley as an endless strip of fast-food stores interspersed with other automobile-oriented activities is largely false. Food stores actually occupy a very small proportion of the retail space of the typical commercial strip and tend to be clustered every couple of miles in response to consumer resistance to driving more than a mile or two to patronize establishments with such a low image differentiation. After all, body food is a necessity, not a luxury.

The range of restaurants found on a classic Hamburger Alley is also much broader than is assumed. The mix of fare varies widely, depending on the demographic profile of those who shop there and the restaurant region in which the strip is located. About half of the restaurants are fast-food stores in the standard suburban alley located in a twentieth-century city. A few chicken and fish outlets are found and, in most areas, a roast beef outlet. Hot dogs are common in Dinerland and Taverntown and, interestingly, in southern California, where the Der Wienerschnitzel chain has been uncommonly successful; they are rare outside the middle city elsewhere in the country. Sub shops have increasingly begun appearing in all alleys in the past few years, partially because of increasing public resistance to fried foods and partially because of the low franchise costs typical of these chains.

There are more sit-down restaurants found in the typical Hamburger Alley than generally assumed. Coffee shops are the most common, followed in frequency by pizza parlors, inexpensive steak places (i.e. Bonanza, Ponderosa, and Sizzler), and a variety of theme restaurants. Most are chain operations. If the neighborhood is sufficiently affluent, some fine-dining restaurants will also appear, but never outside of a cluster of similar places. Thus, a long alley may have a short

Hamburger Alleys appear to be bewildering array of competing restaurants.

section of fine-dining restaurants, often relatively close to an expressway interchange to increase accessibility.

Hamburger Alleys in the West have far more hamburger and roast beef stores than the remainder of the nation, while those in Black, Mexican–American, and select ethnic European residential areas have fewer. More affluent strips tend to replace their Burger King, Hardee's, and Carl's Jr outlets with more upscale "hamburger" units from Chili's, Fuddrucker's, and their imitators. Less affluent areas tend to have fewer chain stores and to replace the more expensive outlets with those perceived to be less expensive. Krystal, Sonic, and Whataburger stores are more common in these areas than are Wendy's and Burger King. Independent grills also are somewhat more common, while such chain coffee shops as Bakers Square, Village Inn, and Denny's are virtually unknown in lower-income strips.

Freeway interchanges are a very specialized type of restaurant cluster. No presumption about the content of interchange clusters can be made on the basis of the surrounding neighborhoods. The interchange merely represents a point at which cars "change mode", and most potential customers are simply passing through. Restaurants that take a long time to prepare food do poorly here while fast-food units thrive. Interchanges also serve residents who get off the through-route at this point before traveling some distance to their homes. This secondary market is often quite important and can have a strong influence on the restaurant character of an interchange. An interchange may be able to support several fine-dining establishments if these restaurants are appropriately shielded from the negative environmental elements and stand between exiting consumers and their upscale residential areas.

The suburban shopping mall food court is coming of age. Initially, shopping malls allocated only a few thousand square feet for food service, but it soon became apparent that more food and relaxation space had to be designated if the shoppers were to be retained for long periods in the mall. The early food courts were rudimentary affairs with small outlets of larger local firms. The fare was often poor, the choices limited, and shoppers' tempers short.

A number of fast-food companies began specializing in mall locations during the 1960s and more than a hundred do so today. Chic-fil-A, for example, began as a food item in the Dwarf House general restaurant in East Point, Georgia. Truitt Cathey attempted to take his chicken sandwich to other free-standing locations with limited success. Cathey then began opening mall locations and now has almost 300 units nationally. Chic-fil-A remained a mall-oriented chain until the mid-1980s, when it again began experimenting with freestanding sites. Orange Julius was originally conceived as a free-standing operation, but it too is largely restricted to food courts today.

The perfect food court store offers finger food which can be served without delay, appears to be relatively inexpensive, and provides some visual adventure. These places are designed to look appetizing to shoppers presented with twenty or more food-stand choices. Especially appetizing to a shopper with several friends, the food court allows each to select appealing meals or snacks, without compromising their personal tastes. Many patrons purchase items at several stalls to create a more complete meal. Younger children love the concept when mom and dad hand them some money to wander from stall to stall to find the most tantalizing morsels. Many come back with foods they would never have eaten if they had been chosen for them; others are never able to make a decision and must eventually be coerced into purchasing their meal.

The major chains have finally realized that these environments are gold mines and they are quickly increasing their exposure in them. Wendy's, McDonald's and others are adding units quickly. Free-standing table-service restaurants, once common in malls, are now returning. The Sunbelt cafeteria chains especially like mall locations. Morrison's Cafeterias of Mobile, Alabama, favored these locations almost entirely during most of the 1960s and 1970s, although they have been moving into commercial strip locations in recent years as well. Interestingly, this company has also been a leader in pioneering other sit-down restaurant concepts in malls with the introduction of its Ruby Tuesday chain. Other even more diverse chains are now joining the mall movement, including such unlikely candidates as Bonanza and some upscale restaurants.

The instant landscape brought about by the creation of a new regional mall and support facilities in previously open fields is one of the most dramatic features of the contemporary suburban landscape. The rapid expansion of the twentieth-century city has meant that such landscapes have become almost common on the fringe of the most rapidly growing metropolitan areas. Typically, instant land-scapes start many years before development begins with the acqui-sition of a site of several hundred acres near an expressway interchange in the projected growth path of a nearby city. Zoning changes, permits for alterations in traffic flow, new streets, traffic adjustments, and leases for the major anchor stores in the proposed mall—all are acquired before the first shovel of dirt is turned, indeed often before the first subdivision is started within miles of the site under development. The developer attempts to lock up the particular sector of the city as early as possible before competitors can go through the same planning stages. Competition is intense, and entire projects can be halted after years of pre-development if other developers successfully near the final stages simultaneously and lessees become unwilling to commit to what could be the wrong site.

Construction takes several years. Typically, the development plan includes not only the mall itself, but also several subsidiary strip centers for retailers, an automobile row, several office-park sites, a zone for hotel development, and as many as ten home subdivision sites targeted to draw consumers with the correct demographic profile for the mall. Provisions for restaurants include the typical mall food court, several freestanding food courts for sit-down restaurants around the mall, and out-parcels in the associated strip retail developments for the creation of an instant Hamburger Alley. The creation of these places is not restricted to twentieth-century cities, but the community must be sustaining major growth.

The engulfed village is another suburban environment which is playing an increasingly important role in fast-growing metropolitan areas. The tidal wave of suburbanization each year engulfs dozens of villages in new subdivisions and shopping centers. These village communities generally do not disappear; rather, they take on new roles. Many suburban home purchasers search for such communities in the belief that they serve as the basis of a sense of community and provide an enhanced suburban lifestyle.

The aging retail core of the engulfed village often undergoes a complete face-lift, which increasingly means peeling back the generations of previous change and restoring the shops to something approaching their original design. Additional shops and offices soon appear nearby, often attempting to emulate the core's adopted style, if not its architecture. A strip generally appears on the through street nearest the city core, and traditional suburban fast-food and other services not suited to older architecture soon find their way to these sites.

Engulfed village cores are increasingly perceived as assets for the

Planning began on Gwinnett Place near Atlanta, Georgia, long before development could support such a facility. It quickly attracted residential, office, factory, and business developments that have made it into an important regional mall. (Scott Slade)

development of shopping areas that draw consumers from beyond the traditional trade-area limitations of similar retail centers. Many are further perceived as being positive environments for the development of a soul food cluster. The nostalgic combination of renovated stores along a quiet old-time shopping street, a variety of gift and antique stores, and one or two fine-dining restaurants makes this a natural site for success.

Many restaurants well beyond the urban fringe are as much a part of the city as those located in its central business district. The rationale of these distant locations is both simple and complex. City families have always taken Sunday trips to the country to breath fresh air, see the sights, and have an adventure. For many, a meal at a simple country inn after visiting antique stores caps the perfect day. How better to end a visit to an historic site with the children than to stop at a charming country restaurant serving historic food in a pleasant setting? Increasingly, country restaurants are becoming destinations in themselves. How better to one-up business associates than to take them out to a quiet dinner at a previously undiscovered country restaurant? How better to visit with your lady friend, without encountering others you know, than go to a rural inn? What better way for a woman to spend some time with visiting relatives than to go shopping in the country and have a light lunch at a tea room among the gift shops and antique stores?

Created and enhanced village environments are springing up throughout the nation to "improve" the quality of this concept. Amana, Iowa (actually, a group of villages), represents a classic example of how a simple community became an entertainment complex. Amana gained national fame from the production of high-quality home appliances. Add to this core some Germanic restaurants, factory outlets, antique shops, junk stores, and gift places and you have the closest thing to Disneyland found in Iowa. Thousands jam the streets on a summer Sunday to enjoy the food, the shops, and the camaraderie.

Helen, Georgia, mirrors the other spectrum. Helen began as an unpretentious mountain community lying between Atlanta and the Smokies. There was little to attract visitors and few stopped, though many passed through on their way to nearby Franklin and Highlands, North Carolina. Local entrepreneurs decided to restyle the community in the 1960s into an alpine village. The earliest attempts were pitiful, but the community's developers were determined to succeed.

The outside restaurants of Helen, Georgia, are quiet only during a summer rain.

New buildings, new hotels, new restaurants, and new attractions were built each year. Today it has become virtually impossible even to venture into that section of Georgia during the fall weekends of Oktoberfest. The explosion of German restaurants, beer gardens, and other vaguely Teutonic food emporiums has been truly remarkable.

Conclusions

The cluster has become the dominant restaurant locational environment during the past twenty years. The demands of contemporary business organization, financing, and the decreasing ability of the consumer to be able to keep track of the constantly changing retail environment have all contributed to this change. It is impossible to determine the relative goodness or badness of this almost universal trend, but some significant negative elements do accompany it. Clustering inevitably supports the continuing rise of the national chains which now dominate the restaurant industry. Opportunities for individual innovators to bring totally new concepts to the marketplace are decreasing rapidly as consumers continually raise their expectations, not so much of food quality, but of the decor and accessories associated with these ventures. The current minimum standards for new restaurants have become so high that initial investment costs bar all but the well financed entrepreneur from the marketplace.

Pig barbecue (FSA, Library of Congress)

9

Feeding the soul: some last thoughts

THE RESTAURANT IS simply a place where, for a fee, one may dine away from home; a modest concept which has taken on literally thousands of expressions in the world around us. This apparent chaos of expression leads us to believe that the institution itself is complex. Nothing could be further from the truth. The restaurant is after all only a mirror of its society—its complexity or simplicity is only a reflection of society's complexity or simplicity.

The distribution of restaurants is largely predictable. Specific environments attract specific types of restaurants. Yet, these businesses fail at such a high rate that it is clear that our understanding of them is faulty. This would appear to stem largely from our concentration upon the effects of the dining out transaction, rather than its causes. What is it about a place that causes people to frequent it? Why do consumers select some places and not others? There is insufficient space to explore fully these questions here, but some things may have been made clear by the preceding discussions.

First, we must recognize that each of us has differing goals at differing times when we dine away from home. Sometimes we select a restaurant because we are concerned primarily with fueling the body. Our goal is to eat and go. Other times our intent is to make ourselves feel better, to celebrate, or to impress others. On these occasions our goal is to feed our souls. Each of these goals has discrete requirements. These may be one and the same, but they rarely are.

Many factors come together to create an individual image of what is

body food and what is soul food. Our decision process is the product
of our socioeconomic status, our cultural origins and our experiences. Socioeconomic status plays a role in that few of us can enjoy a
meal that is partaken too far below or above our normal lifestyle. We
feel uncomfortable when we do not fit our surroundings.

Individual culture determines what we will find good and bad, and
what is soul food and what is not. My Italian–American wife views a
week without pasta as a week without food. Pasta for her is a
necessity for survival—body food. Raised in California, I rarely
encountered pasta while growing up. Pasta for me is soul food.
Dining in the Italian village for my wife is going home; for me it is an
adventure.

Environmental setting is the last great element coloring our duality
of restaurants. From a regional perspective this means that biscuits
and fried chicken are body food in Alabama and soul food in Oregon.
Fresh berry cobbler in Oregon is a delicacy, but it's still body food.
The very same dish in southern California is something else again.
The individual place also defines environmental setting. A fish
dinner at Charleston's Cappy's becomes a little more exquisite as the
sailboats in the marina across the marsh turn brilliant red as the sun
nears the horizon. Dinner at New York City's Russian Tea Room is
made a little more posh as you pass Carnegie Hall to enter. Dinner at
Trader Vic's in the basement of a faceless post-modern Hilton Hotel
in any-city America somehow never achieves the concept of the
original in California.

Rapid change appears to be taking place in the restaurant industry
today, yet diet is highly resistant to change. This seeming contra-
diction is possible only because much of the change is cosmetic. Most
Americans still live on much the same bread, meat, and vegetable diet
consumed by their medieval ancestors, even if the form of these foods
has been altered. Cosmetic or real, these changes are gathering
momentum as the traditional regional cultures, which have served
the populace for more than two hundred years, are being replaced by
a national culture. The concepts of New England, Middle Atlantic,
and Southern cultures are quickly becoming more historic and less
contemporary. Each year it is becoming a little more difficult to find
honest shoefly pie and scrapple, and a little easier to find a Big Mac.

This is not to suggest that America is becoming an homogeneous
society. If anything, it is more diverse than ever. The problem is that
the new subcultures do not lie about in nice neat place-packages as in

the past. They are becoming more and more difficult to identify as the mingling and interchange process of assimilation speeds us ever faster toward a national style. Last week at the grocery store I stood in the checkout line behind a Vietnamese woman. I marvelled at her choice of groceries. A large jar of peanut butter, a family pack of corn chips, a large mound of hamburger, two gallons of whole milk, and a frozen duck. That's America today, or at least tomorrow.

I live in a community that many would describe as yuppie and certainly is located in Chain Alley. My neighbors drive Volvos and BMWs, wear clothes with the label more often on the outside than the inside, play tennis with an intensity that cannot be put to words, and take their summer vacations at the condo at Hilton Head. All were born somewhere else.

There are yuppies in every community in America. Indeed, the concept of a yuppie culture possibly has more validity than that of being a Southerner or a Westerner. But yuppies do not live nicely packaged lives, herded into cultural compounds as subcultures once were. They live in scattered, but quite distinct, locations in my city and others. Whether living in Atlanta or Westchester County, New York, or Orange County, California, they patronize the same kinds of stores, read the same *New York Times* best sellers, vacation in the same places, and form as coherent a geographic place—albeit discontinuous—as any cultural group in history.

These voluntary associations are becoming the core of contemporary American culture. Their habitués may or may not live in close proximity, but they do tend to utilize the same services. They hold many of the same beliefs, and, indeed, they form as viable a cultural cast as any that our society has ever spawned.

The Virginia Highlands section of Atlanta is a classic example of a community formed by such a voluntary association. It is an area of homes built primarily in the 1920s and 1930s. Residential and commercial rehabilitation became popular here in the 1960s. While this area is far from posh, it is one of the most desirable middle-income, inner-city areas in Atlanta today. The lifestyle and retail services found here reflect the subculture, which eschews the facelessness of suburbia, abhors the destruction of the environment, is somewhat artsy-craftsy, or at least eclectic, in its view of beauty, tells itself that it is more interested in quality of life than in possessions . . . and the list could go on forever.

We had dinner last night with friends in a small, crowded bistro in

Virginia Highlands. The menu was a strange but predictable affair, featuring rotisserie chicken, grilled fish, and pasta. The forté of this particular place is its dessert tray. Death by Chocolate, Sinfully Delicious, and Double Dutch Chocolate mousse cake are only a few of its offerings. After dinner we strolled along crowded North Highland among the groups of amiable people drinking white wine and waiting for their names to be called so they could dine in the small cafes along the street. We stopped at a gift store run by two young men, and sorted through their eclectic selection of Italian alabaster, pressed-board cut-out babies for the too-busy family feeling a little guilty, and some very "smart" cards. Later we crossed the street, skirted a New Age bookstore, and wandered into an art gallery where we discovered some paintings by a friend of ours.

Some of the people we encountered on our evening stroll lived there in Virginia Highlands, but most did not. The resurrection of old housing stock is not a prerequisite for enjoying this somewhat camp lifestyle. People come from all over the city to shop and enjoy for a few moments the ebb and flow of life and culture that emanates from this place. Walking along the street, peering into the antique and other specialty shops, brings a sense of community in the same way that the Hajj brings a community experience to Moslems. One need not live there to be a member of the subcultural milieu that created it or to enjoy the rhythm and pace of this special place.

Voluntary associations cannot demand that its members live in a ghetto. Some do, and more would like to. Unfortunately, the needs of city life often require us to live in homes far distant from our soul-mates. The cultural geography of the city thus becomes a complex amalgam of cultural associations which may be expressed in coherent residential patterns or, more frequently, only by the evolution of places where individuals may come together, mingle, and commune to reassert their beliefs and desires. The concept of omniscient culture regions covering vast parts of the nation may be relevant today, but not in our cities.

Edward Hall tells us in *The Silent Language* that culture is communication. He suggests that communication takes place in a myriad of ways, from our facial expressions to how we eat. Increasingly, the restaurant is dominating our dietary life, and our dietary culture is becoming not what we purchase at the supermarket, but where we go and what we order at the restaurant. In Snow White the mirror looks into the soul and tells the viewer who is the fairest of them all. Each year this restaurant mirror becomes a little clearer as it shows us not only how we look, but how we wish to appear.

It should be clear by now that this book isn't really about restaurants. It is about undertanding the geography of the new American culture. The traditional regional subcultures are mostly gone now, the remnants often retained as much from nostalgia as from reality. Mass media, immigration, and accessibility have modified and nationalized almost all of the traditional ways of life that we know. The South is easily the most identifiable of the old culture regions, yet even a short visit to its regional capital in Atlanta indicates that finding tradition in that city requires a special search. Visitors and residents alike must seek out Mary Mac's, Aunt Fanny's Cabin, or Deacon Burton's to have a down-home meal. The accent is mostly gone now, the pace is quickening, and the gentility of old Atlanta is disappearing.

The rise of the national culture, however, has not meant the demise of all subcultures. New subcultures are appearing with increasing intensity throughout the nation, but within new contextual settings. We have called them voluntary associations here, but they actually are subcultures which are as real as any that have gone before them—even if they are not arranged around traditional geographic and ethnic affiliations and locations. Their distribution is tied more to the diffusion of innovations down the hierarchical chain of cities than to past migrations. Their expression on the landscape is in clusters and pockets, not broad geographic zones. Yet that expression is just as persuasive as the Pennsylvania Dutch and Puritan landscapes of old.

Sandwich stand (FSA, Library of Congress)

Bibliographic sources

THIS STUDY BEGAN in the early 1980s with a simple inquiry into the distribution of Atlanta restaurants to determine if there was a geographic relationship between socioeconomic characteristics and restaurant fare. Several earlier attempts had been made to examine the urban landscape through studies of church membership patterns, grocery store shelf-space allocations, and television viewing patterns, with little success. The restaurant study soon became a fascinating adventure in itself.

It was soon clear that the analysis needed to be extended to ascertain which of the patterns discovered were city-specific, which were region-specific, and which were national in character. Analyses of Portland (Oregon), Salem (Oregon), Oklahoma City, Pittsburgh, Providence (Rhode Island), and Orange County (California) were completed to answer these questions. These field surveys included visiting each restaurant in the designated city, mapping its location, and assigning it to a restaurant category. Information on more than 12,000 restaurants was entered into a database and a variety of associations examined. Several thousand inverviews of patrons, restaurant personnel, restaurant owners, and others were conducted about consumer behavior, locational strategies and utilities, and general restaurant lore.

This information was supplemented with additional, less intensive, field surveys in Manhattan, Baltimore, Washington, DC, Phoenix, Chicago, Seattle, and dozens of small towns in every corner of the nation. Return visits to portions of Pittsburgh, as well as continuous viewing of the changing restaurant scene in Atlanta, completed the field information.

Original data used in this study came primarily from the Annual Reports of almost a hundred public restaurant companies, the extensive city directory collection of the University of Pittsburgh library, and the Sanborn Fire Insurance maps at the Library of Congress. The corporate Annual Reports proved to be an invaluable source of the changing thinking of corporate planners and the changing reality under which these companies operate. The city directories were irreplaceable sources for the reconstruction of past restaurant patterns. Several dozen nineteenth-century cities were mapped to give an indication of the restaurant distributions of that period. The Sanborn Fire Insurance maps supplemented this information by allowing the development of an understanding of the contextual setting of late nineteenth-century restaurants.

Telephone directories were an important beginning point for fieldwork, and their value as a source of information on contemporary society cannot be overemphasized. They can be misleading, however, and as much as 15 percent of all restaurants listed—primarily among the lowest economic groups—were found to be missing in a few of the cities surveyed.

Research into contemporary American restaurant patterns must rely heavily upon *Restaurants and Institutions, Restaurant Business,* and *Restaurant Hospitality* magazines. The annual surveys of these magazines are invaluable in developing national studies of restaurants, while their unpublished files, though not used here, are the finest in the nation for this work. Similarly, the various publications of the National Restaurant Association are invaluable in defining the changing character of the restaurant industry.

Several books are of special interest to anyone wishing to learn more about the American restaurant. Philip Langdon's *Orange Roofs, Golden Arches* is the best architectural history of the evolution of restaurant buildings and contains the most comprehensive history of the industry available in a single source. It should be on the reading list of everyone with an interest in the topic. The second invaluable source is Love's *McDonald's: Behind the Arches,* which is ostensibly a history of McDonald's Corporation, but is actually the best contextual history of the fast-food revolution that has been written to this time. Two other books are also of note. Emerson's *Fast Food: The Endless Shakeout* is a business history of the fast-food industry from a somewhat more academic point of view. Wyckoff and Sasser's *The Chain-Restaurant Industry* is another somewhat academic overview of the contemporary period in the restaurant industry. Finally, Mariani's *The Dictionary of American Food and Drink* is a fascinating compendium of our nation's food trivia. If one can afford to purchase only a single book on American food, this somewhat eclectic and obscure paperback is it.

Information on taverns and boarding houses is fragmentary, and there are no great sources for it. The Batterberry's study of New York restaurants is of some interest for that city, while Taylor's *Eating, Drinking and Visiting in the South* is especially good for that region.

The diner has fascinated writers for decades. Diner life was especially well depicted in several recent movies, including *Diner* and *Tin Men* which were both set in Baltimore, not a great diner town. Gutman and Kaufman's *American Diner* is without equal in developing the history and times of this type of restaurant and compulsory reading for those finding this phenomenon fascinating. Actually, a visit to Providence, which seems to be the home of the finest selection of unchanged diners in the nation, is a prerequisite for anyone with even a passing interest in this topic. Hirshorn and Izenour's *White Towers* stands above all others in the depiction of the evolution of the "white box" phenomenon.

The literature on American diet has exploded during the last decade, yet three sources remain as most important: Root and de Rochemont's *Eating in America,* Tannahill's *Food in History,* and Cummings's *The American and His Food.* Simoons's *Eat Not this Flesh* deals with food avoidances, and while not directly relevant is especially helpful in gaining an understanding of the larger issues. The various publications of the United States Department of Agriculture and the National Conference Board also give detailed statistics which are invaluable.

Two works were of special interest in the study of national restaurant patterns. Zelinsky's study of ethnic restaurants in *Geoforum* is an ambitious attempt to utilize telephone directory information to ascertain ethnic restaurant patterns. Zelinsky is a peripatetic observer of the American condition and this study is typical of his careful, far-reaching style. Michael Roark's research on the distribution of fast-food restaurants, his maps of restaurant patterns, and the panel discussions during the annual meeting of the Society for the North American Cultural Survey hosted at Nichols State University by Randall Detro in the mid-1980s were magnificent. Panel participants included Zelinsky, Roark, Roseanne Bye of Denny's, the editor of *Restaurants and Institutions* magazine, Grady Clay; and a variety of specialists— anthropologists, culture historians, and geographers —on American diet and restaurants were without equal as they explored the changing nature of the American diet.

The single most important sources on retail clusters and their character are based on the work of Brian J. L. Berry and his students over the years. While fieldwork and painstaking handmapping was the basis for the development of the restaurant cluster concept discussed here, Allen Pred's ground-breaking analysis of the differing character of the Black shopping street in Chicago proved to be an important intellectual foundation for these ideas. The concept of voluntary associations was first introduced to me in Robert Riley's work in *Landscape* and later in Wilbur Zelinsky's pioneering research on popular culture listed in the bibliography. Also important conceptually was Chris Winters's paper on conscious neighborhood association and development, which also originally appeared in *Landscape*. Indeed, anyone who finds the themes expressed in this book interesting will find *Landscape* the most thought-provoking magazine on the American scene today.

Bibliography

Selected data sources

Annual Reports, various years: BAT Industries, Carroll's, Church's Fried Chicken, Collins Foods, Inc., Dairy Queen International, Denny's Restaurants, Diversified Foods, D'Lites, Dunkin Donuts, General Foods, General Mills, Godfather's Pizza, Howard Johnson's, Jerrico, K-Mart, Manor Care, Marriott Corporation, McDonald's, Morrison's, Piccadilly, Pantera Corporation, PepsiCo, Pillsbury Company, Ponderosa, Ramada, R. J. Reynolds Company, Ralston Purina Company, Rusty Pelican, Sambo's Restaurants, Shoney's, Showbiz Pizza Time Inc., Southland Corporation, Tastee-Freez International, Tombrock, USA Restaurants, VICORP, Victoria Station, Wendy's, White Castle, W. R. Grace.

Bittinger, Janie and Gill, Katie, "The Top 500 Restaurants," *Restaurant Hospitality*, June 1966, pp. 101–32.

Farkas, David, Soeder, John, and Smith, Katie, "The Top 100 Chains," *Restaurant Hospitality*, August 1988, pp. 93–116.

"Foodservice Trends," *Restaurants USA*, June/July 1988, pp. 36–44.

Glazer, David, "11th Annual Restaurant Growth Index-1978," *Restaurant Business*, September 1, 1978, pp. 182–208.

Hall, Jeffrey, "17th Annual Restaurant Growth Index," *Restaurant Business*, September 20, 1984, pp. 157–216.

Kass, Monica and Bertagnoli, Lisa, "R & I's Top 100 Independents: America's Highest-Grossing Restaurants," *Restaurants & Institutions*, March 6, 1989, pp. 46–51.

Pratscher, Maureen et al., "How America Loves to Eat Out," *Restaurants & Institutions*, December 9, 1987, pp. 30–91.

"R & I Choice in Chains," *Restaurants & Institutions*, February 6, 1989, pp. 56–106.

"R & I '400'," *Restaurants & Institutions*, July 1, 1982, pp. 77–117.

"R & I's Top 100 Independents," *Restaurants & Institutions*, March 6, 1989, pp. 46–51.

"Tastes of America," *Restaurants & Institutions*, December 9, 1988, pp. 43–69.

"The Top 100 Chains," *Restaurant Hospitality*, August 1987, pp. 90–116.

"The Top 100 Restaurant Chains," *Restaurant Business*, November 20, 1988, pp. 89–140.

"21st Annual Restaurant Growth Index," *Restaurant Business*, September 20, 1988, pp. 131–222.

US Census Bureau, *Compendium of the Tenth Census* (Washingon: US Government Printing Office, 1884).

US Census Bureau, *Abstract of the Twelfth Census, 1900* (Washington: US Government Printing Office, 1904).

US Census Bureau, *Twelfth Census of the United States, 1900* (Washington: US Government Printing Office, 1906).

US Census Bureau, *Fourteenth Census of the United States, 1920* (Washington: US Government Printing Office, 1924).

Selected city directories

Atchison City Directory, and Business Mirror, for 1859–60 . . . (St Louis: Sutherland & McEvoy Publishers, 1859).

The Boston Directory (Boston: John H. A. Frost and Charles Stimpson, Jr, 1825).

Boyd, William H. (compiler), *Boyd's Rome Directory* (Rome, NY: Abbott & Redway, 1859).

Charlestown Directory (Charlestown, Mass: Adams, Sampson, & Co., 1860).

Commercial Advertiser Directory for the City of Dubuque to which is added a Business Directory, 1858–59 (Dubuque: Webster & Co., 1858–9).

Diffenbacher, J. F., *Directory of Pittsburgh and Allegheny Cities for 1884* (Pittsburgh: Diffenbacher & Thurston, 1884).

Directory of Pittsburgh and vicinity (Pittsburgh: George H. Thurston, 1859).

Jones, John F. (ed.), *Jones's New York Mercantile and General Directory* (New York: printed by the editor, 1805).

Langley, Henry G., *The San Francisco Directory for the Year Commencing July 1860* (San Francisco: Valentine & Co., 1860).

New Trade Directory for Philadelphia, anno 1800 (Philadelphia: 1799).

New York Business Directory for 1840 & 1841 (New York: Publication Office, 1840).

O'Brien's Wholesale Business Intelligencer and Southern & Western Merchants Pocket Directory (Philadelphia: John G. O'Brien, 1839).

Philadelphia As It Is & Citizens Advertising Directory (Philadelphia: P. J. Gray, 1833).

Providence Directory & City Record . . . 1860 (Providence: Adams, Sampson & Co., 1860).

Sacramento City Directory, for the Year AD 1860 (Sacramento: D. S. Cotter & Co., 1859).

Sketches & Business Directory of Boston and its Vicinity (Boston: Damrell & Moore and George Collidge, 1860).

Stimpson's Boston Directory (Boston: Charles Stimpson, Jr, 1834).

Thurston, George H., *Directory of Pittsburgh & Vicinity for 1859–60* (Pittsburgh: George H. Thurston, 1859).

Williams' Atlanta Directory, City Guide, and Business Mirror, Vol. 1 (1859–60) (Atlanta: M. Lynch, 1859).

Wilson's Business Directory of New York City (New York: John F. Trow, Printer and Publisher, 1860).

Williams, Edwin, *New York as it is, in 1834* (New York: J. Disturnell, 1834).

General

Abbott, Carl, *Portland: Planning, Politics, and Growth in a Twentieth-Century City* (Lincoln: University of Nebraska Press, 1983).

Audubon, John J., *Delineations of American Scenery and Character* (London: Simpkin, Marshall, Hamilton, Kent & Co., 1926).

Best, James, and Turner, Eugene, *We the People: An Atlas of America's Ethnic Diversity* (New York: Macmillan, 1988).

Boorstin, Daniel J., *The Americans: The Colonial Experience* (New York: Random House, 1965).

Boorstin, Daniel J., *The Americans: The Democratic Experience* (New York: Random House, 1973).

Guiness, Desmond, and Sadler, Julius T., *Newport Preserv'd: Architecture of the 18th Century* (Newport: Newport Restoration Foundation, 1982).

Hall, Edward, *The Silent Language* (New York: Doubleday & Company, Inc., 1959).

Horwitz, Richard, *The Strip: An American Place* (Lincoln: University of Nebraska Press, 1985).

Jackson, J. B., "The Stranger's Path," in E. H. Zube, *Landscapes: Selected Writings of J. B. Jackson* (Amherst: University of Massachusetts Press, 1970), pp. 92–106.

Martin, Jane, *Talking With . . .* (New York: Samuel French, n.d.).

Pred, Allan, "Business Thoroughfares as Expressions of Urban Negro Culture," *Economic Geography*, 39 (1963), 217–33.

Relph, Edward, *Place and Placelessness* (London: Pion Ltd, 1976).

Riley, Robert B., "Speculation on the New American Landscapes," *Landscape*, 24 (1980), 1–9.

Rooney, John F., Jr et al., *This Remarkable Continent: An Atlas of United States and Canadian Society and Cultures* (College Station: Texas A & M University Press, 1982).

Seamon, David, *A Geography of Lifeworld: Movement, Rest, and Encounter* (New York: St. Martin's Press, 1979).

Snyder, Eugene E., *Early Portland: Stump-Town Triumphant* (Portland, Ore.: Binsford & Mort, 1970).

Weiss, Michael, *The Clustering of America* (New York: Harper & Row, 1988).
Winters, Christopher, "The Social Identity of Evolving Neighborhoods," *Landscape*, 23 (1979), 8–14.
Zelinsky, Wilbur, "Selfward Bound? Personal Preference Patterns and the Changing Map of American Society," *Economic Geography*, 50 (1974), 144–79.

Diet

American Dietetic Association, *Cultural Food Patterns in the U.S.A.* (Chicago: American Dietetic Association, 1976).
Arnott, Margaret L. (ed.), *Gastronomy: The Anthropology of Food and Food Habits* (The Hague: Mouton, 1974).
Bennett, John, "Food and Social Status in a Rural Society," *American Sociological Review*, 8 (1943), 561–9.
Brewster, Letitia, and Jacobson, M. F., *The Changing American Diet* (Washington: Center for Science in the Public Interest, 1978).
Brown, Linda K., and Mussell, Kay (eds.), *Ethnic and Regional Foodways in the United States: The Performance of Group Identity* (Knoxville: University of Tennessee Press, 1984).
Burke, Padraic, "Rolling Carts and Songs of Plenty: The Urban Food Vendor," *Journal of American Culture*, 2 (1979), 480–7.
Camp, Charles, "Federal Foodways Research, 1935–1943," *The Digest*, 2 (Summer 1979), 4–17.
Camp, Charles, "Food in American Culture: A Bibliographic Essay," *Journal of American Culture*, 2 (1979), 559–70.
Camp, Charles, "Foodways," in M. Thomas Inge (ed.), *Handbook of American Popular Culture*, Vol. 2 (Westport, Conn.: Greenwood Press, 1989), pp. 141–61.
Camp, Charles, "Foodways in Everyday Life," *American Quarterly*, 34 (1982), 278–89.
Co, Michael, and Co, Sophie, "Mid-Eighteenth Century Food and Drink on the Massachusetts Frontier" (Dublin Seminar for New England Folklife, Annual Proceedings, 25–27 June 1982), *Foodways in the Northeast* (Boston: Boston University, 1982), pp. 39–46.
Committee on Food Habits, *Manual for the Study of Food Habits* (Washington: National Research Council Bulletin, no. 111, 1945).
Conlin, Joseph, "Did Your Get Enough Pie? A Social History of Food in Logging Camps," *Journal of Forest History*, 23 (1979), 165–85.
Cummings, Richard O., *The American and His Food: History of Food Habits in the United States*, reprint of revised edition (New York: Arno Press, 1943).
Cussler, M., and de Give, M. L., *Twixt the Cup and the Lip: Psychological and Socio-Cultural Factors Affecting Food Habits* (Twayne, NY: 1952).
de Give, Mary L., and Cussler, Margaret, *Bibliography and Notes on German Food Patterns* (Washington: National Research Council Committee on Food Habits, 1944).
Dervin, Daphne, "Wholesome, Toothsome, and Diverse: Eighteenth-Century Foodways in Deerfield, Massachusetts" (Dublin Seminar for New England Folklife: Annual Proceedings, 25–27 June 1982), *Foodways in the Northeast* (Boston: Boston University, 1982), pp. 47–63.
The Digest: A Newsletter for the Interdisciplinary Study of Food (Philadelphia: American Folklore Society, Foodways Section, 1977).

Douglas, Mary, and Nico, Michael, "Taking the Biscuit: The Structure of British Meals," *New Society*, 39 (1974), 744–7.

Fleigel, Frederick, *Food Habits and National Background* (State College: Pennsylvania State University Agricultural Experimental Station Bulletin, no. 684, 1961).

Gizelis, Gregory, "Foodways Acculturation in the Greek Community of Philadelphia," *Pennsylvania Folklife* 19 (1970–1), 9–15.

Gizzardini, G., and Joffe, N., *Italian Food Patterns and their Relationship to Wartime Problems of Food and Nutrition* (Washington: National Research Council Committee on Food Habits, 1942).

Gottlieb, David, *A Bibliography and Bibliographic Review of Food and Food Habits* (Washington: Quartermaster Food and Container Institute for the Armed Forces, 1958).

Hilliard, Sam B., *Hog Meat and Hoecake: Food Supply in the Old South 1840–1860* (Carbondale: Southern Illinois University Press, 1972).

Jerome, Norge, "Diet and Acculturation: The Case of Black-American In-Migrants," in N. Jerome, R. Kandel, and G. Pelto (eds), *Nutrition Anthropology* (New York: Redgrave, 1979).

Jerome, Norge, "Northern Urbanization and Food Consumption Patterns of Southern Negroes," *American Journal of Clinical Nutrition*, 22 (1969), 1667–9.

Joffe, Natalie, "Food Habits of Selected Subcultures in the United States," in *The Problem of Changing Food Habits* (Washington: National Research Council Bulletin, no. 108, 1943).

Jones, Evan, *American Food: The Gastronomic Story*, 2nd edition (New York: Random House, 1981).

Kraut, Alan M., "The Significance of Food in the Designation of Cultural Boundaries Between Immigrant Groups in the US, 1840–1921," *Journal of American Culture*, 2 (1979), 409–20.

Linden, Fabien, and Axel, Helen (eds), *Consumer Expenditure Patterns* (New York: Conference Board, 1978).

Lloyd, Timothy C., "The Cincinnati Chili Culinary Complex," *Western Folklore*, 40 (1981), 28–40.

Lowenberg, Miriam E. et al., *Food & People*, 3rd edition (New York: John Wiley, 1979).

Mariani, John, *The Dictionary of Food and Drink* (New York: Ticknor & Fields, 1983).

McKenzie, J. C. "Social and Economic Implications of Minority Food Habits," *Proceedings of the Nutrition Society*, 26 (1967), 197–205.

Mead, Margaret, *Food Habits Research: Problems of the 1960s* (Washington: National Research Council Bulletin, no. 1225, 1964).

Mead, Margaret, "The Problem of Changing Food Habits," in *The Problem of Changing Food Habits* (Washington: National Research Council Bulletin, no. 108, 1943).

Pangborn, Rose Marie, and Bruhn, Christine, "Social Process and Dietary Change," in *The Problem of Changing Food Habits* (Washington: National Research Council Bulletin, no. 108, 1943).

Pendery, Steven R., "The Archeology of Urban Foodways in Portsmouth" (Dublin Seminar for New England Folklife, Annual Proceedings, 25–27 June 1982), *Foodways in the Northeast* (Boston: Boston University, 1982), 9–27.

Pirkova-Jaokbson, Svatava, and Joffe, N., *Some Central European Food Patterns and Their Relationship to Wartime Problems of Food and*

Nutrition (Washington: National Research Council Committee on Food Habits, 1943).

Revel, Jean-Francois, *Culture and Cuisine: A Journey Through the History of Food* (Garden City, NY: Doubleday, 1982).

Root, Waverley, and de Rochemont, Richard, *Eating in America: A History* (New York: William Morrow and Company, 1976).

Simmons, Amelia, *American Cookery, 1796*, reprinted with introduction by Iris I. Frey (Greenfarms, Conn.: Silver-leaf Press, 1984).

Simoons, Frederick, *Eat Not this Flesh: Food Avoidance in the Old World* (Madison: University of Wisconsin Press, 1963).

Society for Nutrition Education, *Food Habits: A Selected and Annotated Bibliography* (Washington: Society for Nutrition Education, 1973).

Soulsby, T., "Russian–American Food Patterns," *Journal of Nutrition Education*, 4 (1972), 170–2.

Tannahill, R., *Food in History* (New York: Stein & Day, 1973).

Taylor, Joe, *Eating, Drinking, and Visiting in the South: An Informal History* (Baton Rouge: Louisiana State University Press, 1982).

Trillin, Calvin, *American Fried: Adventures of a Happy Eater* (New York: Vintage Books, 1974).

Weaver, William W., "Food Acculturation and the First Pennsylvania–German Cookbook," *Journal of American Culture*, 2 (1979), 432–52.

Wilson, Christine S., "Food Habits: A Selected Annotated Bibliography," *Journal of Nutrition Education*, 5 (1973), 39–72.

Selected regional cookbooks

American Heritage Cookbook and Illustrated History of American Eating and Drinking (New York: Simon & Schuster, 1964).

Anderson, Jean, *Recipes from America's Restored Villages* (Garden City, NY: Doubleday, 1975).

Barrow, Mary, *The Virginia Beach Harvest Cookbook* (Norfolk, Va.: Donning Company, 1985).

Centenary Cookbook (Winston Salem, NC: Centenary Methodist Church, 1928).

Centre St. Cookery (Fernandina Beach, Fla.: Magnolia Garden Club, 1978).

Cheney, Winifred, *The Southern Hospitality Cookbook* (Birmingham, Ala.: Oxmoor House, 1970).

Clements, Cherry, *Monga Ma's Legacy* (Atlanta: Eason Publishing, 1974).

The Cotton Country Collection (Monroe, La.: Junior Charity League, 1982).

Cracker Cookin' and Other Favorites (St Petersburg, Fla.: LaFray Publishing Company, 1977).

Dent, Huntley, *The Feast of Santa Fe: Cooking of the American Southwest* (New York: Simon and Schuster, 1985).

Derbytown Winners Cookbook (Louisville, Ky.: Crescent Hill Woman's Club, 1971).

Evans, Rosemary, *Back-Home Cuisine* (Swainsboro, Ga.: Magnolia Press, 1983).

Farmer, Cheryl (compiler), *Milson S. Jones Family Receipts* (Lenexa, Kan.: Cookbook Publishers, 1983).

Favorite Recipes in Paris Kitchens (Paris, Tenn.: Westminster Guild of the First Presbyterian Church, 1923).

Flexner, Marion, *Out of Kentucky Kitchens* (New York: American Legacy Press, 1981).

Frey, Iris (ed.), *American Cookery, 1796* by Amelia Simmons (Green Farms, Conn.: Silverleaf Press, 1984).

Georgia Recipes for Family Fun & Food (Atlanta: Women's Auxiliary to the Medical Association of Georgia, 1974).

Glenn, Camille, *The Heritage of Southern Cooking* (New York: Workman Publishing, 1986).

Greater Slidell Council of Garden Clubs, Inc. (compilers), *The Recipe Garden* (Lenexa, Kan.: Cookbook Publishers, 1984).

Jeffries, Bob, *Soul Food Cookbook* (Indianapolis: Bobbs-Merrill, 1969).

Jordan, Mildred, *The Distelfink Country of the Pennsylvania Dutch* (New York: Crown Publishers, 1978).

Junior League of Houston, Inc. (compilers), *The Star of Texas Cookbook* (New York: Doubleday, 1983).

Marshall, Lillian, *Southern Living Cooking Across the South* (Birmingham, Ala.: Oxmoor House, 1980).

Mickler, Ernest, *White Trash Cooking* (Berkeley: Ten Speed Press for the Jargon Society, 1986).

The Nashville Cookbook: Specialties of the Cumberland Region (Nashville: Nashville Area Home Economics Association, 1976).

Nathan, Joan, *An American Folklife Cookbook* (New York: Schocken Books, 1984).

Old Capitol Cook Book, 2nd edition (Milledgeville, Ga.: Parent-Teachers Association, Georgia Military College, 1947).

Quail Country (Albany, Ga.: Junior League of Albany, Georgia, 1983).

Randolph, Mary, *The Virginia House-Wife*, 2nd edition (Washington: Way & Gideon, 1825).

River Road Recipes (Baton Rouge: Junior League of Baton Rouge, 1963).

Villas, James, *American Taste: A Celebration of Gastronomy Coast to Coast* (New York: Arbor House, 1982).

Waldrop, Annie Archer, *My Family's Favorite Recipes* (Conyers, Ga.: Annie Archer Waldrop, 1976).

"The War to End all Barbecue Wars: It's time to take a stand and choose sides in a matter of utmost urgency," *Atlanta Journal/Constitution*, September 1, 1985.

Weaver, William W. (ed.), *A Quaker Woman's Cookbook: The Domestic Cookery of Elizabeth Ellicott Lea* (Philadelphia: University of Pennsylvania Press, 1982).

Restaurants

Arreola, Daniel, "Mexican Restaurants in Tucson," *Journal of Cultural Geography*, 3 (1983), 108–14.

Baeder, John, *Gas, Food, and Lodging* (New York: Abbeville Press, 1982).

Batterberry, Michael, and Batterberry, Ariane, *On the Town in New York: From 1776 to Present* (New York: Charles Scribner's Sons, 1973).

Belasco, Warren J., "Toward a Culinary Common Denominator: The Rise of Howard Johnson's, 1925–1940," *Journal of American Culture*, 2 (1979), 503–18.

Berlinksi, Pete, "Tastee-Freez puts ADI markets up for sale," *Restaurant Business*, September 1, 1978, pp. 151–2.

Bernstein, Charles, *Great Restaurant Innovators: Profiles in Success* (New York: Lebhar-Friedman Books, 1981).

"Buffalo Restaurants at a Glance," *American Restaurant*, (May 1926), 42–3

Bye, Roseann, "North American Foodways as Viewed by the Food Industry," *North American Culture*, 2 (1985), 37–42.

Carstensen, Laurence W., Jr, "The Burger Kingdom: Growth and Diffusion of McDonald's Restaurants in the United States, 1955–78," *Geographical Perspectives*, no. 58–9 (1986–7), 1–8.

Chakravarty, Subrata N., "Pizzas, anyone? Hamburgers? Trout Amandine?" *Forbes*, September 9, 1985, pp. 74–5.

Cox, James A., "How Good Food and Harvey 'Skirts' Won the West," *Smithsonian*, 18 (1987), 130–9.

Cummings, Richard, *The American and His Food: A History of Food Habits in the United States*, rev. edn (Chicago: University of Chicago Press, 1941).

Editorial, *Journal of Home Economics*, July 1925, pp. 390–3.

Emerson, Robert L., *Fast Food: The Endless Shakeout* (New York: Lebhar-Friedman Books, 1979).

Fishwich, Marshall, *Ronald Revisited: The World of Ronald McDonald* (Bowling Green, Ohio: Bowling Green University Popular Press, 1983).

Gutman, Richard J. S., and Kaufman, Elliott, *American Diner* (New York: Hagerstown, 1979).

Hanson, Alice C., "Restaurants" *International Encyclopedia of Social Sciences* Vol. XIII (New York: Macmillan, 1979), p. 337.

Henderson, James D., *"Meals by Fred Harvey:" A Phenomenon of the American West* (Fort Worth: Texas Christian University, 1969).

Hirshorn, Paul, and Izenour, Steven, *White Towers* (Cambridge, Mass.: MIT Press, 1979).

Jackson, E. Christine, "Ethnology of an Urban Burger King Franchise," *Journal of American Culture*, 2 (1979), 534–9.

Kovacik, Charles, "Eating Out in South Carolina's Cities: The Last Fifty Years," *North American Culture*, 4 (1988), 53–64.

Kroc, Ray, *Grinding it Out: The Making of McDonald's* (Chicago: Henry Regnery Company, 1977).

Krueger, Gene E., "The Ethnology and Spatial Distribution of Restaurants: Pennsylvania" (MS thesis, Pennsylvania State University, 1970).

Langdon, Philip, *Orange Roofs, Golden Arches* (New York: Alfred A. Knopf, 1986).

Lohof, Bruce A., "Hamburger Stand: Industrialization and the American Fast-Food Phenomenon," *Journal of American Culture*, 2 (1979), 519–33.

Love, John, *McDonald's: Behind the Arches* (New York: Bantam Books, 1986).

"Lowly Hamburger Raised to New Heights," *American Restaurant Magazine*, July 1956, pp. 68–9.

Luxenburg, Stan, *Roadside Empires: How the Chains Franchised America* (New York: Viking, 1985).

"Major Chains Learn Courtly Manners," *Restaurants and Institutions*, July 10, 1989, pp. 125– .

Meyer, J. W., and Brown, L. A., "Duffusion Agency Establishment: The Case of Friendly Ice Cream and Public Sector Diffusion Processes," *Socio-Economic Planning Sciences*, 13 (1979), 241–9.

O'Brien, Robert, Marriott, *The J. Willard Marriott Story* (Salt Lake City: Desert Book Co., 1977), pp. 111–14.

"Origin of the Cafeteria System," *Journal of Home Economics*, 17 (1925), 391–2.

Paul, Ronald N., "Mr. Midscale's Neighborhood," *Restaurant Hospitality*, April 1988, pp. 130–6.

Pearce, John (ed.), *The Colonel: The Captivating Biography of the Dynamic Founder of a Fast Food Empire* (Garden City: Doubleday & Company, 1982).

"The Perils of Pearl Street," *New York Mirror*, March 15, 1834, p. 295; from R. Cummings on 1830s boarding-house fare.

Pillsbury, Richard, "From Hamburger Alley to Hedgerose Heights: Toward a Model of Restaurant Location Dynamics," *Professional Geographer*, 39 (1987), 326–44.

Ranhofer, Charles, *The Epicurean* (New York: 1893).

Roark, Michael, "Fast Foods: American Food Regions," *North American Culture*, 2 (1986), 24–36.

Rushmore, Stephen, *Hotels, Motels, and Restaurants: Valuations and Market Studies* (Chicago: American Institute of Real Estate Appraisers, 1983).

"Sales and Sanitation Go Hand in Hand," *American Restaurant Magazine*, October 1956, pp. 62–3.

Sanders, Col. Harland, *Life as I have Known it Has Been Finger Lickin' Good* (Carol Stream, Ill.: Creation House, 1974).

Savan, Glenn, *White Palace* (New York: Bantam Books, 1987).

Stern, Jane, and Stern, Michael, "Cafeterias," *The New Yorker*, August 1, 1988, pp. 37–54.

"Streamlined for Fast Service," *American Restaurant Magazine*, February 1956, p. 65.

Tyre, Peg, and Walls, Jeannette, "Restaurant Notes from All Over," *New York*, February 13, 1989, p. 14.

Yoder, Paton, *Taverns and Travelers: Inns of the Early Midwest* (Bloomington: Indiana University Press, 1969).

Woodson, LeRoy, Jr et al., *Roadside Food: Good Home-Style Cooking Across America* (New York: Stewart, Tabori and Chang, 1986).

Wyckoff, D. Daryl, and Sasser, E. Earl, *The Chain-Restaurant Industry* (Lexington, Mass.: D. C. Heath, 1978).

Zelinsky, Wilbur, *The Cultural Geography of the United States* (Englewood Cliffs, NJ: Prentice-Hall, 1973).

Zelinsky, Wilbur, "The Roving Palate: North America's Ethnic Restaurant Cuisines," *Geoforum*, 16 (1985), 51–72.

Retail location

Berry, Brian J. L., *Geography of Market Centers and Retail Distribution* (Englewood Cliffs, NJ: Prentice-Hall, 1967).

Craig, C. Samuel, Ghosh, Avigit, and McLafferty, Sara, "Models of the Retail Location Process: A Review," *Journal of Retailing*, 60 (1984), 5–36.

Davies, R. L., *Marketing Geography* (London: Methuen, 1977).

Davies, R. L., (ed.), *Retail Planning in the European Community* (Farnborough, Hampshire, UK: Saxon House, 1979).

Dawson, J., *Retail Geography* (London: Croom Helm, 1980).

Dent, Borden D., "Metropolitan Retail Structure," in Truman Hartshorn, *Interpreting the City: An Urban Geography* (Chicago: University of Chicago Press, 1964).

Eaton, B., and Lipsey, R., "Comparison Shopping and the Clustering of Homogeneous Firms," *Journal of Regional Science*, 19 (1981), 421–35.

Garner, Barry, *The Internal Structure of Retail Nucleations*. Northwestern University Studies in Geography, no. 12 (Evanston, Ill.: Northwestern University Press, 1966).

Hartshorn, Truman A., *Interpreting the City: An Urban Geography* (New York: John Wiley, 1980).

Hise, R. T. et al., "Factors Affecting the Performance of Individual Chain Store Units: An Empirical Analysis," *Journal of Retailing*, 59 (1983), 1–18.

Hubbard, R., "A Review of Selected Factors Conditioning Consumer Travel Behavior," *Journal of Consumer Research*, 5 (1978), 7–21.

Jakle, John A., "Gasoline Stations in the Champaign–Urbana Landscape: 1920 to 1970," *Bulletin* (Illinois Geographical Society), 20 (1978), 3–15.

King, Leslie J., *Central Place Theory* (Beverly Hills: Sage Publications, 1984).

Nevin, J. R., and Houston, M. J., "Image as a Component of Attractiveness to Intra-Urban Shopping Areas," *Journal of Retailing*, 56 (1980), 77–93.

Potter, Robert B., *The Urban Retailing System: Location, Cognition, and Behavior* (Aldershot, Hampshire, UK: Gower Press, 1982).

Rees, Philip H., *Residential Patterns in American Cities: 1960*, Department of Geography Research Papers, no. 189 (Chicago: University of Chicago Press, 1979).

Rees, Philip H., and Kirby, D. A., "Urban Retail Provision and Consumer Behaviour: Some Examples from Western Society," in D. T. Herbert and R. J. Johnson (eds), *Geography and the Urban Environment: Progress in Research and Applications*, Vol. III (New York: John Wiley, 1980).

Stanley, T. J., and Sewall, M., "Image Inputs to a Probablistic Model: Predicting Retail Potential," *Journal of Marketing*, 40 (1976), 48–53.

General index

A & W Root Beer 2, 57, 75–6, 100, 176
Anderson, Walter 49, 67, 100
Applebee's Neighborhood Grill & Bar 195
Arctic Circle 176, 178

Baby Doe's Matchless Mine 152–3
Baker's Square 142, 217
Baltimore Dairy Lunch 59
Barbecue Pit (restaurant region) 116–17, 150, 161–2, 171–2, 202, 224
Battisone, Sam, Sr 100, 102
Beefhouse (restaurant region) 161–2, 175, 177, 179–81
Bell, Glen 94
Bennigan's 9, 151, 195
Bickford's 59–60
Bishop's Cafeteria 62
Blue Fox 5
boarding house 17–18, 20, 22, 31, 36–7, 53, 215, 233
Bob Evans Farms Restaurants 103, 105
Bob's Big Boy 57, 102
body food 4–6, 196–201, 225–6
Bohnett, Newell 100, 102
Bonanza Family Restaurants 215, 218
Boo's Brothers Cafeterias 61
Boulanger, M. 23
Bressler Ice Cream Company 94
Brinker, Norman 150–1
Brown, George 28
Burger Chef 97, 139
Burger King 73, 96, 107, 139, 151, 176, 195, 217
Buckley, T. H. 38

Cajunland (restaurant region) 162, 173
California Dreaming (restaurant region) 162, 202
Capitol Lunch System 59
Captain Anderson's Seafood Restaurant 88
Captain D's Seafood Restaurants 194
Carl's Jr 217
Carney, Frank 155, 158
Carrol's Hamburgers 94
Chain Alley 161–2, 186–7, 202, 227

Chatterbox Cafe 2–3
Chi Chi's Mexican Restaurant 155
Chic-fil-A, Inc. 195, 217–18
Childs, William and Samuel 46
Child's Unique Dairy Lunch 59, 61
Chili's Bar & Grill 195, 213, 217
Chuck E. Cheese Pizza 85
Chuck's Steak House 151
Church's Chicken 194
Collins, James 93–4
Collins Foods International (see also Hamburger Handout, Sizzler Restaurants) 94
Conscience Joint 48
Cork and Cleaver 151

Dairy Queen 6, 55, 57, 76–7, 135
Davenport, Rody, Jr. 73
Delmonico, John 23
Delmonico, Peter 23
Delmonico's Restaurant 24–5, 27–8, 30, 43, 49, 53, 120
Denny's 102, 135–9, 142, 147, 217
Der Wienerschnitzel 215
Dinerland (restaurant region) 161–8, 170, 202, 215
Dinerland South (restaurant region) 162, 175
Dobb's-Hull House 67
Domino's Pizza 50, 97, 135, 168
Dorgan, T. A. 50
Downing, Thomas 27
Dunkin' Donuts 147

Edgerton, David 95, 139
Elby's 144
El Chico Mexican Restaurants 155
engulfed village 200, 219
Ethnic Restaurants
    Chinese 3, 52–3, 80, 129–30, 154, 164–5, 167, 170, 172, 177, 181, 190, 192, 196, 213
    French 3, 26, 31, 52, 152, 170, 193
    Italian 3, 80, 124, 164–5, 167, 170, 172, 177, 181, 198
    Mexican 167, 170, 172, 177, 181, 190, 192, 196, 202, 213

Exchange Buffet 465

57th Fighter Group Restaurants 5–6
Filetti's 163
food court 204–5, 217–19
Fog City Diner 43, 133
Forum Cafeterias 62, 66
Foster's Freeze 2
Franklin Restorator 26
Fraunces Tavern 16, 21
Friendly Restaurants 80, 142
Fuddrucker's 195, 213, 217
Furr's Cafeterias 62, 64, 66

General Equipment Company 139–40
General Foods (see also Burger Chef) 140
General Mills (see also Italian Garden)
    155
gentrifying neighborhood 200, 208
Godfather's Pizza 50, 168
Golden Point 94

hamburger alley 63, 66, 71, 156, 170,
    183–4, 187, 193–5, 204, 215–17, 219
Hamburger Handout 82, 93–4
Hardee's System 140, 176, 217
Harmon, Pete 95
Hartford Lunch 59
Harvey, Fred 44
Harvey House 44–6
Hayes Lunch System 59
Henry's Hamburgers 94
Horn & Hardart 204
Hot Shoppe 77
Hovan Gourmet 195
Hoyt's Cafe 1–3, 142
Howard Johnson's 57, 80, 97, 100, 142
Huddle House 143

Ingram, Edgar "Billy" 49, 67, 100
inn 13, 15–16, 19–20, 221
InstaBurger King Company 95
instant landscape 218
International House of Pancakes 147
Italian Garden 155

Jack in the Box 140, 151
Johnson, Howard 30
Jolly Ox 151

Kelsey, Harry 59
Kenny's Kitchen 168
Kentucky Fried Chicken 94–5, 97, 107,
    135, 194, 197
Kettle Restaurants 142
Kinney-Kelley 59
Krispy Kreme Doughnuts 147
Kroc, Ray 30, 46, 93–4, 98

Krystal Company 54, 67, 73–4, 217
Kullman Dining Car 39
Kutztown Folk Festival 114

L & K Cafeteria 172
Le Panier 195
Le Peep Restaurants 195
Little Caesar's Pizza 50–1, 168
Little Tavern 67, 89
Lombardi, Gennaro 50
Long John Silver's Seafood Shoppes 97,
    194
Louis' Lunch 49
Luby's 65
Luchow's 5

Mariani, John 155
Marie Callender Pie Shops 103, 105
Marriott, J. Willard 46, 57, 75, 77, 87,
    100, 204
Mazzio's Pizza 50, 168
McDonald brothers 51, 93
McDonald's Restaurants 4, 9–10, 30, 43,
    66, 80, 83–5, 93–5, 97–9, 101, 103,
    107, 135, 139, 157, 168, 171, 195,
    197, 213, 218, 232
McLamore, James 95, 139
Megalopolis (restaurant region) 161–2,
    175
Merchant's Coffee House 26
Mister Donut 147
Mobile Module Company 40
Modern Diner 39
Morrison's Cafeterias 62, 64, 66, 218
Morton's of Chicago 5, 206

Norske Nook 168

O'Mahony Company 39
Orange Julius 218
Original Pancake House 180

Pacific Fishhouse (restaurant region)
    162, 179
Palmer, Charles H. 38
Park n' Eat 144
PepsiCo 94, 172
Perkin's Family Restaurants 144, 147,
    195
Piccadilly Cafeterias 62–3, 65–6
Pig & Whistle 76
Pig Stand 75
Pillsbury Company (see also Bennigan's,
    Burger King, Jolly Ox, Poppin'
    Fresh Pie Shops, Steak & Ale) 140, 151
Pizza Hut 50, 135, 158–9, 167, 171–2, 197
Pizza Inn 51
Pizzeria Uno 195

Po Folks 73, 103–5
Ponderosa Steakhouses 140, 215
Popeye's Famous Fried Chicken 194
Poppin' Fresh Pie Shops 151
porter houses 31

Rainbow Inn 120–1
Ralston Purina Company (*see also* Jack
    in the Box) 140
Ranhofer, Charles 24
regional malls 187, 195–6, 204, 217–19
Restaurant Activity Index (RAI) 86
restaurant clusters 191, 203, 206, 215
restaurants
    barbecue 150, 164, 167, 171–3, 177, 195
    beer garden 122–3, 146, 168
    Brownivorous 28
    cafeteria 46, 48, 52–3, 58, 61–2, 64–6,
        77, 119, 143, 164, 167, 172–3, 177,
        181, 203
    Cajun 3, 120
    coffee house 22–3, 26, 29–31
    coffee shops 4, 31, 52, 102, 105, 108,
        137, 142, 202, 205, 215, 217
    Delmonican 28
    diners 34–5, 37–9, 41–3, 80, 125,
        144–5, 162, 166, 233
    dining hall 23
    dining room 23, 30
    drive-in 56, 75–6, 93, 98, 178
    eating house 23, 29–30, 33
    hamburger 58
    lunch counters 80
    lunchroom 32, 38, 46–8, 52–3, 58, 60–1
    lunch-wagon 37–8, 40, 52
    oyster house 22–3, 26–31, 33
    pancake house 147
    pizza 4, 50, 91, 162–4, 167, 170, 172,
        177, 181, 192–3, 195–7, 202, 215
    restorator 23
    sandwich shop 52–3, 60, 164, 167,
        172, 181, 195–6, 202, 229
    six-penny house 28
    Sweeneyorium 28, 32
    sub shop 3–4, 163, 181–2, 202, 215
    tea garden 26
    victualing house 23, 26
Ritz-Carlton Hotels 206
Roark, Michael 156
Robin's Gourmet Burgers and Spirits 180
Ruby Tuesday 218
Russian Tea Room 226
Ruth's Chris Steakhouse 206

S & W Cafeterias 62
sailor's boarding house 21
saloons 31
Sambo's 97, 100, 102

Sanders, Col. Harland 94
Scott, Walter 37
Shakey's Pizza 96
Shoney's Restaurants 103
Showtime Pizza 85
Sizzler Restaurants 94, 215
Skipper's Seafood 180
Sonic Industries 7, 96, 176, 217
soul food 4–6, 196–201, 225–6
Soup Plantation 3
Specialty Restaurants Inc. (*see also* Baby
        Doe's Matchless Mine, 57th Fighter
        Group Restaurants) 5, 152
Stan's Drive-In 2
Steak & Ale 151, 195
Sterling Diners 39
street vendor 31, 36–7
Stuart Anderson 151

Taco Bell 94, 172
Taco John's 176
Taco Stand (restaurant region) 161–2,
        180, 202
tavern 13–18, 20, 22, 31, 35, 37, 53, 151,
        215, 233
Taverntown 161, 167–8, 170, 215
Tennessee Restaurants 143
Thompson, John R. 58
P. J. Tierney & Sons Company 38–9
Toddle House 67
Tombrock Corporation 71
Tontine Coffee House 26–7

Victoria Station 96–7, 151
VICORP 142
Village Inn 9
voluntary associations 227–9

Waffle House 73, 143–4, 147, 195
Waldorf Lunch 59
Ward & Dickinson 39
Wendy's Old Fashioned Hamburgers 73,
        176, 195, 197, 213, 217–18
Whataburger 6, 217
white box 54, 73–5, 77, 98, 143–4, 233
White Castle System 49, 55, 57, 67,
        71–3, 76–7, 98, 100, 143, 168
White Hut 67
White Tavern 67
White Tower 67, 69, 71, 73, 80, 143,
        201, 233
White Horse Tavern 16, 35
Winchell's Donuts 147
Willow Inn 9
Woodward Inn 19, 114
Worcester Lunch Car Company 39

Yasin's Fish Supreme 194

Geographical
index

Albuquerque, NM 45, 119
Allentown, Pa 76
Amana, Iowa 221
Ann Arbor, Mich 88
Ash Fork, Kan 45
Atlanta, Ga 40, 74, 76, 88, 100, 143, 154,
    157, 172, 186–7, 192–3, 201, 212,
    220–1, 227, 229

Bakersfield, Calif 181
Baltimore, Md 40, 75, 89, 121, 163, 196,
    231, 233
Baton Rouge, La 62
Bayonne, NJ 39, 106, 165
Belleville, Pa 114
Boca Raton, Fl 175
Bordentown, NJ 41
Boston, Mass 26, 30, 32, 49, 52, 57,
    59–62, 111, 120–1, 149, 161, 196, 206
Bremerton, Wash 177
Buffalo, NY 52, 57, 59, 122
Butte, Mon 121

Camden, NJ 164
Casper, Wy 167, 177, 181
Castine, Me 112
Charleston, Mass 30, 226
Charleston, SC 171
Charlotte, NC 62
Chattanooga, Tenn 54, 67, 73
Chicago, Ill 5, 53, 61–2, 85, 88, 94, 98,
    100, 121–2, 124–5, 128, 149, 154,
    175, 231
Chico, Calif 93
Cincinnati, Ohio 100, 121
Cleveland, Ohio 100, 128
Clovis, NM 181
Columbia, SC 171
Columbus, Ga 88
Columbus, Miss 171–2
Columbus, Ohio 57, 71, 73, 105
Concord, NH 164
Corbin, Ky 94

Dallas, Texas 75, 100, 151, 154, 158,
    186–7

Darlington, SC 119
Denver, Col 142, 158, 186
Des Moines, Iowa 129
Des Plaines, Ill 98
Deston, Fl 86
Detroit, Mich 62, 67, 100, 122, 124–5,
    128
Dubuque, Iowa 52–3

East Point, Ga 217
Edison, NJ 134

Fall River, Mass 80
Flint, Mich 57
Florence, Kan 44
Florence, SC 172–3
Fort Walton, Fl 86
Fort Wayne, Ind 75, 167
Franklin, NC 221
Fresno, Calif 98
Fulton County, Ga 157

Gainesville, Ga 172
Greenville, SC 171

Hamtramck, Mich 122
Helen, Ga 221–2
Highlands, NC 221
Honolulu, Hawaii 86
Houston, Texas 67, 186–7

Johnstown, Pa 53, 91–2, 126, 163–4, 203

Kankakee, Ill 57
Kansas City, Mo 62
Kutztown, Pa 114

Lafayette, La 172–3
La Mirada, Calif 142
Lawrence, Kan 88
Lodi, Calif 57, 75
Los Angeles, Calif 45, 61–2, 76, 85,
    98–9, 129, 175, 202–3, 210
Louisville, Ky 67, 128, 155

Madison, Wis 168

Manhattan, NY 16, 18, 23, 27–9, 149,
    156, 231
Marietta, Ga xii, 153
Memphis, Tenn 67, 80
Merrimac, Mass 39
Miami, Fl 59, 88, 95, 186
Milwaukee, Wis 57, 67, 80, 121–2, 125,
    168
Minneapolis, Minn 147, 168, 186
Mobile, Ala 62, 218
Montreal, Quebec 204
Morgan City, La 174
Myrtle Beach, SC 87

Nashville, Tenn 74, 105, 142
New Bedford, Mass 209
New Castle, Pa 124
New Haven, Conn 49
New Orleans, La 44, 80, 120, 206
New Rochelle, NY 38
New York, NY 5, 16, 20–1, 26–7, 30, 32,
    44, 46, 50, 53, 56, 59–62, 80, 85,
    111–12, 120–2, 124–5, 129, 149, 154,
    164, 175, 188, 190, 203–4, 226, 233
Newark, NJ 1, 39
Newport, RI 16, 35

Oklahoma City, Okla 52–3, 80, 181, 231
Omaha, Neb 50, 80
Orange County, Calif 211, 231
Osseo, Wis 168, 175

Panama City, Fl 86, 88
Pawtucket, RI 37, 39
Philadelphia, Pa 16–17, 20, 26, 28, 30–2,
    56, 59, 61–2, 121, 152
Phoenix, Ariz 184, 186, 231
Pierre Part, La 120–1
Pittsburgh, Pa 9, 33, 57, 59, 80, 122,
    124–5, 128, 164, 200, 207, 209, 231
Pompano Beach, Fl 172
Portland, Me 162
Portland, Ore 40, 101, 129, 177, 186,
    191, 202, 205, 231
Providence, RI 1, 33, 35, 37–8, 50, 52,
    57, 59, 129, 164, 210, 231

Quincy, Mass 80, 147

Raleigh/Durham NC 88

Redding, Calif 93
Revere, Mass 147
Richmond, Va 75, 162
Rochester, NY 57
Rome, NY 33

Sacramento, Calif 57, 75, 102, 129
Salem, Ore 202, 231
Salt Lake City, Utah 75, 80, 94–5
St Louis, Mo 44, 121, 128
San Antonio, Texas 62, 154–5
San Bernadino, Calif 51, 93–4
San Diego, Calif 186
San Francisco, Calif 5, 32, 43, 52, 59–60,
    93, 129, 154, 200, 206
Santa Barbara, Calif 100, 142
Sante Fe, NM 119
Saugus, Mass 149
Sausalito, Calif 133
Scranton, Iowa 123
Seattle, Wash 142, 186, 231
Shawnee, Ok 96
Shelbyville, Tenn 67
Silver Creek, NY 39
Sioux City, Iowa 167, 170
Springfield, Mass 59
Stamford, Conn 71, 80
State College, Pa 19, 88
Stockbridge, Mass 112

Tacoma, Wash 80
Tampa, Fl 140
Thibídoux, La 173
Toledo, Ohio 67
Topeka, Kan 44–5

Utica, NY 33, 57

Visalia, Calif 93

Wallace, Kan 45
Washington, DC 57, 61–2, 75, 100, 161,
    231
Waukegan, Ill 100
Waynesburg, Pa 8–9
West Palm Beach, Fl 175
Wichita, Kan 49–50, 67, 75, 80, 100
Wollaston, Mass 57
Worcester, Mass 37–9
Wren, Ore 202